# F R E S H
## *from the*
# FREEZER

November 7, 1990,

to Danette

chill out!

Also by Michael Roberts
*Secret Ingredients*

# FRESH
## *from the*
# FREEZER

Michael Roberts

*with Janet Spiegel*

WILLIAM MORROW AND COMPANY, INC., NEW YORK

Recognizing the importance of preserving what has been written, it is the policy of William Morrow and Company, Inc., and its imprints and affiliates to have the books it publishes printed on acid-free paper, and we exert our best efforts to that end.

Library of Congress Cataloging-in-Publication Data

Roberts, Michael, 1949–
    Fresh from the freezer / Michael Roberts
        p.    cm.
    ISBN 0-688-08543-1
    1. Make-ahead cookery.   2. Frozen foods.   3. Cookery (Frozen foods)   I. Title.
    TX652.R635   1990
    641.5′55—dc20                                        90-5750
                                                         CIP

Printed in the United States of America

First Edition

1 2 3 4 5 6 7 8 9 10

BOOK DESIGN BY KATHLEEN HERLIHY-PAOLI

*For Diane and Clifford*

# ACKNOWLEDGMENTS

Thank you, Ann Bramson, for suggesting this book and for all your help in pulling the manuscript together. And for having Laurie Orseck looking over our shoulders.

My agents, Maureen and Eric Lasher—as always.

At Trumps—in the kitchen especially: Lil Miller, Nan Wilkinson, William Barr, Bobbie Nieves and Steve Maxey. And in the dining room, Rebecca Clark, Lesleigh Thoms, Ramon Martin, and Beverley Goodwin. And Lucy Farmer, too.

Big thanks to Harvey Gussman of Guss Meat Company. Also to Dennis Wax and Gordon's Fish Market; Mary Grigsby and Universal Cheese; Merle Tays and Highland Plastics; Lauren Ryan at Dow Brands.

Linda Zimmerman tested and retested all the recipes. Her expertise made the food better and my work much easier.

And, of course, Daniel and Otto.

# CONTENTS

# THE
# FREEZER
# GOURMET

As both a restaurant chef and a home cook, my primary concern has always been to find fresh, quality ingredients and capture that freshness in delicious meals. In business it's quite easy— we buy food every day. At home, though, it's a bit harder to organize, because I don't want to shop for each meal. For a long time I didn't realize that a freezer could help me.

However, I've learned otherwise. When I was testing the recipes for my first cookbook, *Secret Ingredients*, I couldn't use up all the food coming out of the kitchen. So, having been raised to finish everything on my plate, I haphazardly stored the extras in the freezer. When I reheated them, I was amazed to discover how good the dishes tasted (though many of them were pretty sorry to look at), and I began to think that there must be a way of freezing foods that did yield top-quality results.

This book illustrates the many and varied methods I have refined for using the freezer as a basic kitchen tool—like a blender or a stock pot—that can both preserve the perfect freshness of seasonal ingredients and also work to make meal preparation easier and less time-consuming for the cook.

Traditionally, European cooks have shopped daily for food, bringing home fresh vegetables and a loaf of still-warm bread for dinner. On another scale, I shop for my restaurant the same way, choosing the best from the large central and wholesale markets. However, for most of us—and increasingly for the European home cook as well—the supermarket is our main shopping source. In fact, the good supermarkets today resemble the old market streets, with their butchers, fishmongers, produce stalls, and bakeries. And what an abundant selection there is! Shrimp and tomatoes from Mexico, lamb and kiwi fruit from New Zealand, green beans from Kenya, buffalo-milk mozzarella from Italy, along with Texas beef, Maine potatoes, Long Island ducklings, California goat cheese, and Georgia pecans. Instead of shopping for tonight's dinner, we are usually shopping for a week's worth of provisions— so the trick is to preserve the freshness of these ingredients, cooked or uncooked, to enjoy over a period of time.

We also want to capture the freshness of the foods that mark the seasons—soft-shell crabs in May, cherries in June, garden tomatoes in August, cranberries and porcini mushrooms in October, truffles and tangerines in December. We can't rely on the bounty of each season to sustain us—we need ways of making food last throughout the year. And we've been doing that for centuries: salting and smoking meats, marinating cucumbers in vinegar, storing fruit in sugar. We enjoy preserved foods like pastrami, jam, smoked salmon, beef jerky, ham, sauerkraut, pickles, relishes, and spiced apples today. They taste delicious, but we've learned that they aren't particularly good for us. And in fact, we don't need to pump meat full of chemicals to keep it from spoiling. We don't need to salt, smoke, pickle, or dry our fish unless we want a salty, smokey, or pickled taste. For preserving food in a way that best retains its original, fresh flavor, the freezer is unbeatable.

We can enjoy scallops out of season, raspberries in January, tomato preparations year-round, by taking advantage of their peak season and freezing them for later use.

We can also make life easier for ourselves: by cooking a large batch of stew instead of a small one, giving us a meal in reserve; by preparing a dessert in advance of a dinner party, so there's one less thing to think about that day; and by storing odds and ends of leftovers that can be combined to form a last-minute improvised soup when family and friends troop in after the ice-hockey game. And as a bonus, we can learn special freezer techniques: recipes for lasagna, chicken Kiev, and fish sticks, for example, use the freezer as a tool in creating updated versions of these dishes.

Of course the microwave oven, if you have one, makes cooking from the freezer even more convenient. Defrosting and reheating frozen ingredients is fast, simple, clean, and less worrisome as far as spoilage is concerned. And you don't have to plan ahead to defrost something in the refrigerator overnight. The freezer-microwave connection is tailor-made for taking advantage of these techniques.

## HOW TO FREEZE FOODS

The freezer is only as good as the food you put into it. The first rule in freezing food is to buy quality, and buy fresh. Mediocre quality will yield mediocre results.

Freezing food is not difficult, but there are ways of freezing that produce superior results. Specific methods are discussed in the relevant chapters and in the Dictionary. Here are some general rules.

**CHILL FIRST.** Make sure the food is cold before you freeze it. This allows it to freeze faster, reducing the amount of condensation and the amount of drip loss during defrosting.

**Condensation** is the moisture that collects on the surface of the food if it's warm when you put it in the freezer; when you defrost it, the excess water will make the food soggy and tasteless.

**Drip loss** is the term for leakage of natural moisture that occurs during defrosting. Water expands as it turns into ice, causing the food fibers to splinter. This is what causes limp or soggy texture after defrosting. But if the food is chilled before freezing, the ice crystals that form will be smaller, causing less damage to fibers, and less drip loss. The result is better texture and flavor, especially with uncooked meat.

Chill cooked foods uncovered; then cover and seal before freezing to prevent another source of condensation.

**FREEZE SMALL.** The smaller the item, the quicker it will freeze. Whenever possible, freeze portion-size quantities of meat and fish (up to 8 ounces). Store other foods in quantities that suit the size of your household. For example, freeze soup in pint-size containers rather than quart-size if you have a small family.

**Open freezing** is a way of handling small items so they don't freeze in a solid block—gnocchi, Brussels sprouts, choux paste puffs, chocolate truffles. Simply arrange the items with space between them on a baking sheet, and place the tray in the freezer. When the food is frozen, transfer it to a freezer bag, or wrap each item separately and then seal in a freezer bag. You can do the same thing with purées, sauce bases, tomato paste, and other liquids by freezing them first in ice cube trays and then transferring the cubes to freezer bags or containers.

**WRAP WELL.** The goal is to isolate the food from the atmosphere of the freezer, sealing the wrapping tightly to keep out as much air as possible.

Ordinary plastic wrap is too thin and can crack in the freezer. Use heavy-duty or microwave plastic wrap, and use heavy-duty plastic freezer bags rather than the everyday kind. (If you're going to defrost or reheat in a microwave, use microwave plastic bags.) Wrap individual items such as pieces of cheese, loaves of bread, and individual fish fillets in microwave plastic wrap first. Then overwrap them with freezer paper or aluminum foil, or place them in a plastic freezer bag. Seal the package well, squeezing out as much air as possible, and label it clearly.

For liquids, use freezer jars or plastic containers. Remember that liquid expands by over 10 percent when it freezes, so leave ½ to 1 inch of headroom when you are freezing soups, stews, or purées in a rigid plastic container. After the food has cooled, place a layer of plastic wrap directly on the surface; then put the top on the container.

Food that hasn't been properly wrapped will suffer **freezer burn**, which means it is dry, stringy, and may have an off taste. This occurs more often in self-defrosting freezers than in others because the freezer environment is drier. Meat in particular becomes dry and tough. It is still edible, but should be used in a dish cooked in moisture, such as a stew, rather than for grilling or roasting.

**WATCH THE FREEZER TEMPERATURE.** The temperature should remain constant at 0°F (−18°C). Keep a freezer thermometer in the freezer so you can check it periodically. If you are placing a large quantity of food in the freezer at one time, turn the thermostat to its coldest setting until the food is frozen.

**FOLLOW DEFROSTING RECOMMENDATIONS.** These vary from food to food. In general, it's best to defrost in the refrigerator or in a microwave oven. However, large items defrost unevenly in the microwave. With a roast or a family-size quantity of soup, it's best to partially defrost at room temperature (2 hours for a 3-pound block), then transfer the food to the microwave to finish the defrosting. Or you can partially defrost in the microwave and then finish defrosting in the refrigerator.

Liquids can be defrosted under running water. Boil them for 3 minutes after defrosting, to kill any bacteria.

Most foods should be left in their freezer packaging while defrosting. The exceptions are preparations that have a crust or a crispy topping (this includes a number of desserts) that might turn soggy from the condensation that accumulates under the wrapping.

**COOK DEFROSTED FOODS SOON.** Do not let defrosted foods sit around. Microorganisms (yeasts, molds, and bacteria) multiply at temperatures above 50°F.

When I tuck a napkin under my chin, I want an excellent meal. It matters little if the scallops came out of the sea that day or out of my freezer, so long as they taste fresh. If I see raspberries in January I don't crave them unless they promise delicious flavor—I'd rather defrost some fresh-tasting raspberry purée made from last July's crop. For the discriminating home cook the preparation of a meal can begin in a freezer compartment as well as in a market. Sorting through packages of frozen foods doesn't fire up my imagination the way browsing the market stands does, but my freezer allows me to enjoy my own at-home mini-market of both prepared and raw ingredients. With a freezer we can preserve the freshness of the marketplace, prepare our own frozen "convenience" foods, and control the quality—the amount of fat, salt, or sugar, for example—of our meals. And we can improvise meals that utilize a larger repertoire of ingredients than is available at any given time in the market.

Note:

▪ The names of "master recipes"—those that form the base for subsequent recipes—appear in boldface type. See, for example, Chicken and Vegetable Soup, page 20.

▪ The point at which a recipe can be frozen is indicated by the symbol ▨. Instructions for freezing follow the recipe.

# SOUPS

For cooks who are uncomfortable improvising, the freezer can be a breakthrough—especially with soups. You can use your freezer to store bases for a variety of soups, and you can use it to store the ingredients for others.

For example, in this chapter I provide instructions for making four soups —chicken, potato, avocado, and fish—that are complete recipes in themselves but also serve as bases for a variety of other soups: the chicken base can be used in an icy shrimp, coconut, and coriander soup; the potato soup can be transformed into cream of watercress.

Since it takes only a little more time, it makes sense to make large batches of soup and freeze half. When asparagus is in season, don't let a bit go to waste. Prepare plenty of asparagus soup, and freeze what you don't use now. It'll taste even better when you pull it out of the freezer in the dead of winter!

And when you're preparing a vegetable side dish for dinner, make some extra. Steam the whole head of broccoli, and freeze what you don't need, as is or puréed. You'll be ready to defrost it and proceed with broccoli soup when the mood hits. Soon you'll be improvising with the ingredients you have tucked away.

Say you have some puréed broccoli—or carrots, or squash—in the freezer. Here's all you need to do: Defrost the vegetable and add liquid—about twice as much liquid as purée. It can be all-purpose broth (also stored in the freezer), or milk, or cream, or a combination. For a cream of carrot soup, add stock and a little cream if it's to be served hot, more cream and less stock if it's to be served chilled. If cream is too rich for you, substitute milk for all or part of the cream. Try combining purées for more complex flavors.

Never again will you scowl about leftover vegetables. You'll just freeze them to use later in a glorious, satisfying soup.

Because it's more elegant and adds a little drama, I like to arrange the garnish—the solid ingredients—in the individual soup bowls and then pour the broth into the bowls at the table. It's also a way of ensuring that everyone receives equal amounts!

# FREEZING AND DEFROSTING SOUPS

**MEAT AND VEGETABLES IN BROTH.** Soups that are a combination of meat or poultry and vegetables in a broth fare best when the solid and liquid elements are frozen separately. The chunks of meat and vegetables won't become waterlogged, and they won't fall apart when you defrost them. Freezing them separately also gives you the option of using them in other preparations, such as a chicken or vegetable hash; and then the broth can be garnished with other ingredients also.

Strain any chunks of meat and vegetable from the broth. Chill the broth, uncovered, in the refrigerator, allowing approximately 1 hour per pint of liquid. Then remove and discard any fat that has risen to the surface. Place the broth in plastic containers, leaving ½ inch of headroom. Cover, label, and freeze for up to 6 months. Or you can fill freezer bags three-quarters full, squeeze out as much air as possible, and freeze.

Defrost broths in the refrigerator or microwave oven, or under cold running water; or reheat the broth in a saucepan from its frozen state. All soups should be served as soon as possible after defrosting.

Chill the reserved meat until it is completely cold, at least 1 hour. Then place it in a freezer bag, squeeze out as much air as possible, and seal tightly. Freeze for up to 3 months.

Separate cooked poultry from the skin and bones. (Discard the skin and freeze the bones for use in All-Purpose Broth, page 222.) Chill the meat, uncovered, in the refrigerator; then place it in a freezer bag and freeze for up to 6 months.

Refrigerate the reserved vegetables, uncovered, until chilled—about 1 hour per cup. Then place them in a small plastic container or freezer bag, seal, and freeze for up to 3 months.

Defrost meat, poultry, and vegetables, still wrapped, in the refrigerator, at room temperature, or on the defrost setting of a microwave oven.

**VEGETABLE OR BEAN SOUPS.** Though the finished soups freeze well, I find it more convenient to freeze just the soup base (the soup before the addition of the total amount of liquid). It takes up less freezer space than a finished soup, and leaves you with a versatile ingredient that can also be used to make vegetable pancakes or soufflés (see pages 182, 185–187).

Chill the soup base and freeze in freezer bags or plastic containers for up to 6 months. Defrost in the refrigerator, at room temperature, or in the microwave oven (approximately 5 minutes a pint). Reheat as soon as possible after defrosting, thinned to the proper consistency as directed in the recipe. If it contains milk or cream, do not let it boil.

**VELOUTÉ SOUPS.** Velouté soups (and velouté sauces as well) begin with a mixture of butter and flour called *roux*, and are finished with cream and butter, although I substitute milk and omit the butter. Add chunky ingredients to it, and a velouté becomes chowder. When thickened with both *roux* and puréed ingredients, it becomes bisque.

Make the Velouté Soup Base (page 37) and freeze it before adding milk or cream. Defrosted velouté base often looks curdled, but once reheated and finished with milk or cream, it will have the elegant texture that makes these soups so pleasing.

To freeze a completed velouté, chowder, or bisque, place in plastic bags or containers for up to 3 months. When reheating the soup, be very careful not to let the soup boil or you risk curdling.

# CHICKEN AND VEGETABLE SOUP

You'll find that it's easiest to use quartered birds for this chicken soup. If your butcher can sell you the feet, add them—they contribute wonderful flavor and richness to the broth.

2 *boiling chickens (about 4 pounds each), quartered*

10 *cups cold water*

4 *medium carrots, thinly sliced (about 3 cups)*

2 *large onions, finely diced (about 2 cups)*

1 *small bunch celery, thinly sliced (2½ to 3 cups)*

2 *large leeks, green tops and white bottoms separated*

½ *tablespoon whole black peppercorns*

6 *bay leaves*

4 *sprigs fresh thyme, 1½ teaspoons fresh thyme leaves, or ½ teaspoon dried*

1 *tablespoon salt*

1 *tablespoon unsalted butter*

SERVES 8

1. Combine the chicken quarters and the water in a 5-quart stockpot. Cover and bring to a boil over high heat. Reduce the heat to low, and skim off the scum that has accumulated on the surface. Remove the chicken breast pieces and set them aside.

2. Add 2 cups of the carrots, 1 cup of the onions, 2 cups of the celery, the green leek tops, and the peppercorns, bay leaves, thyme, and salt. Cover and simmer for 45 minutes. Then uncover, add the chicken breasts, and continue to cook for another 25 minutes.

3. Meanwhile, slice the white part of the leeks into ¼-inch rounds; you should have about 1 cup. Wash well to remove any sand. Melt the butter in a medium-size saucepan over medium heat; add the leeks and the remaining carrots, onions, and celery. Cover and cook gently until the vegetables are soft, about 5 minutes. Set them aside.

4. Remove the chicken from the liquid and place the pieces on a platter. Strain the liquid through a fine-mesh strainer, discarding the herbs, spices, and vegetables. Skim and discard any fat from the surface of the strained broth.

5. Remove and discard the chicken skin. Remove the meat from the bones, dice it, and set aside. Place the bones in a freezer container and freeze to use in All-Purpose Broth (page 222). ▨

6. Immediately before serving, heat the broth, covered, over high heat. Heat the chicken and reserved vegetables, covered, in a 375°F oven. Decorate each bowl with some vegetables and chicken. Pour the hot broth into a pitcher or soup tureen, and ladle it into the bowls at the table.

▨ To freeze, allow all or part of the chicken meat, broth, and vegetables to cool to room temperature. Refrigerate until thoroughly chilled, then freeze in separate containers for up to 6 months. The defrosted soup can be finished as in Step 6, or as one of the two variations that follow; each calls for half of this recipe.

# SAFFRON CHICKEN AND MUSSEL SOUP

This Mediterranean combination of shellfish and chicken could be Spanish, French, Italian, or Moroccan. Accompanied by a simple green salad, some robust cheese, and crusty bread, this soup can make a meal.

The main ingredients should be arranged in soup bowls and the broth poured into the bowls at the table to ensure that everyone gets the proper mixture of all the ingredients.

½ recipe **Chicken and Vegetable Soup (page 20), frozen or fresh: 3 cups broth, 2 cups diced chicken, 1 cup diced vegetables**

½ cup dry white wine

1 teaspoon saffron threads

1 tablespoon finely minced garlic

**Dash of Pernod**

12 mussels, scrubbed and debearded

1½ teaspoons chopped fresh tarragon leaves, or ¼ teaspoon dried

SERVES 4

1. Defrost the broth, chicken, and vegetables if frozen.
2. Preheat the oven to 375°F.
3. Place the chicken and vegetables in a casserole, cover, and bake for 20 minutes.
4. Meanwhile, combine the wine, saffron, garlic, and Pernod in a 3-quart soup pot and place over high heat. If you are using dried tarragon, add it now. Bring to a boil and cook 1 minute. Add the broth, cover, and bring to a boil again. Add the mussels, cover, and cook until they open, about 3 minutes. Discard any shell that refuses to open.
5. Remove the chicken and vegetables from the oven and arrange them in soup bowls. Remove the mussels from the broth and arrange them around the chicken. Sprinkle with fresh tarragon if you are using it. Pour the broth into a pitcher or soup tureen, and ladle it into the bowls at the table.

# CHILLED CHICKEN, SHRIMP, AND COCONUT SOUP

I'm always pleased when I am able to evoke the flavors of an ethnic cuisine. Coconut and curry—touchstone ingredients in Southeast Asian cooking—identify this nontraditional soup.

Sometimes a chilled chicken soup becomes gelatinous. Simply place it in a blender or processor and pulse until it smooths out.

½ recipe Chicken and Vegetable Soup (page 20), frozen or fresh: 3 cups broth, 2 cups diced chicken, 1 cup diced vegetables

1 tablespoon curry powder

½ teaspoon cayenne pepper

8 cloves garlic, thinly sliced

2 cups unsweetened coconut milk (available in Asian markets)

2 tablespoons rice wine vinegar

2 tablespoons dark sesame oil

8 to 12 jumbo shrimp, shelled and deveined

⅓ cup coarsely chopped cilantro leaves

**1.** Defrost the broth, chicken, and vegetables if frozen. Toss the chicken and vegetables together in a bowl, cover, and set aside in the refrigerator. Place the broth in a soup tureen and set it aside.

**2.** Combine the curry, cayenne, garlic, coconut milk, and vinegar in a medium-size saucepan over medium heat. Whisk well, bring to a boil, and cook 1 minute. Add this mixture to the reserved broth, and place the tureen in the refrigerator. Chill for at least 1 hour.

**3.** Warm the sesame oil in a medium-size skillet over low heat. Add the shrimp, cover, and cook gently for about 5 minutes or until pink and opaque. Transfer the shrimp to a bowl, and place in the refrigerator to chill for at least 1 hour.

**4.** To serve, arrange chicken, vegetables, and shrimp in individual soup bowls, and garnish with the chopped cilantro. Ladle the broth from the tureen at the table.

SERVES 4 TO 6

# POTATO SOUP

Potato starch becomes sticky and elastic when it's beaten—if you've ever attempted mashed potatoes in a food processor, you know what I mean. But once frozen and defrosted, the starch in potatoes loses this quality. So don't be afraid to blend this potato soup when it comes out of the freezer.

Potato soup can be the basis of many superb soups. You might want to triple or quadruple this recipe and freeze the soup in quart containers.

5 *medium leeks*

3 *tablespoons flavorless cooking oil*

12 *cups All-Purpose Broth (page 222) or canned low-sodium chicken broth*

2½ *pounds potatoes, coarsely chopped (about 6 cups)*

1 *teaspoon nutmeg*

1½ *teaspoons salt, or as desired*

½ *teaspoon ground white pepper*

**TO SERVE**

¾ *cup sour cream*

¼ *cup chopped fresh chives*

SERVES 9

1. Trim the leeks, and remove the dark green tops (reserve them for another use). Slice the white part into ½-inch rounds. Rinse thoroughly, and set aside on a plate.

2. Heat the oil in a 5-quart pot over medium heat. Add the leeks and cook, stirring, for 5 minutes.

3. Add the broth, potatoes, nutmeg, salt, and white pepper. Raise the heat to high, cover, and bring to a boil. Then reduce the heat to low, uncover, and simmer for 30 minutes.

4. Remove the pot from the heat, and purée the soup in batches in a blender or food processor. ⊠

5. Transfer the puréed soup to a saucepan and reheat, covered, over low heat. To serve, place a generous dollop of sour cream in the bottom of each soup bowl and sprinkle it with chopped chives. Pour the piping hot soup into a tureen or pitcher and serve it at the table.

⊠ To freeze all or part of this recipe, allow the potato soup to cool to room temperature. Refrigerate until thoroughly chilled, then freeze for up to 6 months. The defrosted soup can be finished as in Step 5, or as one of the three variations that follow; each calls for a third of this recipe.

# CREAM OF WATERCRESS SOUP

⅓ *recipe (3 cups) Potato Soup (page 23), frozen or fresh*

1 *tablespoon flavorless oil*

1 *tablespoon minced garlic*

3 *small bunches watercress, tough stems removed (1½ cups)*

1 *cup buttermilk*

SERVES 4 TO 5

1. Defrost the potato soup if frozen.
2. Heat the oil in a 1-quart saucepan over medium heat. Add the garlic and cook for 1 minute. Then add the watercress and potato soup. Cover and bring to a boil. Add the buttermilk, reduce the heat, and cook for another minute without letting the soup boil.
3. Remove the pan from the heat and transfer the soup to a blender or food processor. Blend until smooth. Serve immediately.

# CREAM OF TURNIP SOUP

⅓ *recipe (3 cups) Potato Soup (page 23), frozen or fresh*

1 *cup diced cooked turnips*

1 *cup milk*

SERVES 4

1. Defrost the potato soup if frozen.
2. Place the potato soup in a blender or food processor, and add the turnips. Purée until smooth.
3. Transfer the purée to a saucepan, cover, and bring to a boil over medium heat. Add the milk, and heat through but do not boil. Serve immediately.

# CHILLED CREAM OF POTATO SOUP

⅓ *recipe (3 cups) Potato Soup (page 23), frozen or fresh*

1 *cup buttermilk*

½ *cup sour cream*

SERVES 4 TO 5

1. Defrost the potato soup if frozen, or prepare from scratch and chill thoroughly.
2. Combine the soup, buttermilk, and sour cream in a blender or food processor, and blend on high speed for 5 minutes. Serve in chilled soup bowls.

# CHILLED PURÉE OF AVOCADO SOUP

Take advantage of the opportunity when avocados are plentiful and cheap—puréed, they freeze without losing any of their subtropical richness.

The exotic colors and textures of this soup will make even a simple meal festive.

2 tablespoons olive oil

1 medium onion, peeled and coarsely chopped

3 ripe or overripe avocados, peeled, seeded, and coarsely chopped

5 cups All-Purpose Broth (page 222) or canned low-sodium chicken broth

1 teaspoon salt, or as desired

½ teaspoon ground white pepper

¼ cup fresh lime juice

TO SERVE

6 thin slices lime

6 thin slices tomato

6 tablespoons plain yogurt

6 teaspoons finely minced red onion

3 tablespoons finely chopped cilantro leaves

1. Heat the oil in a 2-quart saucepan over medium heat. Add the onions and cook, stirring, for 10 minutes or until soft.

2. Add the avocados, broth, salt, and white pepper. Cover, raise the heat to high, and bring to a boil. Reduce the heat and cook for 5 minutes.

3. Remove the pan from the heat and transfer the soup to a food processor or blender. Add the lime juice and purée until smooth.

4. Place the soup in a plastic container and allow it to cool to room temperature. Then refrigerate until chilled, at least 2 hours. (To speed up the chilling process, place the soup in a bowl—metal if possible—and set it in a larger bowl filled with ice. Stir until chilled.) ▨

5. Ladle the chilled soup into chilled soup bowls, and decorate the surface of each with slices of lime and tomato, a dollop of yogurt, 1 teaspoon red onion, and ½ tablespoon chopped cilantro.

SERVES 6

▨ Freeze soup for up to 6 months. The defrosted soup can be finished as in Step 5, or as one of the two variations that follow; each calls for half of this recipe.

# MINTED AVOCADO AND PEA SOUP

½ recipe (3 cups) Chilled
  Purée of Avocado Soup
  (page 25), frozen or fresh
¾ cup cooked fresh peas or
  defrosted frozen peas
1 tablespoon chopped fresh
  mint leaves
½ cup milk

1. Defrost the avocado soup if frozen.
2. Combine the soup, peas, mint, and milk in a blender or food processor, and purée until smooth.
3. Transfer the soup to a pitcher or tureen, and refrigerate for 2 hours or until well chilled.

SERVES 3 TO 4

# CHILLED AVOCADO AND CRAB BISQUE

½ recipe (3 cups) Chilled
  Purée of Avocado Soup
  (page 25), frozen or fresh
¾ cup bottled clam juice
½ cup milk
1 teaspoon minced garlic
¼ pound crabmeat, flaked

1. Defrost the avocado soup if frozen.
2. Combine the soup, clam juice, milk, and garlic in a blender or food processor, and purée until smooth.
3. Transfer the soup to a tureen, stir in the crabmeat, and refrigerate until well chilled.

SERVES 3 TO 4

## VEGETABLE SOUPS

Ideally, vegetables should be completely cooked without liquid before they are turned into soup. This breaks down the cellulose fiber in the vegetable, releasing the sweetness in root vegetables such as carrots, turnips, rutabagas, and celeriac, releasing the flavor in green vegetables such as broccoli, asparagus, and zucchini, and concentrating flavor in leafy vegetables such as spinach, sorrel, and chard. The freezer allows you to keep on hand a supply of leftover cooked vegetables, ready to become soup.

Vegetables cooked in a little fat or oil taste better, when defrosted, than those that have been steamed or boiled. If you have leftover steamed or boiled vegetables, simply cook them gently in a little butter or oil to develop the flavor before you use them in a soup.

The technique for preparing fresh vegetable soups is simple. First cook some onion in a little butter or oil. Add the vegetable of choice—the ingredient that gives the soup its name—and sauté it to intensify the flavor. Add some liquid—broth or milk—and simmer the soup for 10 minutes. You can then either purée the soup or leave the vegetables chunky. You can finish it with cream, or not. You can serve it immediately—or freeze it for another day.

# CREAM OF ASPARAGUS SOUP

Asparagus is another favorite that has a short season. I try always to have some asparagus purée in the freezer for a soup, pudding, or soufflé base. If you freeze some yourself, you can extend the season.

2 tablespoons unsalted butter

1 large onion, coarsely chopped (about 1 cup)

3 pounds asparagus, trimmed, cooked or uncooked

3 cups All-Purpose Broth (page 222) or canned low-sodium chicken broth

½ teaspoon salt

¼ teaspoon freshly ground black pepper

4 cups milk or cream, or a combination

SERVES 8

1. Melt the butter in a 3-quart soup pot over medium heat. Add the onions, cover, and cook, stirring occasionally, for 10 minutes or until the onions are soft.

2. Add the asparagus and continue to cook, covered, another 15 minutes.

3. Add the broth, salt, and pepper. Cover and bring to a boil. Then reduce the heat and cook for 15 minutes.

4. Transfer the mixture to a food processor or blender, and purée until smooth. Strain the purée through a large-mesh strainer to remove any stringy fibers. ⊠

5. Place the purée over medium heat and add the milk and cream. Cover and bring to a boil. Reduce the heat to low and cook, covered, for 5 minutes. Serve piping hot.

⊠ To freeze, allow the puréed asparagus to cool to room temperature. Refrigerate until thoroughly chilled, then freeze for up to 6 months. To serve, defrost and finish as in Step 5.

# MUSHROOM SOUP

This full-bodied soup conjures up flavors of the forest, and although good anytime, is especially satisfying in the fall. It can be made with uncooked mushrooms, cooked mushroom slices, or Mushroom Duxelles (page 240).

¼ cup (½ stick) unsalted butter

2 large onions, finely minced (about 2 cups)

3 cups cooked sliced mushrooms, or 1½ pounds sliced raw mushrooms

1 cup dry sherry or Madeira

2 tablespoons freshly chopped thyme leaves, or 1 teaspoon dried

1 teaspoon salt

Freshly ground black pepper to taste

2 tablespoons flour

4 cups milk

1 cup whipping cream

SERVES 6

1. Melt the butter in a 2-quart soup pot over medium heat. Add the onions, cover, and cook, stirring occasionally, for 10 minutes or until the onions are soft.

2. Add the mushrooms and continue to cook, covered, another 10 minutes. Then add the sherry, thyme, salt, and pepper. Sprinkle the mixture with the flour and cook, stirring, about 1 minute. ▨

3. Add the milk and cream, cover, and simmer an additional 10 minutes (do not let the soup come to a rolling boil or the milk will curdle). Serve immediately, piping hot.

**Mushroom Barley Soup:** Add 6 tablespoons uncooked barley along with the milk and cream. Simmer gently until the barley is soft, about 30 minutes.

▨ To freeze, allow the soup to cool to room temperature. Refrigerate until thoroughly chilled, then freeze for up to 6 months. To serve, defrost and finish as in Step 3.

# CORN CHOWDER

The natural sugar in corn quickly turns to starch after the vegetable has been harvested, so very often frozen corn is sweeter than fresh. For soup making you can use either fresh corn or frozen, cooked or uncooked. Cooked corn will result in a slightly sweeter soup; uncooked corn will make the soup "cornier." In the summer, when corn's at its sweetest, cook up a big batch of this filling chowder.

3 tablespoons unsalted butter

2 large onions, peeled and coarsely chopped (about 2 cups)

4 cups corn kernels

3 cups All-Purpose Broth (page 222) or canned low-sodium chicken broth

½ teaspoon salt

¼ teaspoon ground mace or nutmeg

Freshly ground black pepper to taste

½ teaspoon chopped fresh rosemary leaves, or a pinch of dried

4 cups milk or cream, or a combination

SERVES 6

1. Melt the butter in a 2-quart soup pot over medium heat. Add the onions, cover, and cook, stirring occasionally, until they are soft, about 10 minutes.

2. Add the corn and continue to cook, stirring occasionally, another 8 to 10 minutes.

3. Add the broth, salt, mace, and pepper. Cover, reduce the heat slightly, and cook for 20 minutes.

4. Transfer the mixture to a blender or food processor, and purée until smooth. ▨

5. Return the mixture to the soup pot, place it over medium heat, and add the rosemary and milk. Cover and bring to a boil. Then reduce heat to low and cook 5 minutes. Serve piping hot.

**Succotash Soup:** Add 2 cups cooked lima beans along with the milk.

▨ To freeze, allow the puréed corn to cool to room temperature. Refrigerate until thoroughly chilled, then freeze for up to 6 months. To serve, defrost and finish as in Step 5.

# CREAM OF BROCCOLI SOUP

Anise-flavored Pernod and nutty-flavored walnut oil add depth to this robust soup. Both ingredients are optional, but if you skip one, skip both—they work together.

2 tablespoons unsalted butter

1 large onion, coarsely chopped (about 1 cup)

1½ pounds broccoli, cooked or uncooked, stems peeled, coarsely chopped (about 4 cups)

1 teaspoon salt

2 capfuls Pernod (optional)

5 cups All-Purpose Broth (page 222) or canned low-sodium chicken broth, or water

3 cups milk or cream, or a combination

⅓ cup walnut oil (optional)

SERVES 8

1. Melt the butter in a 6-quart soup pot over medium heat. Add the onions, cover, and cook, stirring occasionally, until they are soft, about 10 minutes. Then add the broccoli, salt, and Pernod. Continue to cook, covered, stirring, for another 15 minutes.

2. Add the stock, cover, raise the heat to high, and bring to a boil. Then reduce the heat to low and simmer for 15 minutes.

3. Transfer the mixture, in batches, to a food processor or blender, and purée until smooth. ▨

4. Combine the purée, cream and milk, and walnut oil in a soup pot. Cover and bring to a boil. Then reduce the heat and cook for 5 minutes. Serve piping hot.

▨ To freeze, allow the puréed broccoli to cool to room temperature. Refrigerate until thoroughly chilled, then freeze for up to 6 months. To serve, defrost and finish as in Step 4.

# CREAM OF CELERY SOUP

Celeriac (root celery) is the best choice for this soup because it has a stronger celery flavor than the stalk variety. Cooked celeriac takes well to freezing, sacrificing none of its flavor or smoothness. Decorate the hot soup with paper-thin slices of cooked stalk celery.

1 medium bulb celeriac
(about 1½ pounds)

¼ cup (½ stick) unsalted butter

1 large onion, coarsely chopped (about 1 cup)

3 cups All-Purpose Broth (page 222) or canned low-sodium chicken broth

½ teaspoon salt

½ teaspoon celery seeds

2 sprigs fresh tarragon, or ½ teaspoon dried

Freshly ground black pepper to taste

6 celery stalks, thinly sliced (about 2½ cups)

3 cups milk

SERVES 8

1. Remove and discard the celeriac tops. Using a small knife, remove and discard the black skin. Dice the white pulp into cubes roughly 1 inch square; you should have about 5 cups. If you're not using it immediately, place the celeriac in acidulated water (1 cup water with 1 teaspoon lemon juice) and refrigerate it for up to 1 hour.

2. Melt 2 tablespoons of the butter in a 2-quart soup pot over medium heat. Add the onions, cover, and cook, stirring occasionally, 8 to 10 minutes or until they are soft. Drain the celeriac, if necessary, and add it to the pot. Cover and cook for 20 minutes.

3. Add the broth, salt, celery seeds, tarragon, and pepper. Bring to a boil. Then cover, reduce the heat, and simmer for another 25 minutes.

4. Transfer the soup to a food processor or blender, and purée until smooth. ▧

5. Melt the remaining 2 tablespoons butter in a 2-quart pot over medium heat. Add the sliced celery and cook, stirring, for 5 minutes.

6. Add the purée and the milk, and bring almost to a boil. Then reduce the heat to low and simmer for 5 minutes (do not let the soup boil or the milk may curdle). Serve piping hot.

▧ To freeze, allow the puréed celeriac to cool to room temperature. Refrigerate until thoroughly chilled, then freeze for up to 6 months. To serve, defrost and finish as in Steps 5 and 6.

# CREAM OF CHESTNUT SOUP WITH BACON AND APPLES

Chestnuts and apples make us think of winter, but coriander and nutmeg add a surprising flavor that we associate with food from warmer climates.

2½ pounds fresh chestnuts; or 1½ pounds bottled or canned cooked chestnuts, drained; or 1 can (15½ ounces) unsweetened chestnut purée

½ pound bacon

2 large onions, coarsely chopped (about 2 cups)

2 cups All-Purpose Broth (page 222) or canned low-sodium chicken broth

½ teaspoon ground coriander

½ teaspoon ground nutmeg

¼ teaspoon ground white pepper

3 cups milk

2 green apples, such as Granny Smith or Pippin

SERVES 6 TO 7

1. If you are using fresh chestnuts, preheat the oven to 350°F. Make a small X in the shell on the flat side of each nut, and place the nuts on a baking sheet. Bake for 20 minutes. Allow to cool slightly, then peel off the shells and the inner brown skin. (Don't let them get too cool, or it will be difficult to remove the inner skins.)

2. Finely chop the bacon. Place a 2-quart soup pot over medium heat, add the bacon, and cook, stirring occasionally, for 5 minutes. Add the onions and cook, stirring occasionally, for another 10 minutes or until the onions are translucent. Remove the pot from the stove, drain the bacon and onions through a strainer, and discard the fat.

3. Return the onions and bacon to the pot and place it over medium heat. Add the chestnuts, broth, coriander, nutmeg, and white pepper. Cover, raise the heat to high, and bring to a boil. Reduce the heat to low and cook for 20 minutes.

4. Transfer the soup to a food processor or blender, and purée until smooth. ▨

5. Place in a saucepan and add the milk. Cover, and place over medium heat.

6. Peel and core the apples, and chop the fruit into ¼-inch pieces. When the soup has come to a boil, add the apples and cook another 2 minutes. Serve piping hot.

▨ To freeze, allow the puréed chestnuts to cool to room temperature. Refrigerate until thoroughly chilled, then freeze for up to 6 months. To serve, defrost and finish as in Steps 5 and 6.

# PURÉE OF GARLIC SOUP

When garlic is cooked for a long time, it surrenders its bite and becomes mellow and nutty. Finished with milk (cream is even better), this is one of the most elegant soups imaginable. To serve it as a main course, garnish the soup with poached eggs and sautéed diced vegetables.

1 *pound garlic (about 8 heads)*

3 *tablespoons olive oil*

2 *large onions, coarsely chopped (about 2 cups)*

3 *cups All-Purpose Broth (page 222) or canned low-sodium chicken broth*

1 *lemon, cut in half*

4 *bay leaves*

4 *sprigs thyme, 1 tablespoon chopped fresh thyme leaves, or ½ teaspoon dried*

4 *cups milk*

SERVES 8

1. Separate the heads of garlic into cloves, but don't bother to peel them.

2. Heat the oil in a 2-quart soup pot over medium heat. Add the garlic and cook, stirring occasionally, for 15 to 20 minutes or until the skins start to turn golden. Then add the onions and cook until soft, another 5 minutes.

3. Add the broth, then the lemon halves, bay leaves, and thyme. Raise the heat to high and bring to a boil. Lower the heat to medium and simmer, covered, for 30 minutes.

4. Remove and discard the lemon halves. Transfer the soup to a food processor or blender, and purée. Strain the purée through a sieve or pass it through a food mill. ▨

5. Place the garlic purée in a saucepan over medium heat. Add the milk, cover, and bring to a boil. Immediately reduce the heat to low and simmer, covered, for 10 minutes. Serve piping hot.

▨ To freeze, allow the puréed garlic to cool to room temperature. Refrigerate until thoroughly chilled, then freeze for up to 6 months. To serve, defrost and finish as in Step 5.

## BEAN SOUPS

Most dried beans, with the exception of lentils, require long cooking even after they have been soaked overnight. That means that preparing a simple bean soup takes several hours. So save yourself time by making some extra for the freezer. Cooked beans are also handy to have around for making pancakes (page 181). And when you are cooking a bean side dish, prepare some extra beans to freeze for later use.

## GARBANZO BEAN SOUP

My friends and I often make a meal of this Italian country mainstay, with nothing more than good bread and a vinegary salad alongside. It's the most comforting of soups after a trying day.

2½ cups dried garbanzo
    beans

3 tablespoons olive oil

1 large onion, finely diced
    (about 1 cup)

1 small carrot, finely diced
    (about ½ cup)

1 stalk celery, finely diced
    (about ½ cup)

9 cups All-Purpose Broth
    (page 222) or canned
    low-sodium chicken broth

¼ cup fresh lemon juice

TO SERVE

⅔ cup sour cream

3 tablespoons chopped
    fresh dill

SERVES 9

1. Place the garbanzo beans in a bowl, cover with 3 inches of water, and soak for at least 8 hours, or up to 10. Or for a quick-cooking method, cover the beans with boiling water and set aside to soak for 1 hour; then continue with the recipe.

2. Place the oil in a 2-quart soup pot over medium heat, add the onions, and cook, stirring occasionally, for 5 minutes. Then add the carrots and celery and cook another 5 minutes.

3. Add the drained beans and 6 cups of the broth. Cover, raise the heat to high, and bring to a boil. Then reduce the heat to low and cook, covered, for 1½ hours.

4. Transfer the beans and liquid to a food processor or blender, and purée until smooth. ▨

5. Combine the purée, remaining 3 cups broth, and lemon juice in a 1-quart pot. Cover, bring to a boil, and then reduce the heat. Simmer for 5 minutes. Place a dollop of sour cream in each soup bowl and sprinkle with some chopped fresh dill. Pour the piping-hot soup into the bowls at the table.

⊠ To freeze, allow the puréed beans to cool to room temperature. Refrigerate until thoroughly chilled, then freeze for up to 6 months. To serve, defrost and finish as in Step 5.

# WHITE BEAN, CHARD, AND PANCETTA SOUP

This soup is a traditional Tuscan one, and is as beautiful to look at as it is satisfying to eat.

If you partially freeze the pancetta first, it will be much easier to dice.

½ *pound pancetta (Italian bacon), finely diced*

1 *large onion, finely diced (about 1¼ cups)*

1 *tablespoon finely minced garlic*

2½ *cups dried white beans (about 1 pound)*

5 *cups All-Purpose Broth (page 222) or canned low-sodium chicken broth*

2 *tablespoons tomato paste*

1 *tablespoon chopped fresh thyme leaves, or 1 teaspoon dried*

½ *pound Swiss chard*

3 *cups water*

6 *tablespoons olive oil*

*Juice of 3 lemons*

*Salt and freshly ground black pepper to taste*

*Grated Parmesan cheese*

1. Place the pancetta in a 5-quart ovenproof pot over medium heat and cook, stirring occasionally, for 5 minutes. Then add the onions and garlic and continue to cook, stirring occasionally, another 5 minutes or until the onions have softened.

2. Add the beans, broth, tomato paste, and thyme. Cover the pot tightly and place it in the oven. Turn the oven on to 350°F, and cook the mixture for 1½ hours or until the beans are soft. ⊠

3. Remove the center stem from the chard leaves, and cut it crosswise into ¼-inch-thick slices. Coarsely chop the leaves. You should have 1½ cups stems and leaves, tightly packed.

4. Place the bean mixture in a soup pot, and add the chard stems and leaves. Add the water, olive oil, and lemon juice. Cover the pot, place it over medium heat, and cook until heated through. Add salt and pepper as desired.

5. Serve the soup piping hot, and offer grated cheese on the side.

SERVES 10

(continued)

White Bean, Chard, and Pancetta Soup   (continued)

⊠ To freeze, allow the cooked beans to cool to room temperature. Refrigerate until thoroughly chilled, then freeze for up to 6 months. To serve, defrost and finish as in Steps 3, 4, and 5.

# VELOUTÉ SOUPS

Velouté—please excuse the lapse into French—means velvety, and, in culinary parlance, can refer to soups or sauces made in the classic way: thickened with a combination of flour and butter called *roux*, and then thinned with some cream and enriched with a nut of butter. But the reputation of veloutés has suffered because of dietary concerns about fat consumption and, quite frankly, due to the heavy-handedness of certain chefs.

The best veloutés are lightly thickened broths that are cooked for a long time, eliminating the flour taste of the *roux* and concentrating the flavor of the broth. I find that finishing a richly flavored velouté with cream and butter is like gilding the lily—the cream and butter actually prevent us from tasting the complexities of the rich broth. (Here's a rare example of something healthier being tastier, too.) Instead, I like to finish the broth with milk and forget the butter enrichment.

Thickened broths become thicker when frozen and defrosted. Freeze the thick broth and add the milk after defrosting when you reheat the soup to prepare a variation.

When chunky ingredients are added to it, a velouté becomes chowder. When thickened with both *roux* and pureéd ingredients it becomes bisque. Generally I freeze a velouté before adding milk, but you should do the convenient thing. Be warned that defrosted veloutés often looked curdled, but once reheated and finished with milk or cream, they will have the elegant texture that makes these soups so pleasing.

# VELOUTÉ SOUP BASE

½ cup plus 2 tablespoons (1¼ sticks) unsalted butter

1 large onion, diced (about 1 cup)

1 small carrot, diced (about ½ cup)

1 stalk celery, diced (about ½ cup)

7 tablespoons flour

9 cups All-Purpose Broth (page 222), or any combination canned low-sodium chicken broth and bottled clam juice

2 cups dry white wine

8 sprigs fresh thyme, or 1½ teaspoons dried

½ teaspoon ground nutmeg

½ tablespoon salt

¼ teaspoon ground white pepper, or as desired

TO SERVE

2 cups milk or cream, or combination

SERVES 8

1. Melt the butter in a 3-quart soup pot over low heat, and add the onions, carrots, and celery. Cook, stirring occasionally, about 5 minutes.

2. Add the flour and cook, stirring, for 1 minute.

3. Add the broth, wine, thyme, nutmeg, salt, and white pepper. Raise the heat to high and bring to a boil. Then reduce the heat to low and simmer for 1½ hours, skimming off the foam occasionally. The mixture should be reduced to 7 cups. ▨

4. Add the milk, bring back almost to a boil, and immediately remove from the heat. Serve piping hot.

**Cream of Chicken Soup:** Use all chicken stock or canned low-sodium chicken broth for the all-purpose broth or clam juice. Garnish the chicken velouté with diced cooked chicken and vegetables.

▨ To freeze, allow all or part of the velouté base to cool to room temperature. Refrigerate until thoroughly chilled, then freeze for up to 6 months. The defrosted base can be served as a cream soup by finishing as in Step 4, or made into one of the following 7 variations; each uses half of this recipe.

# FISH CHOWDER

This is an elegant soup, even when you serve it in order to use up frozen leftover seafood.

½ recipe (3½ cups) Velouté Soup Base (page 37), frozen or fresh

1 medium potato

6 ounces white lean fish, such as sole, flounder, snapper, or bass (cooked or uncooked)

1 cup milk

2 tablespoons unsalted butter

SERVES 4

1. Defrost the Velouté Soup Base if frozen.

2. Wash the potato but don't peel it. Cut off and discard the ends of the potato. Trim slices off four sides to form a block shape. Lay the potato flat, and cut it into ¼-inch-thick slices. Then pile up the slices, two at a time, and cut them into ¼-inch sticks. Cut small piles of the sticks into ¼-inch cubes. Place the cubes in a bowl of cold water as they are cut.

3. Place the velouté base in a 2-quart soup pot over medium heat. Add the potatoes (drained), cover, and cook 10 minutes.

4. Coarsely chop the fish and add it to the hot soup. Add the milk and cook, uncovered, an additional 5 minutes.

5. Remove the pot from the heat and whisk in the butter. Ladle the chowder into bowls and serve immediately.

**Turkey and Oyster Chowder:** Cook the leftover bones from a roasted turkey with the velouté base in step 2, and add 6 ounces combined chopped oysters and turkey meat instead of the fish.

# CHOWDER WITH SALT COD AND ROASTED PEPPERS

A hearty New England–style chowder, this can be a meal in itself. Cod tastes better salted, dried, and reconstituted than it does fresh from the sea. Leave enough advance time to soak it, changing the water twice daily. You can freeze the desalted fish for up to 6 months.

½ pound salt cod

½ recipe (3½ cups) Velouté
Soup Base (page 37),
frozen or fresh

2 medium-size red bell
peppers

1 medium potato

½ cup milk

½ cup whipping cream

2 tablespoons unsalted butter

SERVES 4

**1.** Two days before you'll be serving the soup, prepare the salt cod: Place the cod in a glass bowl or plastic container and cover it with water. Cover the bowl, place it in the refrigerator and allow the cod to soak, changing the water twice, for at least 12 hours or up to 24.

**2.** Meanwhile, defrost the Velouté Soup Base if frozen.

**3.** Drain the cod and discard the water. Remove and discard any bones and remnants of skin. Cut the cod into ½-inch cubes, and set them aside on a plate.

**4.** Prepare the roasted peppers: If you have a gas range, place the peppers directly on the burner over a high flame and cook, turning, until the skins are completely blackened. If you have an electric range, place the peppers on a roasting pan and broil 4 inches from the heat. Immediately place the peppers in a paper bag, close the top, and set aside for 5 minutes. Then rinse the peppers under cold running water, rubbing them to remove all the blackened skin. Slice the peppers in half, and discard the core, stem, and seeds. Place the halves in a food processor or blender, and purée until smooth. Reserve the purée in a small bowl.

**5.** Wash the potato but don't peel it. Cut off and discard the ends of the potato. Trim slices off four sides to form a block shape. Lay the potato flat, and cut it into ¼-inch-thick slices. Then pile up the slices, two at a time, and cut them into ¼-inch sticks. Cut small piles of the sticks into ¼-inch cubes. Place the cubes in a bowl of cold water as they are cut.

**6.** Place the velouté base in a 2-quart soup pot and bring it to a boil over medium heat. Add the potatoes (drained) and salt cod, cover, and cook 10 minutes. Remove the pot from the heat and add the pepper purée, milk, cream, and butter. Return to a boil. Transfer the chowder to a soup tureen or individual bowls, and serve.

# SCALLOP CHOWDER

½ *recipe (3½ cups) Velouté Soup Base (page 37), frozen or fresh*

½ *cup dry white vermouth*

1 *teaspoon grated orange rind*

¾ *pound bay scallops or halved large sea scallops*

1 *cup milk*

SERVES 4

**1.** Defrost the Velouté Soup Base if frozen.

**2.** Combine the vermouth and the orange rind in a 2-quart soup pot over high heat. Bring to a boil, cook 1 minute, and then whisk in the velouté base. Reduce the heat to medium and bring almost to a boil.

**3.** Add the scallops and milk and cook 1 to 2 minutes, depending on the scallops' size. (They may appear undercooked, but will finish cooking in the hot velouté.) Pour the chowder into a tureen and serve immediately.

# RED SHRIMP BISQUE

Cloves can become bitter in the freezer, so if some of this soup is destined for the freezer, add the spice after defrosting.

½ *recipe (3½ cups) Velouté Soup Base (page 37), frozen or fresh*

1 *pound uncooked shrimp*

1 *tablespoon olive oil*

2 *plum tomatoes, preferably overripe, quartered*

2 *tablespoons finely minced shallots*

¼ *teaspoon ground cloves*

¼ *cup brandy*

2 *cups milk*

2 *tablespoons unsalted butter*

SERVES 4

**1.** Defrost the Velouté Soup Base if frozen.

**2.** Peel and devein the shrimp, and set aside the shells. Chop the shrimp very fine and set aside.

**3.** Combine the olive oil, shrimp shells, tomatoes, shallots, cloves, and brandy in a large soup pot over medium heat. Cover and cook until the shells turn red, about 5 minutes. Add the velouté base, cover, and simmer for 5 minutes.

**4.** Pass the soup though a medium-mesh strainer, pressing hard to extract the tomato pulp; or pass it through a food mill.

**5.** Return the velouté to a clean pot, add the milk, and place over medium heat. Add the shrimp to the soup and cook for 3 minutes. Then remove the pot from the heat, whisk in the butter, and serve immediately.

# LOBSTER BISQUE

Lobster bisque used to be a complicated soup, but the freezer lets us prepare it in two stages.

Offer this as a first course for a very important meal, or increase the amount of lobster to 1 pound per person and serve it as a main dish. (The vanilla intensifies the lobster flavor.)

½ *recipe (3½ cups) Velouté Soup Base (page 37), frozen or fresh*

*Shells of a 1-pound lobster (about ½ pound)*

¼ *cup brandy*

½ *cup dry sherry*

1 *drop vanilla extract*

2 *tablespoons tomato paste*

½ *pound cooked lobster meat*

1 *cup whipping cream or half-and-half*

SERVES 4

1. Defrost the Velouté Soup Base if frozen.

2. Preheat the oven to 375°F.

3. Place the lobster shells in a roasting pan, and bake for 30 minutes or until the edges begin to brown. Transfer the shells to a 2-quart soup pot, and add the brandy, sherry, vanilla, and tomato paste. Cover, place over medium heat, and cook for 5 minutes.

4. Add the velouté and bring to a simmer. Then reduce the heat to low and cook, uncovered, for 10 minutes.

5. While the soup is cooking, finely chop the lobster meat.

6. Strain the soup through a sieve and discard the lobster shells. Return the soup to a clean pot, add the lobster meat and cream, and cook for 5 minutes. Serve immediately.

# CURRIED TURKEY BISQUE

This is a sophisticated combination that's easy to love. Yellow and orange make a beautiful presentation, and the curry gives an unusual kick to an otherwise subtle bisque.

½ *recipe (3½ cups) Velouté Soup Base (page 37), frozen or fresh*

1 *cup dry white wine*

1 *tablespoon tomato paste*

2 *tablespoons curry powder*

½ *teaspoon grated orange rind*

¾ *pound raw or cooked turkey, diced*

½ *cup milk*

¼ *cup whipping cream, or ¾ cup half-and-half*

½ *tablespoon chopped fresh dill*

1 *tablespoon unsalted butter*

SERVES 4

1. Defrost the Velouté Soup Base if frozen.
2. Combine the wine, tomato paste, curry, orange rind, and turkey in a 2-quart pot over high heat. Cover, bring to a boil, and cook for 5 minutes.
3. Reduce the heat to medium, add the velouté base, and simmer 15 minutes, partially covered.
4. Add the milk and cream to the velouté base and bring to a simmer over medium heat. Immediately remove the pot from the heat. Add the dill and whisk in the butter.
5. Pour the soup into a tureen or individual bowls, and serve immediately.

# CHICKEN AND CRAB SOUP WITH ROASTED GARLIC

The gentle nutty flavor of roasted garlic contrasts with the sweet chicken and crabmeat.

½ *recipe (3½ cups)* **Velouté**
    **Soup Base (page 37),**
    *frozen or fresh*

2 *tablespoons olive oil*

16 *cloves garlic, unpeeled*

3 *tablespoons water*

½ *cooked chicken, diced*
    *(about 1 cup)*

½ *pound cooked crabmeat,*
    *flaked (about 1¼ cups*
    *tightly packed)*

1 *cup milk*

2 *tablespoons chopped fresh*
    *chives*

SERVES 4

**1.** Defrost the Velouté Soup Base if frozen.

**2.** Preheat the oven to 375°F.

**3.** Combine the olive oil, garlic, and water in a small baking dish. Bake for 30 minutes, or until garlic cloves are soft and the skins are golden.

**4.** Meanwhile, place the velouté in a 1-quart pot over medium heat. Bring it to a simmer and cook for 10 minutes. Then remove the pot from the heat and transfer the velouté base to a food processor or blender. Add the garlic cloves and purée until smooth.

**5.** Strain the velouté base through a sieve into a clean soup pot. Add the chicken and crabmeat and milk, place over medium heat, and return the soup almost to a boil.

**6.** To serve, pour the soup into a tureen and garnish with the chopped chives.

# STEWS

A stew, by definition, is a dish requiring long cooking. Why go through the process two or three times when you can do the work just once? Increasing the quantity during preparation is a fraction of the bother it would be to re-create the dish every time. And, if a stew is better the second day—and indeed it is—then it is even better the second month if you have frozen and defrosted it properly. The freezing and defrosting process actually aids in the blending and development of the various flavors.

I have developed what I call "mother" recipes for chicken, beef, veal, and pork stews. The mother recipe turns out a large quantity that can be divided into smaller portions—ready to be finished for the meal at hand or to go into the freezer. The ingredients that make a dish different from the mother recipe—that turn a basic veal stew into a veal paprika, for instance—are added when the mother batch is defrosted.

Here's how it works: You cook a mother recipe for stewed veal, let's say, and then freeze the meat and the sauce separately. Then you reheat some sauce and meat, and add shallots, celeriac, cream, and sage. The fresh flavors and crunch of the quickly cooked vegetables and herbs accent the mellow flavors of the long-cooked veal and sauce—and no one will ever suspect that the stew came from the freezer. Serve it to the haughtiest purist, your most sophisticated friend, or an intimidating business associate. Will you feel guilty for not having spent all day cooking? What do you think?

## REFRIGERATING AND FREEZING STEWS

The key to freezing stews is to separate the meat from the sauce. When they are frozen and defrosted separately, the sauce remains limpid—clear and attractive—and the chunks of meat retain their shape and texture. Of course this also allows us to complete the dish in a variety of ways.

Separate the meat and vegetables from the sauce while the stew is still hot. This is most easily done in a colander or large sieve placed over a bowl. Then separate any vegetables from the meat. Place the meat and the sauce in separate freezer containers, filling them to within 1 inch of the top. Let them cool completely in the refrigerator (about 2 hours for meat, 1 hour for sauce). Discard the vegetables. Cover containers tightly, label, and refrigerate for up to 3 days or freeze for up to 3 months.

# DEFROSTING

It is best to defrost the stews slowly and evenly. Try to plan ahead and defrost them overnight in the refrigerator. Or use the defrost setting of a microwave oven, especially for small quantities. Never defrost by placing a freezer container in a bowl of hot water—the meat becomes stringy and tends to fall apart and the sauce tends to separate when they are unevenly defrosted. Remove fat, and cook as soon as possible after defrosting.

# REHEATING

Place the defrosted stew meat in an ovenproof dish along with ¼ cup chicken stock or low-sodium chicken broth. Cover the dish and bake in a preheated 325°F oven for 20 minutes or in a microwave.

Meanwhile, heat the sauce, covered, in a small heavy saucepan over low heat for 10 minutes.

You may notice that I usually do not indicate to preheat the oven. Preheating is necessary for roasting, because you want the heat to quickly form a crust and seal in the juices, and it's necessary in baking, in order for the cake batter or pastry crust to start cooking before the butter can run out of the dough. But for general cooking, preheating just wastes energy. (If the habit dies hard, however, don't worry. It won't hurt anything if the oven is preheated.)

**CREAM SAUCES.** Often a cream- or milk-based sauce will separate after having been frozen and defrosted. Freezing the liquid before its final reduction to saucelike consistency helps avoid this problem. But if it does happen, there are a couple of ways of bringing back a broken or separated sauce.

The easiest method, as long as the sauce has no garnish ingredients in it, is to place the reheated sauce in a blender and blend at high speed.

Another method—not quite as foolproof but the only chance you have if there is a garnish in the sauce—is to add some stock to the sauce and then boil it down to its proper consistency. Then remove the sauce from the heat and whisk in 1 tablespoon of room-temperature butter for each pint of stew sauce.

# FRICASSEED CHICKEN

Chicken that is cooked on the bone is creamier in texture than boneless chicken because it benefits from the proteins—albumin and gelatin— that the bones exude during cooking. Although a boneless cut may be your preference when cooking for a quick meal, the bone-in slow-cook method becomes very important when some of the chicken is destined for the freezer. Chicken that is frozen on the bone freezes much better than boneless.

Sautéed Green Beans with Mushrooms and Pine Nuts (page 155) and Rice Pilaf (page 175) go well with this fricassee.

2 chickens (3½ to 4 pounds each), cut up, or 7 to 8 pounds chicken pieces

Salt and freshly ground black pepper to taste

3 tablespoons unsalted butter or margarine

2 large onions, coarsely chopped (about 2 cups)

2 large carrots, coarsely chopped (about 2 cups)

1 stalk celery, coarsely sliced (about ½ cup)

¼ cup flour

3 cups All-Purpose Broth (page 222) or canned low-sodium chicken broth

3 cups milk

⅛ teaspoon ground nutmeg

4 bay leaves

6 sprigs fresh thyme, or 1 teaspoon dried

SERVES 6 TO 8

1. Preheat the oven to 375°F.

2. Rinse the chicken pieces and pat them dry. Sprinkle with salt and pepper. Melt the butter in a large flameproof casserole or Dutch oven over low heat. Add the chicken pieces and cook on all sides without browning, about 7 minutes (do this in batches to avoid crowding the pan). Remove pieces to a plate as they are done, and set aside.

3. Add the onions, carrots, and celery to the casserole and cook about 5 minutes. Sprinkle the flour over the vegetables and cook, stirring, for 30 seconds.

4. Add the broth, milk, nutmeg, bay leaves, and thyme. Raise the heat to high, cover the casserole, and bring to a boil. Add the thighs and drumsticks to the casserole, and transfer it to the oven. Bake for 25 minutes. Then add the breasts and cook for another 15 minutes.

5. Remove the casserole and turn off the oven. Remove the chicken pieces and set them aside. Strain the sauce through a fine-mesh sieve into a clean pot, and discard the vegetables and herbs. ▨

6. Keep the chicken pieces warm in the oven while you finish the sauce: Place the sauce over medium heat and cook for 10 to 15 minutes, or until the liquid is thick enough to cling to a wooden spoon.

7. To serve, arrange the chicken on a deep platter and ladle the sauce over it.

(continued)

Fricasseed Chicken (continued)

▨ To freeze all or part of this recipe, allow to cool to room temperature. Refrigerate until thoroughly chilled, then freeze the chicken and sauce in separate containers for up to 3 months. The defrosted dish can be finished as in Steps 6 and 7, or as one of the following 6 variations; each uses half of this recipe.

# BALSAMICO CHICKEN WITH OLIVES

My Italian friends think we Americans are a bit crazy to cook with balsamic vinegar—they use this dark brown, mild, aged-in-oak vinegar only in salads. But it's such sweet nectar that I can't resist using it. Of course it's still vinegar and is capable of "cooking" foods that sit in it. So add the vinegar to the meat after defrosting.

Polenta makes an interesting accompaniment for this dish—or you can serve noodles tossed with olive oil.

½ *recipe Fricasseed Chicken (page 47), frozen or fresh*

3 *tablespoons Fresh Tomato Paste (page 227) or canned*

½ *cup All-Purpose Broth (page 222) or canned low-sodium chicken broth*

½ *cup balsamic vinegar*

¾ *cup pitted green olives, drained*

1 *tablespoon chopped fresh parsley*

SERVES 3 TO 4

1. Defrost the Fricasseed Chicken if frozen.
2. Arrange the chicken pieces in an ovenproof casserole or Dutch oven. Combine the tomato paste, broth, and vinegar in a small bowl, and add to the chicken. Add the olives, cover, and place in the oven. Turn the oven on to 375°F.
3. Meanwhile, place the fricassee sauce in a small saucepan over medium heat, and cook until it is thick enough to coat a wooden spoon, about 5 to 10 minutes.
4. Uncover the casserole and strain the sauce over the chicken. Continue to bake, uncovered, another 5 minutes.
5. To serve, arrange the chicken and sauce in a serving bowl or on a deep serving platter, and sprinkle with the parsley.

# CHICKEN WITH BROCCOLI AND CREAMY WALNUT PESTO

Most of us have used pesto only as a sauce with pasta, but it is exceptional when added to a cream sauce—and we get to sop it up with some bread!

If you have regular pine nut pesto in the freezer, certainly substitute it for the listed pesto ingredients and add it in the final step. But if you have fresh basil, or puréed basil from last summer's garden, in the freezer, try making the pesto with walnuts. In this variation the walnuts add more than texture to the ensemble—you'll be surprised.

½ *recipe* **Fricasseed Chicken** (*page 47*)*, frozen or fresh*

2 *cups* **broccoli florets** (*about* ¾ *pound*)

½ *cup* **All-Purpose Broth** (*page 222*) *or canned low-sodium chicken broth*

**PESTO**

1 *cup* **walnut pieces**

2 *cloves* **garlic**

2 **anchovy fillets**

2 *tablespoons* **grated Parmesan cheese**

¼ *cup* **olive oil**

1¼ *cups* **tightly packed fresh basil leaves**

SERVES 3 TO 4

1. Defrost the Fricasseed Chicken if frozen.

2. Place the chicken pieces, broccoli florets, broth, and ½ cup of the walnuts in an ovenproof casserole or Dutch oven. Cover the casserole, place it in the oven, turn the oven on to 375°F, and bake for 20 minutes.

3. Meanwhile, make the pesto: Combine the remaining ½ cup walnuts, garlic, anchovies, cheese, and olive oil in a blender or food processor and process until blended. Add the basil leaves and purée to a coarse paste. Scrape the pesto into a small bowl and set aside.

4. Place the fricassee sauce in a small saucepan over medium heat, and cook until it is thick enough to coat a wooden spoon, about 10 minutes.

5. Pour the sauce over the chicken and continue to bake, uncovered, another 5 minutes.

6. Remove the casserole from the oven and transfer the chicken and broccoli to a serving dish. Add the pesto to the sauce and mix well. Pour the creamy pesto over the chicken and serve immediately.

# PAPRIKA CHICKEN WITH ROASTED PEPPERS

Paprika must be cooked for its flavor to develop. Tomatoes and coriander actually bring out the paprika flavor. Serve over buttered noodles.

½ recipe Fricasseed Chicken (page 47), frozen or fresh

½ cup All-Purpose Broth (page 222) or canned low-sodium chicken broth

4 large red bell peppers (about 1 pound)

2 tablespoons paprika (preferably Hungarian sweet paprika)

½ teaspoon ground coriander

1 tablespoon Fresh Tomato Paste (page 227) or canned

SERVES 3 TO 4

1. Defrost the Fricasseed Chicken if frozen.

2. Arrange the chicken pieces in a casserole or Dutch oven, cover, and place in the oven. Turn the oven on to 375°F.

3. Meanwhile, place the peppers over the flame of a gas range or under a preheated broiler, and cook, turning, until the skin is completely blackened. As they are done, place the peppers in a paper bag, close tightly, and set aside for 5 minutes. Then rinse the peppers under cold running water, rubbing them to remove all the blackened skin. Split the peppers lengthwise, remove the seeds, core, and stem, and cut into thirds. Add the peppers to the chicken.

4. Place the fricassee sauce in a saucepan over medium heat, and add the paprika, coriander, and tomato paste. Cook until the mixture is thick enough to cling to a wooden spoon, about 5 minutes.

5. Strain the sauce over the chicken and peppers, cover, and bake another 5 minutes.

6. Transfer the stew to a serving bowl, and serve piping hot.

# GINGER CHICKEN AND VEGETABLES

Sometimes I'm in the mood for something vaguely Chinese but more intimate than take-out. Fricasseed chicken is easily adapted to make this "pretend" Asian dish.

½ recipe **Fricasseed Chicken (page 47), frozen or fresh**

2 large **leeks, white part only**

2 stalks **celery**

¼ pound **snow peas**

¼ cup **All-Purpose Broth (page 222) or canned low-sodium chicken broth**

2 tablespoons fresh lemon juice

2 tablespoons finely minced fresh ginger, or ¼ teaspoon powdered

1 teaspoon chopped fresh tarragon leaves, or ½ teaspoon dried

1 tablespoon flavorless cooking oil

2 tablespoons soy sauce

SERVES 3 TO 4

1. Defrost the Fricasseed Chicken if frozen.

2. Slice the leeks into ½-inch-thick rounds and rinse them well under cold water; set them aside. Holding your knife at a 45° angle, cut the celery into ½-inch-thick diagonal slices; add them to the leeks. Trim off the tips of the snow peas, and remove the strings. Set them aside.

3. Arrange the chicken in an ovenproof casserole or Dutch oven, and add the broth and lemon juice. Cover the casserole, place it in the oven, and turn the oven on to 375°F. Bake for 20 minutes.

4. In the meantime, combine the fricassee sauce and ginger in a small saucepan. If you are using dried tarragon, add it now. Place the pan over medium heat, bring to a boil, and simmer until the sauce is thick enough to coat a wooden spoon, about 5 minutes.

5. Remove the casserole from the oven. If you are using fresh tarragon, sprinkle it over the chicken. Strain the sauce over the chicken, discarding the fresh ginger and dried tarragon. Return the casserole to the oven and continue to bake, uncovered, for another 10 minutes.

6. Heat the oil in a large skillet over high heat, and add the leeks and celery. Cook, stirring, for 3 minutes. Add the snow peas and cook another 2 to 3 minutes. Stir in the soy sauce and remove the skillet from the heat.

7. To serve, make a bed of the vegetables on a deep serving platter. Arrange the chicken pieces on the vegetables, and ladle the sauce over the top.

# CHICKEN AND GREEN BEANS WITH FOIE GRAS PURÉE

No one will imagine that the chicken came out of the freezer because it's bathed in such an elegant sauce. Use tiny French green beans called *haricots verts* if you can, or substitute frozen French-style green beans. Serve this with Rice Pilaf (page 175) and Mushroom Duxelles (page 240).

½ *recipe Fricasseed Chicken (page 47), frozen or fresh*

1½ *cups dry sherry or Madeira*

1 *pound haricots verts, or 1 package (10 ounces) frozen French-style green beans*

4 *ounces cooked foie gras or tinned pâté de foie gras*

SERVES 3 TO 4

1. Defrost the Fricasseed Chicken if frozen.

2. Arrange the chicken in an ovenproof casserole or Dutch oven, and add the sherry. Cover the casserole, place it in the oven, and turn the oven on to 375°F. Bake for 10 minutes.

3. If you are using fresh haricots verts, trim off the tips and discard the strings; add the beans to the chicken. If you are using frozen beans, add them to the chicken without defrosting. Cover the casserole and continue to cook for another 10 minutes.

4. Meanwhile, place the fricassee sauce in a small saucepan over medium heat, bring it to a boil, and cook for 5 minutes. Transfer the sauce to a blender or food processor, add the foie gras, and blend until smooth.

5. Pour the sauce over the chicken and beans. Bake, uncovered, another 5 minutes.

6. To serve, arrange the chicken and beans in a deep serving dish, and ladle the sauce over the top.

# CHICKEN, COUNTRY HAM, AND PEAS

This is also terrific served over pasta—a variation of spaghetti carbonara.

½ recipe **Fricasseed Chicken** (page 47), frozen or fresh

½ cup milk

**Small pinch of ground cloves**

¼ pound **Virginia ham** or prosciutto, cut into ½-inch dice

1 package (10 ounces) frozen peas

1 tablespoon chopped fresh parsley

SERVES 3 TO 4

1. Defrost the Fricasseed Chicken if frozen.
2. Arrange the chicken pieces in a casserole or Dutch oven, cover, and place in the oven. Turn the oven on to 375°F.
3. Meanwhile, combine the fricassee sauce, milk, and cloves in a saucepan over medium heat. Bring to a boil. Then remove the pan from the heat.
4. Stir the ham and peas into the sauce and place over medium-high heat. Cook for about 5 minutes, or until the sauce is thick enough to coat a wooden spoon. Pour the sauce, ham, and peas over the chicken and continue to bake for 5 minutes.
5. To serve, arrange the chicken and sauce in a serving bowl or on a deep serving platter, and sprinkle with the parsley.

# PAN-BRAISED CHICKEN

In contrast to the almost sweet, lemony poultry flavor of a fricassee (page 47), this dark stew has a sultry personality—it's quite remarkable how browning the pieces of chicken in a little oil thoroughly changes the character.

I prefer drinking a red wine with these nutty, bold French-style stews. In fact the color of a sauce better determines the color of the wine to choose than does the color of the meat. Mashed potatoes are perfect with this subtly flavored sauce.

(continued)

Pan-Braised Chicken   (continued)

2 chickens (3½ to 4 pounds
    each), cut up
Salt and freshly ground
    black pepper to taste
⅓ cup flavorless cooking oil
2 large onions, coarsely
    chopped (about 2 cups)
2 large carrots, coarsely
    chopped (about 2 cups)
1 stalk celery, thickly sliced
    (about ½ cup)
1 tablespoon minced garlic
¼ cup flour
2 cups All-Purpose Broth
    (page 222) or canned
    low-sodium chicken broth
1 tablespoon tomato paste
2 bay leaves

SERVES 6 TO 8

1. Preheat the oven to 325°F.

2. Rinse the chicken pieces and pat them dry. Sprinkle with salt and pepper. Heat the oil in a large flame proof casserole or Dutch oven over medium-high heat. Add the chicken pieces and brown well on all sides, about 7 minutes (do this in batches to avoid crowding the pan). Transfer the chicken to a plate as the pieces are done.

3. Discard all but 2 tablespoons oil, reduce the heat to medium, and add the onions, carrots, celery, and garlic to the casserole. Cook about 3 minutes. Then sprinkle the vegetables with the flour and cook, stirring, 1 minute longer.

4. Add the broth, tomato paste, and bay leaves. Place the chicken thighs and drumsticks in the casserole, along with any accumulated juices. Cover and bring to a boil. Then transfer the casserole to the oven and bake for 15 minutes.

5. Add the chicken breasts, cover, and cook another 25 minutes.

6. Remove the chicken from the casserole and set it aside. Strain the sauce through a fine-mesh sieve into a clean pot, and discard the vegetables. ▨

7. Keep the chicken pieces warm in a 250°F oven. Skim off any fat that has risen to the surface of the sauce, and reheat the sauce over medium heat. Arrange the chicken on a deep serving platter, ladle the sauce over the top, and serve immediately.

▨ To freeze all or part of this recipe, allow to cool to room temperature. Refrigerate until thoroughly chilled, then freeze the chicken and sauce in separate containers for up to 3 months. The defrosted dish can be finished as in Step 7, or as one of the 4 variations that follow; each uses half of this recipe.

# CHICKEN AND SAUSAGE STEW

Manufacturers of both sausages and freezers say that cured meats should not be frozen for more than a few weeks because they change flavor in the freezer. I find this to be a problem only when the cured meat has been cooked in sauce and then frozen—and even then, it's the sauce that changes flavor more than the meat. At any rate, this dish combines defrosted chicken with fresh sausages. The ingredients do not become muddled, nor do their flavors alter in the freezer. Serve this over Rice Pilaf (page 175) or buttered noodles so you can enjoy every bit of the flavorful sauce.

½ *recipe* **Pan-Braised Chicken** *(page 53), frozen or fresh*

1 *pound hot Italian sausages*

3 *-inch strip of orange rind*

1 *cup Tomato Concassée (page 223), or 2 tablespoons tomato paste*

½ *cup dry white wine*

SERVES 4

1. Defrost the Pan-Braised Chicken if frozen.

2. Slice the sausages into 1-inch pieces, place them in an ovenproof casserole or Dutch oven, and add the chicken. Cover the casserole, place it in the oven, and turn the oven on to 375°F. Bake for 20 minutes.

3. Meanwhile, make sure all white pith is removed from the orange rind, and combine the tomato concassée, wine, braising sauce, and orange rind in a small saucepan. Cook over medium heat for 10 minutes.

4. Remove the casserole from the oven and pour off the accumulated fat. Spoon the tomato mixture over the chicken and sausages, and bake, uncovered, another 10 minutes.

5. To serve, arrange the chicken and sausages in a serving bowl or deep serving platter and pour the sauce over the top.

# SPICY CHICKEN WITH DATES

Creamy-textured sweet dates become swollen with the spicy flavors of this stew while it cooks. Personally, I prefer even more kick—another teaspoon of cayenne—especially when the weather is hot and humid. But start with 1 teaspoon and see how you like it. You can always make it hotter.

(continued)

Spicy Chicken with Dates   (continued)

½ *recipe Pan-Braised Chicken (page 53), frozen or fresh*

½ *cup All-Purpose Broth (page 222) or canned low-sodium chicken broth*

¼ *pound pitted dates, coarsely chopped*

1 *teaspoon cayenne pepper*

½ *teaspoon ground cumin*

*Juice of two lemons (½ cup)*

2 *tablespoons finely chopped fresh parsley*

SERVES 3 TO 4

1. Defrost the Pan-Braised Chicken if frozen.

2. Combine the chicken, broth, dates, cayenne, and cumin in an ovenproof casserole or Dutch oven. Cover the casserole, place it in the oven, and turn the oven on to 375°F. Bake for 20 minutes.

3. Meanwhile, combine the braising sauce and lemon juice in a small saucepan and place over medium heat. Cook, covered, for 5 minutes.

4. Strain the sauce over the chicken and dates, and bake, uncovered, another 10 minutes.

5. To serve, arrange the chicken and dates on a deep serving platter and ladle the sauce over the top.

# MISO CHICKEN WITH CARROTS

The salty flavor of miso, a fermented soybean paste, is softened by the addition of a fortified wine, such as sherry or Madeira.

½ *recipe Pan-Braised Chicken (page 53), frozen or fresh*

4 *large carrots, thinly sliced (about 3 cups)*

1 *cup whipping cream*

2 *cups All-Purpose Broth (page 222) or canned low-sodium chicken broth*

2 *tablespoons miso paste*

1 *cup Madeira or dry sherry*

SERVES 3 TO 4

1. Defrost the Pan-Braised Chicken if frozen.

2. Arrange the carrots in an ovenproof casserole or Dutch oven. Add the cream, and then arrange the chicken on top. Cover the casserole, place it in the oven, and turn the oven on to 375°F. Bake for 20 minutes.

3. Meanwhile, combine the braising sauce, broth, miso, and Madeira in a saucepan over medium heat. Bring to a boil. Then reduce the heat and simmer until the mixture is thick enough to coat a wooden spoon, 15 to 20 minutes.

4. Strain the sauce over the chicken and carrots, and bake, uncovered, 10 minutes.

5. Transfer the stew to a serving bowl or deep platter, and serve immediately.

# HUNTER CHICKEN

*Chasseur* in French, *Cacciatore* in Italian—this dish is delicious, and it's nothing like the chicken-stewed-in-tomato-sauce I remember eating in school cafeterias.

½ *recipe Pan-Braised Chicken (page 53), frozen or fresh*

½ *pound slab bacon, cut into ½-inch cubes*

½ *pound mushrooms, sliced*

1 *tablespoon Fresh Tomato Paste (page 227) or canned*

¼ *cup brandy*

¼ *cup milk*

¼ *cup whipping cream*

1 *tablespoon chopped fresh tarragon leaves*

SERVES 3 TO 4

**1.** Defrost the Pan-Braised Chicken if frozen.

**2.** Place the bacon in a flameproof casserole or Dutch oven over medium heat, and cook, stirring occasionally, for 5 minutes. Pour off the excess fat, and add the mushrooms, tomato paste, and brandy. Mix well.

**3.** Place the chicken pieces on the bacon/mushroom mixture, cover, and transfer to the oven. Turn the oven on to 375° and bake for 20 minutes.

**4.** Meanwhile, combine the milk, cream, and braising sauce in a small saucepan over medium heat. Cover and bring to a boil; then reduce the heat to low and simmer for 5 minutes.

**5.** Strain the sauce over the chicken and mushrooms and bake, uncovered, another 10 minutes.

**6.** To serve, arrange the chicken pieces on a platter and spoon the bacon, mushrooms, and sauce over the top.

# STEWED VEAL

Cuts of veal that are less desirable for quick cooking develop excellent character when stewed. Long, slow cooking extracts flavor by dissolving the meat proteins and softening the fibers. In fact, a frozen and defrosted veal stew has better flavor than one served directly from the stove.

Serve this on a bed of buttered noodles or Rice Pilaf (page 175) to enjoy the sauce.

(continued)

Stewed Veal   (continued)

3½ *pounds boneless veal stew meat*

8 *cups All-Purpose Broth (page 222) or canned low-sodium chicken broth*

1 *medium onion, coarsely chopped (about ½ cup)*

2 *stalks celery, sliced (about 1 cup)*

1 *medium carrot, coarsely chopped (about ½ cup)*

½ *teaspoon salt, or as desired*

½ *teaspoon whole white peppercorns*

¼ *teaspoon ground nutmeg*

1 *small lemon, cut in half*

5 *tablespoons unsalted butter*

6 *tablespoons flour*

SERVES 8

**1.** Combine the veal and 4 cups of the broth in a heavy 5-quart pot. Cover, and bring to a boil over high heat. Remove any scum that accumulates on the top, and then add the remaining broth along with the onions, celery, carrots, salt, white peppercorns, nutmeg, and lemon halves. Reduce the heat to low and simmer, covered, for 1¼ hours or until the meat is just tender.

**2.** Meanwhile, melt the butter in a 3-quart pot over low heat, and whisk in the flour. Cook, stirring, for 2 minutes, and then remove the pan from the heat. Set aside until the meat is cooked.

**3.** When the meat is done, use a slotted spoon to remove it from the liquid and set it aside. Pick off and discard any vegetables that cling to the veal.

**4.** Place the butter/flour mixture over medium heat, and strain the cooking liquid into it, whisking constantly. Discard the vegetables. Cook, stirring, until the mixture has thickened, about 3 to 5 minutes. Then continue to cook, skimming off any residue that rises to the surface, for 15 minutes. ▧

**5.** Cook the sauce over medium heat until it has reduced to about 5 cups and is thick enough to coat a wooden spoon, about 15 minutes. Add the meat to the sauce and heat through, another 5 minutes.

**6.** Pour the meat and sauce into a bowl or deep platter, and serve.

▧ To freeze all or part of this recipe, allow to cool to room temperature. Refrigerate until thoroughly chilled, then freeze the veal and sauce separately for up to 3 months. The defrosted dish can be finished as in Steps 5 and 6, or as one of the following 4 variations; each uses half of this recipe.

# VEAL STEW WITH CELERIAC AND SHALLOTS

Most root vegetables became unfashionable about twenty years ago, it seems—or perhaps it's because the makers of frozen vegetables don't process them that we seem to have forgotten them.

½ *recipe Stewed Veal (page 57), frozen or fresh*

24 *shallots (about ¾ pound)*

1¼ *pounds celeriac*

1 *teaspoon flavorless cooking oil*

½ *cup All-Purpose Broth (page 222) or canned low-sodium chicken broth*

1 *cup whipping cream*

1 *teaspoon minced garlic*

1½ *teaspoons chopped fresh sage leaves, or ½ teaspoon dried*

¼ *cup fresh lemon juice*

¼ *teaspoon ground nutmeg*

**Salt to taste**

SERVES 4

1. Defrost the Stewed Veal if frozen.

2. Place the shallots in a bowl, cover with warm water, and set aside for 30 minutes to soften the skins. Then drain and peel the shallots. Cut an X in the root tip of each one. Set them aside.

3. While the shallots are soaking, remove and discard the celeriac tops. Using a paring knife, remove and discard the black skin of the celeriac bulb. Dice the white pulp into ½-inch pieces, and set them aside. (If you are not using them immediately, squeeze some lemon juice over the celeriac to prevent discoloration.)

4. Heat the oil in a skillet over medium heat. Add the shallots and celeriac and cook, tossing, for 5 minutes. Transfer to a plate and set aside.

5. Place the veal and sauce in a large flameproof casserole or Dutch oven. Add the broth, cream, garlic, sage, lemon juice, nutmeg, and salt. Stir well and bring to a boil over medium heat. Then add the celeriac and shallots, and transfer the casserole to the oven. Turn the oven on to 375°F and bake for 25 minutes.

6. Remove the casserole from the oven, transfer the stew to a serving dish, and serve immediately.

# VEAL AND PEPPER GOULASH WITH DUMPLINGS

In Hungary, where goulash is the national dish, paprika comes in many varieties from sweet to hot and always adds strong character to a recipe. Good-quality Hungarian paprika isn't widely available here, so I have added dried tomatoes and Tabasco sauce to give this variation more personality and depth. The dumplings soak up some of the sauce while they cook, adding to the charm of this dish.

½ recipe Stewed Veal (page 57), frozen or fresh

1 medium russet potato (about 8 ounces), baked

1 tablespoon unsalted butter

½ cup finely diced onion

½ cup flour

1 egg

½ teaspoon baking powder

1 teaspoon salt

1 tablespoon tomato paste

2 tablespoons red wine vinegar

2 tablespoons paprika (preferably Hungarian sweet paprika)

¼ teaspoon Tabasco sauce

½ cup All-Purpose Broth (page 222), canned low-sodium chicken broth, or water

2 ounces dehydrated tomatoes, cut into small pieces

4 small red bell peppers, roasted (see page 171) and chopped

½ cup sour cream

1. Defrost the Stewed Veal if frozen.

2. Make the dumplings: Scoop the pulp out of the baked potato, mash it in a mixing bowl, and set aside. (Discard the skin.) Melt the butter in a small skillet over medium heat, add the onions, and cook 5 to 7 minutes or until the onions are translucent. Add them to the potato pulp. Add the flour, egg, baking powder, and salt, and mix well. Turn the dough out onto a floured work surface, and flatten it out until it is 1 inch thick. Using a knife or cookie cutter, cut the dough into 12 pieces. Cover with a damp cloth and set aside.

3. Prepare the goulash: Place the stewing sauce in a saucepan over medium heat, and bring to a boil. Reduce the heat and heat through, skimming off any foam that appears on the surface, 7 to 10 minutes.

4. Meanwhile, combine the tomato paste, vinegar, paprika, Tabasco, and broth in a deep ovenproof dish. Stir thoroughly, and then add the veal. Cover the casserole, place it in the oven, and turn the oven on to 375°F. Bake for 10 minutes.

5. Strain the sauce over the veal. Add the dried tomatoes and roasted peppers, and mix gently. Arrange the 12 pieces of dumpling dough on the surface of the goulash, and return the casserole to the oven. Bake, uncovered, until the dumplings are done, about 25 minutes.

SERVES 4

**6.** Transfer the dumplings to a warmed plate. Stir the sour cream into the goulash, and then pour the mixture into a serving dish or deep platter. Replace the dumplings on top, and serve immediately.

# VEAL AND CRAYFISH STEW

Today's culinary vocabulary includes many bizarre combinations— ingredients borrowed from different cuisines to create dishes with a polyglot background. We sometimes forget that culinary experimentation has a long history, as evidenced in this updated freezer version of Veal Marengo. Legend has it that this dish was created for Napoleon Bonaparte out of odds and ends after the long battle of Marengo— apparently there was nothing left in the larder except a lobster and some veal. Serve this rich stew over a bed of rice or buttered noodles.

½ *recipe Stewed Veal*
    *(page 57), frozen or fresh*
½ *cup dry sherry*
1 *cup whipping cream*
24 *small mushroom caps,*
    *wiped clean*
24 *cooked crayfish tails,*
    *shelled, or ¾ pound*
    *cooked lobster meat*

**1.** Defrost the Stewed Veal if frozen.

**2.** Place the stewing sauce in a saucepan over medium heat, and add the sherry. Bring to a boil and cook for 20 minutes or until reduced by one third. Then add the cream, meat, and mushrooms. Cover, and cook until heated through, another 10 minutes.

**3.** Add the crayfish and cook over low heat for 5 minutes. Serve immediately.

SERVES 4

## VEAL BLANQUETTE À L'ANCIENNE

A *blanquette* is a white, creamy French stew. It's meant to be very rich, and in classic recipes the sauce was often thickened with egg yolks as well as cream. I don't use yolks at all, and you can lighten the blanquette further by using half-and-half or milk instead of cream.

½ recipe Stewed Veal
  (page 57), frozen or fresh
24 pearl onions
1 teaspoon sugar
¼ teaspoon salt
1 tablespoon unsalted butter
½ cup water
1 cup whipping cream, half-
  and-half, or milk
24 small mushroom caps,
  wiped clean

SERVES 4

1. Defrost the Stewed Veal if frozen.
2. Place the onions in a bowl, cover with warm water, and soak for 15 minutes. Then drain and peel the onions. Cut an X in the root end of each onion. Place the onions in a medium saucepan, and add the sugar, salt, butter, and water. Cook over medium heat for 10 minutes or until almost all the water has evaporated. Gently toss the onions to coat them with the buttery syrup that has formed in the pan. Remove the pan from the heat, transfer the onions and syrup to a small bowl, and set them aside to keep warm.
3. Meanwhile, place the veal sauce in a saucepan over medium heat and bring to a boil. Cook until the sauce has reduced by one third, 15 to 20 minutes. Then add the cream, meat, and mushrooms and cook another 10 to 15 minutes, or until the ingredients are heated through.
4. Using a slotted spoon, transfer the meat and mushrooms to a serving dish. Add the reserved onions and mix together. Strain the sauce over the stew, and serve.

## STEWED LAMB

Red meats such as lamb should be cooked into a dark-colored stew, so brown the meat well before adding liquid. Not only is the resulting flavor more intense, but the meat also freezes better. If you have bones in the freezer, from cooked lamb chops or a leg of lamb, add them to the stew for a stronger lamb flavor.

4 *pounds boneless lamb
  shoulder, cut into 2-inch
  cubes*

½ *teaspoon salt, or as
  desired*

*Freshly ground black pepper
  to taste*

¼ *cup vegetable oil*

1 *medium onion, quartered*

2 *medium carrots, coarsely
  chopped (about 1 cup)*

2 *stalks celery, each cut into
  4 pieces*

1 *tablespoon finely minced
  garlic*

2 *tablespoons tomato paste*

¼ *cup flour*

1 *cup dry white wine*

5 *cups All-Purpose Broth
  (page 222) or canned
  low-sodium chicken broth*

½ *tablespoon whole black
  peppercorns*

2 *tablespoons chopped fresh
  thyme leaves, or 1
  teaspoon dried*

SERVES 8

1. Preheat the oven to 325°F.

2. Pat the meat dry and sprinkle it with salt and pepper. Heat the oil in a large flame-proof casserole or Dutch oven over high heat. Add the meat and brown well on all sides, 5 to 7 minutes (do this in batches to avoid crowding). Remove the pieces to a plate as they are done, and set aside.

3. Pour off any remaining fat, and place the casserole over medium heat. Add the onions, carrots, celery, garlic, and tomato paste. Cook, stirring, for 5 minutes. Use your spoon to loosen and dissolve any brown bits stuck to the bottom of the casserole. Sprinkle the flour over the vegetables and cook, stirring, 1 more minute.

4. Add the wine, and cook for about 1 minute to burn off the alcohol. Then add the meat (and any juices that have accumulated on the plate) and add the broth, peppercorns, and thyme. Cover and bring to a boil. Then transfer the casserole to the oven and bake for 1¼ to 1½ hours or until the meat is tender.

5. Remove the casserole from the oven. Using a slotted spoon, remove the meat from the sauce and place it in a bowl. Pour the sauce through a fine-mesh strainer into another bowl, and discard the vegetables and spices. ▨

6. Place the meat in a serving bowl, spoon the sauce over it, and serve piping hot.

---

▨ To freeze all or part of this recipe, allow to cool to room temperature. Refrigerate until thoroughly chilled, then freeze the lamb and sauce in separate containers for up to 3 months. The defrosted dish can be finished as in Step 6, or as one of the following 4 variations; each uses half of this recipe.

# LAMB AND SAUSAGE COUSCOUS

If you can't find *merguez*, a North African lamb sausage redolent of cumin, garlic, and hot peppers, use a hot Italian sausage.

½ recipe Stewed Lamb (page 62), frozen or fresh

6 spicy sausages, preferably merguez style, cut into ½-inch pieces

1 cup Tomato Concassée (page 223), or drained, chopped canned tomatoes

1 large onion, sliced into ½-inch rings

2 medium zucchini, cut into 1-inch rounds

2 cups All-Purpose Broth (page 222) or canned low-sodium chicken broth

1 teaspoon ground cumin

¼ teaspoon cayenne pepper

1½ cups couscous, uncooked

SERVES 6

1. Defrost the Stewed Lamb if frozen.
2. Place the meat in an ovenproof casserole or Dutch oven, cover, and bake in a 375°F oven for 20 minutes.
3. Meanwhile combine the sausages, tomatoes, onion, and zucchini in a baking dish, cover, and bake until the sausages are cooked, about 20 minutes.
4. While the meat and vegetables are in the oven, combine the broth, stewing sauce, cumin, and cayenne in a 2-quart saucepan. Cover, and bring to a boil over medium heat. Remove the pan from the heat and keep warm.
5. Cook the couscous according to package directions. Or line a large strainer or colander with a damp kitchen towel or napkin and add the couscous; place over a pot of rapidly boiling water, cover tightly, and steam for 30 minutes or until soft.
6. Remove the dishes from the oven. Pour off and discard any excess fat from the sausages, and combine the sausages, vegetables, and lamb in a serving dish. Place the couscous in another serving dish. Pour the broth into a pitcher or soup tureen. Each diner places some couscous in a soup bowl, tops it with meat and vegetables, and moistens it with broth.

# PROVENÇAL LAMB STEW

Anchovies provide a better-tasting salty element in this dish than table salt could, and you can't detect any fishy flavor. Baked polenta is the traditional accompaniment.

½ recipe Stewed Lamb
(page 62), frozen or fresh
12 anchovy fillets
1 tablespoon minced garlic
1 cup Tomato Concassée
(page 223), or drained,
chopped canned tomatoes
1 cup dry white wine
1 cup pitted green olives
(14½-ounce jar), drained
1 bunch parsley, leaves
finely chopped (about
½ cup)

1. Defrost the Stewed Lamb if frozen.

2. Combine the anchovies, garlic, to-matoes, wine, olives, and lamb in an 2-quart pot. Cover and place over medium-low heat.

3. Place the stewing sauce in a small pot over medium heat. Bring it to a simmer, strain over the lamb mixture, and cook until bubbling, about 20 minutes.

4. Remove the stew from the heat, add the parsley, and mix well. Transfer the stew to a dish, and serve immediately.

SERVES 4

# YANKEE LAMB STEW

½ recipe Stewed Lamb
(page 62), frozen or fresh
2 medium carrots, cut into
½-inch rounds (about
1 cup)
1 medium potato, cut into ½-inch cubes (about 1 cup)
2 tablespoons unsalted butter
½ cup water
2 medium turnips, cut into
½-inch dice (about 1½
cups)
½ cup fresh peas or defrosted
frozen peas

1. Defrost the Stewed Lamb if frozen.

2. Combine the lamb and sauce in a 2-quart ovenproof casserole or Dutch oven, cover, and bake in a 375°F oven for 25 minutes.

3. Combine the carrots, potatoes, butter, and water in a saucepan over medium heat, and cook, uncovered, for 5 minutes. Add the turnips and peas and cook, stirring occasionally, until all the water has evaporated, leaving the vegetables bathed in butter, about another 5 minutes.

4. Remove the casserole from the oven, stir in the vegetables, and transfer the stew to a large serving dish. Serve immediately.

SERVES 4

# LAMB CURRY

Curry powder is a blend of many herbs and spices. It develops a good flavor only when cooked, and is particularly complementary with lamb. Don't forget the chutney (page 230). And if you like your curry very hot, accompany it with a side dish of plain yogurt.

½ recipe Stewed Lamb
   (page 62), frozen or fresh

1 large onion, finely diced
   (about 1 cup)

1 tablespoon vegetable oil

⅛ teaspoon cayenne pepper,
   or more as desired

½ teaspoon ground coriander

3 tablespoons curry powder,
   or to taste

½ cup All-Purpose Broth
   (page 222), canned low-
   sodium chicken broth, or
   water

SERVES 4

1. Defrost the Stewed Lamb if frozen.

2. Combine the onions, oil, cayenne, coriander, and curry powder in an 2-quart pot over medium heat. Cook, stirring, 2 minutes. Add the broth and cook another 2 minutes.

3. Add the lamb and sauce. Reduce the heat to low, cover, and cook until bubbling hot, about 25 minutes.

4. Remove the pan from the heat, transfer the mixture to a serving dish, and serve immediately.

# STEWED BEEF

When seared properly, the cubes of beef in a beef stew glisten with a dark golden crust. Stewing cuts of beef—shoulder, brisket, rump, and chuck are the most common—have the best flavor. They require long cooking, but at serving time the pieces of meat should be tender, not dry or falling apart. Browning the meat concentrates the flavor, and cooking in liquid draws the flavor back into the gravy.

4 pounds boneless beef stew
  meat, cut into 2-inch
  chunks

Salt and freshly ground
  black pepper to taste

¼ cup flavorless cooking oil

1 medium onion, quartered

2 medium carrots, cut into 1-
  inch pieces

2 stalks celery, coarsely
  sliced (about 1 cup)

4 tablespoons flour

2 cups dry red wine

6 cups All-Purpose Broth
  (page 222) or canned
  low-sodium chicken broth

1 tablespoon fresh thyme
  leaves, or 1 teaspoon
  dried

SERVES 8

1. Pat the meat dry and sprinkle it with salt and pepper. Heat the oil in a large flameproof casserole or Dutch oven over high heat. Add the meat and brown very well on all sides, 7 to 10 minutes (do this in batches to avoid crowding the pan). Remove the pieces to a plate as they are done, and set aside.

2. Pour off all but 2 tablespoons fat from the casserole, place it over medium heat, and add the onions, carrots, and celery. Cook, stirring, for 5 minutes or until the vegetables have softened. Sprinkle the flour over the vegetables and cook, stirring, 1 minute longer. Then add the wine, meat, and any juices that have accumulated on the plate. Add the broth and thyme, cover, and raise the heat to high. Bring to a boil.

3. Transfer the casserole to the oven, turn the oven on to 375°F, and cook for 1¼ hours or until the meat is tender.

4. Remove the casserole from the oven and using a slotted spoon, carefully remove the meat from the sauce and place it in a bowl. Strain the sauce, discarding the vegetables and spices, into another bowl. ▨

5. If the sauce seems a little thin, boil it down quickly until it has the right consistency.

6. Pour the sauce over the beef, and serve.

▨ To freeze all or part of this recipe, allow to cool to room temperature. Refrigerate until thoroughly chilled, then freeze the beef and sauce in separate containers for up to 3 months. The defrosted dish can be finished as in Steps 5 and 6, or as one of the following 2 variations; each uses half of this recipe.

# BEEF AND ONIONS IN BEER

Vegetable Pancakes (page 182) are wonderful with this full-bodied stew—or serve it over buttered noodles.

½ *recipe Stewed Beef*
  *(page 66), frozen or fresh*
4 *medium onions, thinly*
  *sliced lengthwise*
1 *can (12 ounces) dark beer*

SERVES 4

1. Defrost the Stewed Beef if frozen.
2. Preheat the oven to 375°F.
3. Combine the onions, beef, and beer in an ovenproof casserole or Dutch oven, and bake for 30 minutes.
4. Meanwhile, place the stewing sauce in a small saucepan over medium heat and bring to a boil. Reduce the heat and simmer until the sauce has reduced, about 15 minutes. Strain the sauce over the meat and onions, and bake, uncovered, 5 minutes.
5. To serve, remove the casserole from the oven and transfer the stew to a serving dish.

# BOEUF À LA BOURGUIGNON

Boeuf à la Bourguignon conjures up memories of one's first meal in a French restaurant. Of course, it's simply beef stew fortified with red wine. Serve it over buttered noodles.

½ *recipe Stewed Beef*
  *(page 66), frozen or fresh*
20 *pearl onions*
¼ *pound bacon, cut into 1-*
  *inch pieces*
1 *pound small*
  *mushroom caps*
1 *tablespoon tomato paste*
½ *cup red wine*

SERVES 4

1. Defrost the Stewed Beef if frozen.
2. Place the onions in a bowl, cover with warm water, and soak for 30 minutes. Then drain and peel the onions. Cut an X in the root tip of each one.
3. Place a skillet over medium heat, add the bacon, and cook 5 minutes. Drain off the fat, add the mushrooms and onions, and cook another 5 minutes.
4. Transfer the contents of the skillet to an ovenproof casserole or Dutch oven, and add the meat. Cover the casserole, place it in the oven, and turn the oven on to 375°F.

Bake for 20 minutes.

**5.** Meanwhile, combine the stewing sauce, tomato paste, and wine in a 1-quart saucepan over medium heat, and cook until the sauce has reduced by half or it thick enough to coat a spoon, 10 to 15 minutes.

**6.** Strain the sauce over the meat, replace the cover, and bake another 5 minutes.

**7.** Transfer the stew to a serving bowl and serve immediately.

# STEWED PORK

For people trying to reduce their intake of calories, stewing is the preferred method of cooking pork. The marbling fat is cooked out of the meat and can be skimmed off the top; if you refrigerate or freeze the stew before serving it, you can extract virtually all the fat.

*4 pounds boneless pork shoulder, trimmed of fat, cut into 1-inch cubes*

*½ tablespoon salt*

*½ teaspoon freshly ground black pepper*

*¼ cup vegetable oil*

*1 large onion, coarsely chopped (about 1 cup)*

*3 tablespoons flour*

*2 cups dry white wine*

*4 cups All-Purpose Broth (page 222) or canned low-sodium chicken broth*

*2 bay leaves*

*4 sprigs fresh thyme, or ½ teaspoon dried*

SERVES 8

**1.** Preheat the oven to 375°F.

**2.** Pat the pork dry with paper towels and sprinkle it with the salt and pepper.

**3.** Heat the oil in a flameproof casserole or Dutch oven over medium-high heat. Add the pork and brown it well on all sides, 7 to 10 minutes (do this in batches to avoid crowding the pan). Remove the pieces to a plate as they are browned. Pour off all but about 2 tablespoons fat from the casserole.

**4.** Reduce the heat to low, add the onions to the casserole, and cook for 5 minutes, scraping up any brown bits that cling to the bottom. Sprinkle the flour over the onions and cook 1 more minute, stirring.

**5.** Add the wine and broth and bring to a boil. Add the pork along with any juices that have accumulated, and the bay leaves and thyme. Cover tightly and transfer to the oven. Bake for 1¼ hours or until the meat is tender.

**6.** Remove the stew from the oven, and

(continued)

Stewed Pork   (continued)

using a slotted spoon, remove the meat from the sauce and set it aside. Strain the sauce through a fine-mesh sieve, discarding the onions and herbs. ▨

**7.** Place the meat in a serving dish and ladle the sauce over it. Serve immediately.

---

▨ To freeze all or part of this recipe, allow to cool to room temperature. Refrigerate until thoroughly chilled, then freeze the pork and sauce in separate containers for up to 3 months. The defrosted dish can be finished as in Step 7, or as one of the following 3 variations; each uses half of this recipe.

---

# PORK AND MUSTARD PICKLE STEW

Salty sweet pickles accompany the rich pork flavor of this stew. I like dishes that make the mouth pucker with each bite. Serve boiled new potatoes alongside.

½ *recipe Stewed Pork (page 69), frozen or fresh*

12 *cornichons or 1 dill pickle, finely chopped*

¼ *cup tarragon vinegar*

½ *cup dry white wine*

1 *tablespoon Dijon mustard*

½ *cup whipping cream*

3 *medium carrots, cut into 1-inch rounds (about 1½ cups)*

½ *pound Brussels sprouts, rinsed and halved (about 1 cup)*

1. Defrost the Stewed Pork if frozen.

2. Combine the cornichons, vinegar, wine, and mustard in an ovenproof casserole or Dutch oven. Place over medium heat and cook for 5 minutes.

3. Add the pork, its sauce, and the cream; mix well. Cover, transfer to the oven, and bake at 375°F for 30 minutes or until bubbling hot.

4. Meanwhile, bring a medium-size pot of salted water to a boil, and cook the carrots for 7 minutes. Add the Brussels sprouts and cook another 5 minutes. Drain the vegetables well, and add them to the stew for the last 5 minutes of cooking.

5. To serve, remove the pot from the oven and transfer the stew to a serving dish.

SERVES 4

# PORK COLLIOURE

Collioure is a small town on the French Riviera. This combination of horseradish and mustard sparked by lemon is a classic of the area. It's more often used to accompany swordfish, but I find it equally charming in this creamy pork stew. Serve it on a bed of buttered noodles.

½ recipe Stewed Pork
  (page 69), frozen or fresh

2 tablespoons freshly grated
  or good-quality bottled
  horseradish

2 tablespoons whole-grain
  mustard

Juice of 2 lemons (about
  ½ cup)

½ cup whipping cream

2 medium parsnips, cut into
  1-inch rounds (about 1½
  cups)

SERVES 4

1. Defrost the Stewed Pork if frozen.

2. Combine the stewing sauce, horseradish, mustard, lemon juice, and cream in a 3-quart ovenproof pot. Place over medium heat and bring to a low boil. Decrease the heat to low and simmer, uncovered, for 10 minutes.

3. Place the pork in an ovenproof casserole or Dutch oven, cover, and bake in a 375°F oven for 15 minutes.

4. Meanwhile, fill a medium saucepan with salted water, bring to a boil, and add the parsnips. Boil for 5 minutes. Drain the parsnips and add them to the pork. Pour the sauce into the casserole and continue to bake, covered, another 10 minutes.

5. Transfer the stew to a serving dish and serve immediately.

# CHOUCROUTE GARNIE

This dish is a brasserie favorite in France, and similar dishes are popular in Germany and Eastern Europe. It's a dish of preserved ingredients—salted and cured pieces of pork combined with sauerkraut—that adapts perfectly to a twentieth-century method of conserving food: the freezer. Serve mustard, or better yet a selection of mustards, with the choucroute. The accompanying cooking liquid is delicious mashed with your potatoes or for sopping up with bread.

½ **recipe Stewed Pork (page 69), frozen or fresh**

2 **pork sausages, such as knockwurst, cut into 3 pieces each**

12 **small new potatoes, unpeeled**

6 **cups drained sauerkraut**

½ **pound piece of ham, cut into 6 equal pieces**

1 **cup All-Purpose Broth (page 222) or canned low-sodium chicken broth**

4 **whole cloves, or ¼ teaspoon ground**

SERVES 6

1. Defrost the Stewed Pork if frozen.
2. Preheat the oven to 375°F.
3. Place the sausages and potatoes in an ovenproof casserole or Dutch oven, cover, and bake for 15 minutes.
4. Remove the casserole from the oven and pour off any fat. Add the sauerkraut, pork, and ham. Cover and bake for 20 minutes.
5. Meanwhile, combine the stewing sauce, broth, and cloves in a medium saucepan. Cover and bring to a boil over medium heat; cook for 5 minutes.
6. Strain the sauce over the stew, discarding the whole cloves. Bake, uncovered, for another 15 minutes.
7. To serve, mound the sauerkraut on a large serving platter and arrange the potatoes and meats around it and on top. Pass any remaining sauce on the side.

# SEAFOOD

There are some foods and prepared dishes that we freeze ahead because they require long preparation—but fish isn't one of them. It takes so little time to sauté, grill, broil, or steam fresh fish or shellfish that one may wonder why freeze it at all. But of course there are reasons.

Often we freeze fish because a favorite uncle or next-door neighbor is an avid angler, occasionally sharing a bountiful catch. We may be known to reel in a big one ourselves from time to time. The freezer lets us freeze some or all of the catch for another meal.

Another reason is health-related: Fans of sushi, sashimi, and rare tuna are learning that in this era of pollutants, raw fish is safer to eat after it has been frozen briefly because freezing kills ocean parasites.

The best reason to freeze fish is to suspend its preparation so that a desired effect can be achieved later: improving the flavor and/or texture of a seafood dish, for example, or making the final steps particularly quick and easy. In this way the freezer becomes just another tool like a knife, a food processor, or a skillet in the evolution of a dish from market basket to serving plate.

Historically, commercially frozen fish has had an advantage over home-frozen fish in that it is flash-frozen. This means that the size of the ice crystals that form in the flesh is much smaller, creating less disturbance in the texture. We can't flash-freeze at home, but we can compensate for it through several techniques.

The first technique is dehydrating: removing most of the moisture that would otherwise form large ice crystals, break the fish fibers, and upon defrosting, make a thorough exit, leaving the flesh dry and stringy. Dehydrating works particularly well on large steak fish like swordfish, tuna, and mahi-mahi, and on fatty fish like salmon, mackerel, bluefish, and whitefish.

Delicate fish such as flounder, sole and snapper, whitefish, and cod or scrod become mushy or soggy in the freezer, making them a trial to sauté or grill. Breading them before freezing forms a protective crust, enhances their appeal, and allows us to cook them directly from their frozen state. (It also gives us a convenience food—such as fish sticks—that taste deep-fried without the mess and the calories!)

Firm-fleshed fish like sea bass, catfish, and sturgeon freeze well in a marinade, as do fatty fish such as salmon, bluefish, carp, and shad, because the oil, which does not form ice crystals, protects the texture of the fish.

We can't flash-freeze, but do try to freeze these fish preparations as quickly as possible by placing them in a fast-freeze spot near the bottom of the freezer, with as much air circulation around them as possible. Once the food is well frozen, it can be moved to a more tightly packed area. If you're freezing a big batch or have no room to make a fast-freeze spot, set the temperature control on high for 24 hours.

The recipes in this chapter produce fresher-tasting, finer-textured fish than many meals prepared from so-called fresh fish, which have spent a few days on a fishing boat, a day or two in the wholesale arena, and a few more days in your supermarket. Unless you have access to fish pulled from the water within hours of consumption, the taste of these freezer preparations will compare favorably with supermarket "fresh."

Still, no freezer technique can improve what was poor quality to begin with. Find a reputable fishmonger, establish a good relationship with him or her, and always ask when and where the fish was caught.

## CURING FRESH FISH FOR FREEZING

A light salt cure prior to freezing draws moisture out of the flesh and results in a smoother, more compact texture when we defrost fatty fish such as salmon, pompano, mackerel, bluefish, whitefish, and swordfish. The flavor is actually enhanced by the salting—the fish have more flavor, yet taste less "fishy."

If you're preparing a large fish—salmon, for example—buy a whole fish, have the fishmonger fillet it, then cut the fillet into serving portions before placing them in the freezer. For smaller fish, try to find fillets that are more or less the same size and shape so you can pair them for salting.

# SALT-CURED FISH

This technique works well even when you're not going to freeze the fish. After Step 2, proceed with your recipe.

**4 pounds boneless fillets of fish (or fish steaks)**
**1 tablespoon salt**
**2 tablespoons sugar**

SERVES 8 TO 10

**1.** Lay the fillets skin side down on a work surface. Mix the salt and sugar together in a small bowl and sprinkle the mixture over the flesh. Put two fillets together flesh to flesh, closing them like a book, and place them on a rimmed plate or in a pie plate. Place another plate over the fish and weight it down with a 2-pound weight (cans from the supermarket or even a clean brick from the garden will work nicely). Refrigerate for 1½ hours.

**2.** Remove the weight and pour off any liquid that has been released from the fish. Turn the fillets over, replace the plate and the weight, and refrigerate for another hour.

**3.** Remove the weight and separate the fillets. Rinse them under cold water and pat dry. If the fillets are large, cut them into serving pieces (about 7 to 8 ounces each).

**4.** Wrap each piece of fish in plastic freezer wrap and place them in a freezer bag (or place each one in a separate freezer bag), pressing out as much air as possible. Freeze for up to 8 weeks. Defrost in the refrigerator before cooking.

# GRILLED SALMON WITH CUCUMBER AND MINT SALSA

When I cook salmon, I always keep it on the rare side. Well-cooked seems chalky to me, especially if it's not the Norwegian variety. Don't believe that you have to overcook this salmon or drench it in sauce to disguise its freezer background—you don't.

(continued)

Grilled Salmon with Cucumber and Mint Salsa   (continued)

This is also a great recipe for tuna. Choose fillets that are 1½ inches thick. Grill them 2 minutes on the first side, then 1 minute on the other side—or longer for well cooked.

**4 salmon fillets (8 ounces each), salt-cured (page 75), frozen or fresh**

**1 teaspoon ground coriander**

**⅛ teaspoon ground allspice**

**1 teaspoon finely minced garlic**

**1 teaspoon finely minced shallots or onion**

**1 cup dry vermouth**

**2 tablespoons flavorless cooking oil**

**Cucumber and Mint Salsa (recipe follows)**

SERVES 4

**1.** Place the salmon flesh side down in a glass baking dish large enough to hold it in one layer. Combine the coriander, allspice, garlic, shallots, and vermouth, pour over the fillets, and cover. If using frozen salmon, defrost the fish in the marinade in the refrigerator. If fish is fresh, marinate for 30 minutes or up to 2 hours in the refrigerator.

**2.** Light a barbecue grill. When the charcoal is coated with white ash, remove the salmon from the marinade. Pat the fillets dry and brush both sides with a little oil. Lightly oil the grill. Place the fish skin side down on the grill.

**3.** Grill the salmon about 4 minutes; then turn and grill another 2 minutes for rare, or up to 6 minutes for well done. Remove the fish from the grill and carefully remove the skin. Arrange the salmon flesh side up on a platter, and serve. Offer the Cucumber and Mint Salsa on the side.

## CUCUMBER AND MINT SALSA

**1 medium cucumber**

**1 tablespoon salt**

**2 tablespoons dark walnut oil**

**2 tablespoons fresh lemon juice**

**1 tablespoon finely chopped fresh mint leaves**

SERVES 4

**1.** Peel the cucumber and cut it in half lengthwise. Scoop out and discard the seeds. Finely chop the flesh and place it in a colander. Sprinkle the cucumber with the salt, and place the colander over a plate to catch the drips. Set aside for 30 minutes.

**2.** Rinse the cucumber under cold water, and press it against the sides of the colander to squeeze out any excess water. Place it in a mixing bowl and add the walnut oil, lemon juice, and mint leaves. Mix well. Pour into a small serving bowl to accompany the fish.

# MILK-POACHED SALMON WITH RED PEPPER PURÉE

The red pepper purée flavors a strong milk broth here—it's not a traditional rich fish sauce. Serve the fish in individual soup bowls with boiled potatoes, and serve a large vegetable accompaniment—perhaps as a separate course.

*4 salmon fillets (8 ounces each), salt-cured (page 75), frozen or fresh*

*1 large red bell pepper (4 to 6 ounces)*

*2 tablespoons olive oil*

*1 medium onion, finely diced (about ¾ cup)*

*1½ cups milk*

*⅛ teaspoon ground mace*

SERVES 4

1. Defrost the salmon fillets if frozen.

2. If you have a gas range, place the pepper directly on the burner over a high flame and cook, turning, until the skin is completely blackened. If you have an electric range, place the pepper on a roasting pan and broil 4 inches from the heat. Immediately place the pepper in a small paper bag, close the top, and set aside for 5 minutes. Then rinse the pepper under cold running water, rubbing it to remove all the blackened skin. Slice the pepper in half, and remove and discard the stem, core, and seeds. Place the halves in a blender or food processor and purée.

3. Set a 3-inch-deep skillet, large enough to hold the salmon comfortably in one layer, over medium heat. Add the olive oil and onions. Cook, stirring, for 5 minutes. Add the pepper purée and cook another 5 minutes.

4. Add the salmon, milk, and mace. Cover the skillet, raise the heat to high, and bring almost to a boil. Immediately remove the skillet from the heat and let the salmon sit covered, for 5 minutes.

5. Carefully remove the salmon from the skillet and remove the skin. Place a piece of salmon in each soup bowl and spoon some of the liquid over it.

# POACHED SALMON WITH CHIVE BUTTER

Fish that has been lightly salt-cured is easier to poach because the risk of its falling apart is greatly decreased. Poaching also removes any vestiges of salty flavor that may remain. In fact, the fish has an especially wonderful aroma when prepared this way.

4 salmon fillets (8 ounces each), salt-cured (page 75), frozen or fresh

1 small carrot, coarsely chopped (about ½ cup)

1 medium onion, coarsely chopped (about ¾ cup)

1 stalk celery, coarsely sliced (about ¾ cup)

1 cup plus 2 tablespoons dry white wine

¼ cup white vinegar

¼ teaspoon salt, or as desired

Pinch of cayenne pepper

6 tablespoons (¾ stick) unsalted butter, room temperature

¼ cup finely chopped fresh chives

SERVES 4

1. Defrost the salmon fillets if frozen.

2. Set a 3-inch-deep lined copper, enamel, or stainless steel skillet on the stove and add the salmon. The skillet should be large enough to hold the salmon comfortably (use two skillets if necessary). Add the carrots, onions, celery, and 1 cup of the wine. Add enough cold water to cover the salmon. Place over medium heat, cover, and bring to a simmer. Then immediately remove the skillet from the heat and let the salmon sit, covered, for 5 minutes. (If you prefer your fish well done rather than slightly pink, let it sit 5 minutes longer.)

3. Meanwhile, combine the vinegar, remaining 2 tablespoons wine, salt, and cayenne in a small saucepan and place over medium heat. Using a small whisk, add the butter, 1 tablespoon at a time, until melted. Immediately remove the pan from the heat and stir in the chives.

4. Remove the salmon from the poaching water, discarding the vegetables, and remove the skin. Arrange the fillets on a serving platter. Pour the sauce into a sauceboat and serve it on the side.

# SAUTÉED POMPANO WITH GRAPEFRUIT

**S**ome people find pompano too strong-flavored for their taste. You will find that a light salting and freezing sweetens the flavor of this Caribbean denizen and gives it a milder flavor. The tart citrus sauce is a good complement to the rather fatty fish.

*4 pompano fillets (7 to 8 ounces each), salt-cured (page 75), frozen or fresh*

*1 cup milk*

*3 tablespoons flour*

*3 tablespoons unsalted butter*

*1 tablespoon flavorless cooking oil*

*1 cup fresh grapefruit juice*

*1 grapefruit, peeled and sectioned*

SERVES 4

**1.** Place the fillets in a glass dish and cover with milk. If using frozen fillets, defrost them in the milk in the refrigerator. If the fish is fresh, let stand in the milk for 30 minutes to 2 hours in the refrigerator.

**2.** Sprinkle the flour on a plate. Remove the fillets from the milk, and if they have skin, remove and discard it. Pat them dry with paper towels, and dust with the flour on both sides.

**3.** Combine 2 tablespoons of the butter with the oil in a large heavy skillet over medium heat. When the butter has melted and the foam has subsided, add the pompano without crowding the skillet (cook the fish in batches if necessary—a crowded skillet will steam the fish and cause it to fall apart). Sauté until golden brown, about 4 minutes. Then turn the fish and cook 5 minutes on the other side.

**4.** As the fillets are done, remove them from the skillet and place them on a plate in a preheated 250°F oven to keep warm.

**5.** Discard the cooking fat and wipe the skillet clean with a paper towel. Replace the skillet on the stove, add the grapefruit juice, and raise the heat to high. Cook until reduced by about half, 5 to 7 minutes. Then remove the skillet from the heat and whisk in the remaining 1 tablespoon butter.

**6.** Remove the fillets from the oven and arrange them on a serving platter. Garnish with grapefruit sections, spoon the sauce over the top, and serve immediately.

# SWORDFISH PASTRAMI

If you're accustomed to buying only individual pieces of fish, usually steaks of salmon and halibut, or individual fillets of smaller fish such as red snapper, carp, and catfish, you'll probably have to search to get the right piece for this recipe. Ask your fishmonger for a 3-pound piece of swordfish or tuna "loin"—one about 1 foot in length and 3 inches in diameter. If you can't obtain such a morsel, you can adapt the recipe for portion-size pieces of fish by simply decreasing the cooking time.

Close your eyes and you'll think you're eating pastrami—but this version is free of the salt, chemicals, and fat of commercial meat varieties.

*3 tablespoons kosher salt*

*¼ cup chopped garlic*

*1 loin of swordfish (3 pounds), skin removed*

*5 tablespoons cracked coriander seed*

*¼ cup cracked black pepper*

*16 charcoal briquettes*

*8 mesquite or hickory wood chips*

*4 lemon wedges*

**Mustard Sauce or Tarragon and Green Peppercorn Sauce (recipes follow)**

SERVES 4

1. The night before you plan to cook, combine the kosher salt and garlic in a small bowl and mix to form a paste. Completely coat the swordfish with the paste. Place the fish in a baking dish, cover, and refrigerate for 8 hours to 12 hours.

2. Remove the swordfish from the dish. Rinse it well under cold water and pat dry. Combine the coriander and peppercorns on a plate, and completely coat the swordfish with that mixture. ▨

3. Light the charcoal briquettes in a smoker or lidded grill. (If your grill doesn't have a lid, you can improvise one using an inverted roasting pan, for example, to catch the smoke.) Soak the wood chips in water. When the charcoal is covered with white ash, push it into a pile on one side of the grill and scatter the wood chips over it.

4. Place the swordfish on the grill, but not directly over the briquettes. Cover immediately and cook for 12 minutes. Then turn the swordfish and continue to cook, covered, for another 10 to 15 minutes. (If you are using tuna, the total grilling time should be 12 minutes—it's best rare.)

5. Remove the swordfish from the grill and cut it into 4 pieces. Arrange them on a serving platter and garnish with lemon wedges. Serve the sauce on the side.

⊠ To freeze, wrap the coated fish tightly in 2 layers of plastic freezer wrap, and freeze for up to 2 months. Partially defrost in the refrigerator (4 hours per pound) before grilling.

# MUSTARD SAUCE

1 *cup All-Purpose Broth (page 222)*

1 *anchovy fillet, coarsely chopped*

2 *tablespoons finely minced shallots*

3 *tablespoons Dijon mustard*

3 *tablespoons plain yogurt*

Combine the broth, anchovy, shallots, and mustard in a small saucepan over medium heat and bring to a boil. Reduce the heat and simmer until the mixture has reduced by about one third and begun to thicken, 5 minutes. Remove the pan from the heat and whisk in the yogurt. Serve immediately or keep warm in a warm water bath (the sauce cannot be reheated because the yogurt will curdle).

SERVES 4

# TARRAGON AND GREEN PEPPERCORN SAUCE

1 *cup dry white wine*

2 *anchovy fillets, coarsely chopped*

2 *tablespoons drained green peppercorns in water*

1 *tablespoon Dijon mustard*

½ *cup whipping cream*

1 *tablespoon chopped fresh tarragon leaves, or 1 teaspoon dried*

Combine the wine, anchovies, green peppercorns, and mustard in a small saucepan. If you are using dried tarragon, add it now. Place the pan over medium heat and cook until the mixture has reduced by one third and begun to thicken, about 7 minutes. Add the cream and continue to cook, reducing again until the sauce has thickened, another 5 minutes. Remove the pan from the heat and stir in the fresh tarragon.

SERVES 4

## MARINATING FRESH FISH FOR FREEZING

I like to marinate lean, meaty fish prior to freezing. Their flesh is softened by the acid in the wine and they become plumper. Try hake, whiting, halibut, John Dory, or grouper. Hawaiian fish—such as opakapaka, mahi-mahi, and ono—and other deepwater dwellers are meatier, but they also benefit from being frozen in a marinade.

## MARINATED FISH

This technique works well even when you're not planning on freezing the fish.

*2 pounds boneless fillets of lean, meaty fish*

*½ teaspoon salt*

*¼ teaspoon freshly ground black pepper*

*1 tablespoon Dijon mustard*

*½ cup dry white wine*

*2 tablespoons minced garlic*

*½ teaspoon ground coriander*

*¼ cup olive oil*

1. Portion the fillets into 8 pieces, and sprinkle them with the salt and pepper.

2. Mix together the mustard, wine, garlic, coriander, and oil. Place the fish in a flat freezer container or in freezer bags, and pour the marinade over the fish. Cover and refrigerate for up to 4 hours or freeze for up to 2 months.

SERVES 4

## SEARED MARINATED TUNA WITH TOMATO TARRAGON SAUCE

Tuna is quite terrible when it is cooked well-done. You might as well open a tin and make a salad. In fact, fresh red-fleshed tuna can be treated almost like red meat. The nice thing is that it doesn't have the calories, fat, or cholesterol of red meat.

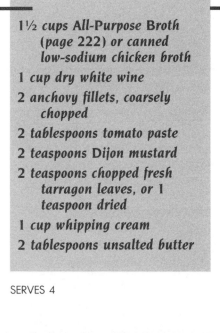

4 tuna fillets (7 to 8 ounces
    each), marinated (page
    82), frozen

2 tablespoons flavorless
    cooking oil

4 lemon wedges

Tomato Tarragon
    Sauce (recipe follows)

SERVES 4

1. Partially defrost the tuna and pat dry.

2. Heat the oil in a large heavy skillet over medium-high heat. When the oil is hot, add the frozen tuna and cook for 3½ minutes. The fish will stick slightly to the pan, but as it sears, it will loosen itself.

3. Carefully turn the tuna and continue to cook another 5 minutes. The interior should be rare but not cold, and the outside should be charred. (If you prefer your tuna well-cooked, place it in a preheated 375°F oven for 5 minutes before serving.)

4. Arrange the tuna on a serving platter, decorate with lemon wedges, and accompany with the sauce.

# Tomato Tarragon Sauce

1½ cups All-Purpose Broth
    (page 222) or canned
    low-sodium chicken broth

1 cup dry white wine

2 anchovy fillets, coarsely
    chopped

2 tablespoons tomato paste

2 teaspoons Dijon mustard

2 teaspoons chopped fresh
    tarragon leaves, or 1
    teaspoon dried

1 cup whipping cream

2 tablespoons unsalted butter

1. Combine the broth, wine, and anchovies in a small saucepan over medium heat and bring to a boil. Cook for 5 minutes. Then add the tomato paste and mustard. If you are using dried tarragon, add it now. Continue to cook for 10 minutes or until the mixture has reduced by one third.

2. Add the cream and cook until the sauce has thickened, about 6 minutes. Remove the pan from the heat and whisk in the butter, stirring until incorporated. Pour the sauce into a sauceboat and serve on the side.

SERVES 4

# HALIBUT BAKED IN CREAM

**N**o one will guess that the cream in this recipe is really yogurt.

**2 pounds halibut, marinated (page 82), frozen or fresh**

**½ teaspoon salt, or to taste**

**Pinch of cayenne pepper**

**2 tablespoons finely chopped shallots**

**1 tablespoon finely minced garlic**

**½ cup dry white wine**

**½ cup milk**

**½ cup plain yogurt**

**¼ cup chopped fresh chives**

SERVES 4

1. Defrost the halibut if frozen. Remove the fish from the marinade and brush off any remains of the marinade.

2. Preheat the oven to 350°F.

3. Arrange the halibut in a shallow casserole, and sprinkle it with the salt and cayenne. Add the shallots, garlic, wine, and milk. Cover, and bake for 20 minutes.

4. Remove the dish from the oven. Transfer the halibut to a plate and keep warm, covered. Pour the cooking liquid into a saucepan and place it over medium-high heat. Bring to a boil and cook, stirring with a wooden spoon, for 5 minutes or until the liquid has begun to thicken. Then remove the pan from the heat, whisk in the yogurt, and add the chives.

5. Place the halibut on a serving platter and add to the sauce any liquid that may have accumulated on the plate. Spoon a little sauce over each piece of fish, and serve the remaining sauce on the side.

# LEMON-POACHED HALIBUT

**2 pounds halibut, marinated (page 82), frozen or fresh**

**1 cup dry white wine**

**2 cups water**

**½ teaspoon salt**

**¼ cup fresh lemon juice**

**3 tablespoons unsalted butter, cut into 6 pieces**

SERVES 4

1. Defrost the halibut if frozen. Remove the fish from the marinade and brush off any remains of the marinade.

2. Combine the wine, water, and salt in a 3-inch-deep pan large enough to hold the fish in a single layer (or use two pans). Place it over high heat and bring to a boil. Add the halibut, cover, and cook 1 minute. Remove the pan from the heat and let it stand, covered, for 10 minutes.

3. Meanwhile, place the lemon juice in a small saucepan over medium heat and

cook 1 minute. Then add the butter, piece by piece, whisking to incorporate.

**4.** To serve, remove the halibut from the poaching liquid and place it on a serving platter. Pour the lemon butter into a sauceboat and serve it on the side.

# SEAFOOD ESCABECHE

**E**scabeche is a traditional Spanish dish featuring marinated fish or white-meat poultry. This variation is a perfect way to use your frozen marinated fish—and especially welcome in hot weather. All this version needs is a green salad and some good bread.

¼ *cup olive oil*

8 *small new potatoes, quartered*

1 *medium onion, finely slivered lengthwise*

1 *tablespoon finely minced garlic*

1 *cup dry white wine*

¼ *cup white wine vinegar*

½ *cup water*

½ *teaspoon salt, or to taste*

*Freshly ground black pepper to taste*

¼ *cup quartered pitted Niçoise olives*

¼ *cup dehydrated tomatoes (about 1 ounce) or sun-dried tomatoes, cut up*

1 *sprig fresh marjoram leaves, or ½ teaspoon dried*

4 *pieces (7 to 8 ounces each) marinated fish (page 82), frozen or fresh*

**1.** In a large heavy skillet, combine the olive oil, potatoes, onions, garlic, wine, vinegar, water, and salt. Give the mixture a few turns of the peppermill, and place over medium heat. Cover, and cook for 20 minutes.

**2.** Add the fish, cover, and cook for 10 minutes if the fish is still frozen, 5 minutes if fresh or defrosted. Add the olives, tomatoes, and marjoram leaves. Remove the skillet from the heat and let sit, covered, until the fish is cooked as desired.

**3.** Serve the escabeche warm, at room temperature, or chilled, topped with the cooking mixture. ▨

SERVES 4

(continued)

Seafood Escabeche   (continued)

▨ To freeze, place the cooked fish, along with the cooking liquid, tomatoes, and olives, in plastic containers or bags, and freeze for up to 3 months. Defrost and serve chilled or heated.

# PREPARING SCALLOPS FOR FREEZING

The edible part of the scallop is the large muscle that keeps the two shells of the bivalve closed—the equivalent of the foot of an oyster or clam. Fresh scallops are an off-white color; if they are an opaque milky white, they are too old for the freezer or have previously been frozen. Choose the largest sea scallops. If they have been carefully handled, there will be no broken pieces, only whole muscles. They should smell of the sea but without an overpowering odor. Having sampled the commercially frozen variety, I simply assumed that scallops could not be successfully frozen. I was wrong. One of the greatest surprises was the excellent quality scallop that I retrieved from my freezer.

*3 pounds large sea scallops*
*Juice of 1 lemon (about*
*¼ cup)*
*¼ cup flavorless cooking oil*

SERVES 6 TO 8

1. Combine the scallops and lemon juice in a bowl, and mix well. Cover and refrigerate for 1 hour.

2. Lightly brush a baking sheet with oil. Remove the scallops from the bowl and pat them dry. Place them in a clean bowl and toss them with the remaining oil. Then carefully arrange the scallops on the baking sheet, leaving space between them. Place the baking sheet in the freezer and leave it for 1 hour, or until the scallops are frozen.

3. Place portion-size quantities of scallops in freezer bags, and freeze for up to 1 month. Defrost in the refrigerator.

# BROILED SCALLOPS

Scallops taste best when they caramelize on a grill or under a broiler. Cook them quickly by placing them as close as possible to the source of heat; in that way they will become golden on the outside but remain creamy at the center.

1 teaspoon finely minced garlic

1 tablespoon finely minced shallots

¼ teaspoon salt, or as desired

Freshly ground black pepper to taste

¼ cup dry sherry

1 tablespoon fresh lemon juice

2 tablespoons olive oil

1 teaspoon Dijon mustard

1½ pounds large sea scallops, frozen (page 86) or fresh

3 tablespoons unsalted butter

3 tablespoons chopped fresh parsley

3 or 4 lemon wedges

SERVES 3 TO 4

**1.** Combine the garlic, shallots, salt, pepper, sherry, lemon juice, olive oil, and mustard in a glass or ceramic bowl. Stir thoroughly. Then add the scallops and toss them in the mixture. If using frozen scallops, let them defrost in the marinade. If the scallops are fresh, let marinate for 30 minutes to 2 hours.

**2.** Preheat the broiler.

**3.** Oil the broiler pan or a baking sheet. Remove the scallops from the marinade, brush them off, and arrange them on the oiled surface. Broil for 5 minutes without turning.

**4.** While the scallops are broiling, combine the remaining marinade with the butter in a small saucepan. Place it over medium heat and cook until the butter stops foaming. Remove from the heat and add the parsley.

**5.** Pour the butter sauce onto a serving platter, and arrange the scallops on top. Garnish with lemon wedges and serve immediately.

# POACHED SCALLOPS AND MUSHROOMS

This is a lightened version of a school recipe of mine—a "bonne femme" preparation normally laden with cream and butter. Not only does this adaptation use your frozen scallops, it is also virtually fat-free.

1½ *pounds large sea scallops, frozen (page 86) or fresh*

1 *cup dry white wine*

1 *pound mushrooms, finely sliced*

¼ *cup finely minced shallots or onion*

1 *teaspoon fresh thyme leaves, or ½ teaspoon dried*

½ *cup plain yogurt*

SERVES 3 TO 4

1. Defrost the scallops overnight in the refrigerator if frozen.

2. Place the wine in a saucepan over medium heat, cover, and bring to a boil. Add the mushrooms, shallots, and thyme. Return to a boil, cover, and cook for 2 minutes.

3. Add the scallops, cover, and cook another 3 minutes, or until they are medium-rare. Using a slotted spoon, transfer the scallops to a plate or bowl and set aside. Cook the liquid until it has reduced by two thirds.

4. Return the scallops and any juices that have collected to the pan, and cook over high heat for another 2 minutes or until the scallops are cooked as desired.

5. Remove the pan from the heat and stir in the yogurt. Transfer the scallops, mushrooms, and sauce to a serving dish, and serve immediately.

## BREADING FISH FOR FREEZING

Breading and then freezing fish gives us a convenience food without any of the unknowns in the commercially frozen variety (how fresh was the fish before breading? what is in the crust itself? how long has the fish been frozen?) It also allows us the luxury of deep-fried flavor without the mess or the calories, since these breaded fish are actually baked. The preparation takes only a few minutes and lets you prepare a quick, delicious meal on a moment's notice (don't defrost the fish). Flounder, whitefish, catfish, and sole are good choices for breading.

# BREADED FROZEN FISH

4 pounds boneless, skinless
   fish fillets
1 teaspoon salt, or as desired
½ teaspoon cayenne pepper
¼ cup flour
1½ cups fresh bread crumbs
4 to 5 eggs
½ cup (1 stick) unsalted
   butter

SERVES 8

**1.** Cut the fish fillets into 4-ounce serving pieces, and pat them dry with paper towels. Sprinkle them with the salt and cayenne, and set aside on a plate.

**2.** Place the flour on one plate and the bread crumbs on another. Beat the eggs in a shallow bowl.

**3.** Lightly dust a fillet with flour, shaking off the excess. Dip it in the eggs and let the excess drip off. Then dip it in the crumbs and pat gently to make them adhere. Place the fillet on a cookie sheet. Repeat with all the fillets, arranging them in one layer on the cookie sheet. Place the cookie sheet in the freezer for 1 hour.

**4.** Meanwhile, melt the butter in a small saucepan. When the fillets are frozen, remove them from the freezer. Lightly brush the surfaces with the melted butter. Place the frozen fillets between sheets of freezer paper, and place them in plastic bags or containers. Freeze for up to 3 months.

# PARSLEYED WHITEFISH WITH DIPPING SAUCE

These "fish sticks" will please the biggest fans of convenience-food fish dinners. Catfish, bass, and snapper are good to use, too.

2 tablespoons unsalted butter, melted

2 pounds breaded whitefish, frozen (page 89) or fresh

6 tablespoons finely chopped fresh parsley

2 teaspoons prepared grated horseradish

2 teaspoons capers

4 anchovy fillets

¼ cup fresh lemon juice

¼ cup plain yogurt

¼ cup olive oil

3 or 4 lemon wedges

SERVES 3 TO 4

1. Preheat the oven to 400°F.

2. Generously butter a baking sheet with half the melted butter, and arrange the breaded fillets on it without crowding. Using a pastry brush, gently brush the top of the fillets with the remaining butter. Bake 25 minutes for frozen, 12 minutes for fresh.

3. Meanwhile, combine the parsley, horseradish, capers, anchovies, and lemon juice in a blender or food processor; process until blended but still chunky. Scrape the mixture into a bowl, add the yogurt, and mix well. Slowly add the oil in a slow steady stream, mixing until incorporated. Transfer the sauce to a serving bowl and set aside.

4. Arrange the fish on a platter and garnish with lemon wedges. Serve the sauce on the side.

# PREPARING LOBSTER FOR FREEZING

As a rule, we choose live lobsters and either boil or broil them and devour them immediately. Yet lobster meat is also a welcome addition to many preparations, from soups to fancy seafood stews. And it can be delicious in salads, omelettes, and soufflés.

Lobsters are prepared differently for the freezer than for the meal at hand. They are partially cooked by a slow method, ensuring tender meat that can be stored for up to 3 months in the freezer. The shells are indispensable in many soups and sauces, so freeze them too.

4 *live lobsters (1½ to 2*
   *pounds each)*

2 *large onions, coarsely*
   *chopped (about 2 cups)*

1 *carrot, coarsely chopped*
   *(about ½ cup)*

2 *stalks celery, coarsely*
   *sliced (about ½ cup)*

1 *cup white wine*

1 *teaspoon whole black*
   *peppercorns*

1 *tablespoon salt*

4 *bay leaves*

SERVES 4

**1.** Place the live lobsters belly down on a work surface. Take a large chef's knife and insert it in the separation of the shell between the body and the tail of the lobster. (This kills the lobster instantly.)

**2.** Place the lobsters in a large stockpot, add all the other ingredients, and cover with cold water. Cover the pot, place it over high heat, and bring to a boil.

**3.** When the water comes to a boil, immediately remove the pot from the heat and let the lobsters sit in the hot liquid for 5 minutes. Then remove the lobsters and set them aside until they are cool enough to handle. Discard the liquid.

**4.** Remove the lobster meat from the shells: Twist the large claw legs to separate them from the body. Twist the body and tail to separate them. Scoop the green tomalley out of the body cavity and place it in an airtight freezer bag or container. (Female lobsters may have coral, which will be a very dark green, almost black. This turns red when fully cooked. Freeze it separately.) Using a mallet or the side of a large chef's knife, crack the claws and the legs; carefully remove the meat and set it aside. Use poultry shears to cut the underside of the tail. Remove the tail meat in one piece and set it aside.

**5.** Place the heads, along with the claw, leg, and tail shells, in plastic freezer containers; freeze for up to 6 months. Place the lobster meat in plastic containers and freeze for up to 3 months. Defrost in the refrigerator or microwave oven.

# BROILED LOBSTER

Meat of 4 prepared lobsters,
    tomalley, and coral,
    frozen (page 91) or fresh

¼ cup (½ stick) unsalted
    butter, room temperature

1 teaspoon brandy

2 teaspoons Madeira

1 teaspoon salt

¼ cup olive oil

Freshly ground black pepper
    to taste

4 lemon wedges

SERVES 4

1. Defrost the lobster meat for 5 hours in the refrigerator if frozen.

2. Combine the tomalley, coral, butter, brandy, Madeira, and ½ teaspoon of the salt in a blender. Whip until smooth. Transfer to a small serving bowl and set aside.

3. Preheat the broiler.

4. Place the lobster meat in a mixing bowl and add the olive oil. Sprinkle with the remaining ½ teaspoon salt and give a few turns of the peppermill. Toss to coat the meat with the oil.

5. Arrange the lobster meat on a broiling pan, and broil for 3 to 5 minutes or until hot. Transfer the tails to a cutting board and cut them into medallions. Arrange the tail and claw meat on a serving platter, decorate with lemon wedges, and serve immediately. Offer the whipped butter on the side.

# BOUILLABAISSE

**F**reezer technology lets us prepare this classic Mediterranean fish stew on the spot. Save those scraps of fish, shellfish, and shells in the freezer and use them to prepare the soup base. Then add assorted frozen or fresh fish to finish—almost anything except swordfish or tuna (their texture is unpleasant when boiled). Firm-fleshed fish such as monkfish, sea bass, and turbot make serving easier because the fillets don't fall apart easily. You might consider cooking small whole fish, or steaks of fish that flake easily, because the bones help keep the flesh intact. Try whole trout, or halibut steaks, for example. The greater the variety of fish, the greater the richness of the stew. Marinated or salt-cured fish are fine to use.

2 tablespoons olive oil

1 large onion, coarsely chopped (about 1 cup)

1 tablespoon finely minced garlic

¾ pound fish bones

¾ pound lobster heads and shells, or shrimp shells

5½ cups All-Purpose Broth (page 222)

2½ dry cups white wine

1 tablespoon fresh thyme leaves, or 1½ teaspoons dried

½ tablespoon salt, or as desired

½ teaspoon ground white pepper, or as desired

3 pounds potatoes

4 pounds assorted fish (such as monkfish, cod, bass, snapper, halibut), frozen or fresh cut into 2-inch chunks

Aïoli (recipe follows)

1. Heat the olive oil in a 3-quart pot over medium heat. Add the onion, garlic, bones, and shells. Cook, stirring occasionally, for 5 minutes. Then add the broth, wine, thyme, salt, and white pepper. Cover and bring to a boil; then uncover and simmer for 30 minutes.

2. Place a large strainer over a clean pot and strain the broth into it. Use a large wooden spoon to press down on the shells, bones, and vegetables, getting all their pulpy bits into the broth.

3. Peel the potatoes and cut them into 1-inch dice.

4. Combine the broth and potatoes in a large pot over high heat. Cover, bring to a boil, and cook for 2 minutes.

5. Add the fish, lower the heat to medium, and simmer, uncovered, for about 20 minutes or until the fish is done. Frozen fish will take about 5 minutes longer.

6. Using a slotted spoon, remove the fish and potatoes from the broth and arrange in a large serving bowl. Pour the broth into a soup tureen. Serve immediately, and pass the Aïoli.

SERVES 8 TO 10

# Aïoli

16 *peeled garlic cloves*

2 *egg yolks*

2 *tablespoons fresh lemon juice*

¼ *cup dried bread crumbs*

1 *teaspoon salt*

⅔ *cup olive oil*

SERVES 8 TO 10

**1.** Place the garlic, egg yolks, lemon juice, bread crumbs, and salt in a blender or food processor; blend until smooth, scraping down the sides of the container as necessary.

**2.** Slowly add the oil, a drop or two at a time, blending until incorporated. The mixture should have the consistency of a thick mayonnaise. Transfer the aïoli to a bowl and serve.

# POULTRY

In the freezer, birds are protected by their skin in much the same way that they are protected from the cold in nature: a layer of fat between the skin and the meat keeps the flesh from drying out. So even if you plan to remove the skin and/or the fat before cooking or serving, wait until you have defrosted the meat.

Skin and the substantial fat layer on waterfowl such as ducks and geese make them particularly well suited to freezing. It's too bad that the pleasures of these delicious and easy-to-prepare birds are relatively unknown on American tables. Yes, ducks and geese are fatty, but cooking them doesn't have to splatter your oven or dirty your kitchen. Using a simple steaming technique, we can de-fat and precook them in one step before freezing—and later finish them in the oven. Here the freezer works as a valuable tool to transform a tedious preparation into an easy staple of your entertaining repertoire.

Many chicken recipes are found in the chapter on stews, because chicken freezes so well when cooked in sauce. However, freezing poultry without any sauce is pure simplicity, as you'll see here.

## PREPARING UNCOOKED POULTRY FOR FREEZING

It takes up more space, but I prefer to freeze poultry on the bone. The bones flavor the meat and protect the texture during reheating. Of course, boneless cuts—like turkey paillards and chicken breasts—can also be frozen.

Buy fresh birds, and extract the giblets from the cavity. Rinse the bird inside and out, and dry it thoroughly with paper towels. Wrap the bird, whole or in pieces, in two layers of plastic wrap; then wrap it again in freezer paper. If you freeze the giblets in a self-closing freezer bag, you can add to them when you have more; use them in stuffings, pâtés, or confits. Do the same thing with the livers—eventually you'll have enough for a meal or a pâté. And the necks can be frozen to use in making broth. The chicken will keep for up to 3 months in the freezer. Defrost it 5 hours in the refrigerator or on the defrost setting of a microwave oven for 8 to 10 minutes per pound.

**SEASONING.** Seasoning before freezing adds to the flavor of the cooked bird, especially with white-fleshed fowl (chicken, turkey breast, capon, game hens, pheasant, partridge). The seasonings should enhance the chicken flavor, however, not add a competing flavor that will detract from the final dish. Garlic, rosemary, lemon, coriander, and salt and pepper are good choices.

**MARINATING.** The acid in a marinade will toughen white meat if it is in contact with it for more than a few hours. But dark-fleshed fowl (squab, duck, goose, and the dark meat of chicken, capon, and turkey) benefits from a marinade. You can use either a neutral one, such as the gin marinade on page 101, or you can impart a unique flavor, as in the peanut marinade on page 103.

**FREEZING WHOLE BIRDS:** If you have room in the freezer, by all means season and truss a whole bird for freezing (it will defrost and cook more evenly if trussed). I know that many people are afraid of freezing stuffed birds. I have never had a problem with it; I just make sure that the bird is fresh and well chilled and that I use fresh, well-chilled stuffing. The stuffed bird must be defrosted in the refrigerator; it will take at least 24 hours.

# PREPARING COOKED POULTRY FOR FREEZING

If you have leftovers, by all means freeze them. Wherever possible, leave the meat on the bones. The bits and pieces can be used later in salads, pasta dishes, casseroles, or burritos. The bones themselves can be frozen for use in broth. Breast meat, however, is never as good after defrosting. I prefer to use it in salads, pastas, or sandwiches without freezing it.

Boiled chicken doesn't freeze as well as chicken cooked by other methods—it's too waterlogged. If you do freeze boiled chicken, after defrosting roast, grill, broil, or sauté it in a little oil to rescue the flavor.

Cooked poultry can be frozen for 3 months.

# ROAST CHICKEN

Roasting is a dry-heat method of cooking and is particularly good for poultry. The radiant heat in the oven creates a crusty skin, bathing the bird with fat and sealing in moisture. The dark meat of roasted poultry freezes well, but the white meat may be dry after defrosting—use it in dishes where the other ingredients will add moisture.

1 *roasting hen (4 to 5 pounds)*

4 *cloves garlic*

1 *tablespoon fresh rosemary leaves, or 1 teaspoon dried*

*Rind of 1 lemon, all white pith removed*

½ *teaspoon ground coriander*

½ *tablespoon freshly ground black pepper*

1 *teaspoon salt*

½ *cup olive oil*

½ *cup water*

½ *cup dry white wine*

3 *tablespoons white wine vinegar*

2 *tablespoons chopped fresh parsley or chervil*

SERVES 4

**1.** Rinse the bird well under cold running water, pat it dry with a kitchen towel, and truss.

**2.** Combine the garlic, rosemary, lemon rind, coriander, pepper, salt, and 5 tablespoons of the oil in a small food processor or a blender. Purée until it forms a coarse paste. Rub the surface of the bird with the mixture. Place the bird on a plate, cover, and refrigerate for at least 2 hours, or up to 24 hours. ▨

**3.** Preheat the oven to 450°F.

**4.** Place the bird on its side in a roasting pan. Place it in the oven and immediately lower the temperature to 350°F. Cook for 20 minutes. Then turn it on the other side and cook another 20 minutes.

**5.** Turn the bird breast up, cover with a lid or aluminum foil, and bake for 20 minutes. Then remove the cover and cook another 20 minutes. The bird is done when the thigh moves loosely in its joint. Remove the bird from the roasting pan and set it aside on a serving platter.

**6.** Pour the water into the roasting pan, place the pan over medium-high heat, and scrape up any bits that may have stuck to the bottom. Pour the pan juices into a saucepan, and place over medium-high heat. Quickly cook the pan juices so that they caramelize on the bottom of the pan, about 5 minutes. Then pour off and discard any fat in the pan.

**7.** Return the pan to the heat and add the wine, vinegar, and remaining 3 tablespoons olive oil. Cook, scraping up the juices that have concentrated on the bottom of the pan, for 5 minutes or until the liquid has reduced by about one third. Remove the pan from the heat and stir in the parsley.

**8.** Untruss the bird, pour the sauce into a sauceboat, and serve immediately.

(continued)

Roast Chicken   (continued)

**Chicken Provençale:** Add ½ cup Tomato Concassée (page 223) and ¼ cup finely chopped black olives when you add the wine (Step 7).

**Minted Yogurt Chicken:** Remove the saucepan from the heat after the sauce has been reduced (Step 7). Whisk in 1 cup plain yogurt and 1 tablespoon chopped fresh mint leaves in place of the parsley.

**Herbed Chicken:** Substitute 1 tablespoon chopped fresh rosemary, basil, oregano, marjoram, or dill for the parsley.

**Miso Chicken:** Blend 2 tablespoons miso paste with 1 cup Madeira and 1 cup whipping cream. Add this to the pan juices in the saucepan instead of the wine, vinegar, and oil (Step 7). Cook until thickened, and then add the parsley.

**Stuffed Chicken:** Choose one of the stuffings on pages 242–243 and fill the bird either prior to freezing (page 95) or after defrosting. Increase the cooking time by 25 to 30 minutes.

▨ To freeze the uncooked bird, wrap in two layers of plastic wrap, then overwrap with freezer paper. Freeze for up to 3 months. Defrost in the refrigerator or microwave oven. To freeze leftover roast chicken, first cool it, uncovered, in the refrigerator for 1 hour. Then remove the legs from the body and remove any breast meat from the ribs. Place the pieces in freezer bags and freeze for up to 3 months. Use a large knife to break up the bones, and freeze them for later use in making All-Purpose Broth.

Defrost the meat in the refrigerator or microwave oven. For making broth, the bones can be cooked without defrosting.

# PAN-FRIED CHICKEN

The surprise that we've uncovered here is that pieces of pan-fried chicken can be frozen and then reheated, regaining their crispness and even seeming to lose some of the residual frying fat.

The chicken will have even more flavor if you use fat that has a good flavor. This can be leftover fat from Rillettes (page 210) or rendered fat from a steamed duck or goose (page 108). Or combine some bacon fat with the cooking oil.

Don't overcrowd the skillet, or the chicken will steam and not fry —perform this operation in batches if necessary.

Serve a flavored butter (pages 235–237) with the hot chicken.

*2 fryer chickens (3 pounds each), cut into 8 pieces each*

*6 tablespoons flour*

*2 tablespoons cornstarch*

*1½ tablespoons freshly ground black pepper, or as desired*

*1 teaspoon salt, or as desired*

*Cooking oil*

SERVES 8

1. Rinse the chicken pieces under cold running water, pat them dry with a kitchen towel, and set aside.

2. Combine the flour, cornstarch, pepper, and salt in a bowl and mix well. Add the chicken pieces and dust well, shaking off the excess.

3. Meanwhile, heat 1 inch of oil in a large cast-iron skillet over medium heat (the oil is hot enough when a drop of water dances across the surface and evaporates). Carefully place the chicken, skin side down, in the skillet and cook until golden, 8 to 10 minutes. Turn the chicken and cook until the other side is golden, another 10 minutes.

4. Remove the chicken from the skillet as the pieces brown, and place them on a baking sheet. ▨

5. Preheat the oven to 375°F.

6. Bake the white meat pieces for 10 minutes, the dark meat for 15.

7. Arrange a cloth napkin on a serving platter and place the chicken on the napkin. Serve immediately, or let the chicken cool, uncovered, and serve at picnic temperature.

▨ To freeze all or some of the chicken, let it cool to room temperature, then refrigerate, uncovered, until cold. Place the chicken in freezer bags,

(continued)

Pan-Fried Chicken  (continued)

or wrap tightly in two layers of plastic wrap. Freeze for up to 6 months.

Reheat defrosted chicken for 20 minutes in a preheated 375°F oven, or place the still-frozen chicken in a preheated 400°F oven and bake for 35 to 40 minutes, turning once.

# CHICKEN BREASTS STUFFED WITH BUTTER

This dish is also known as Chicken Kiev—a boneless breast rolled around a butter filling, coated with bread crumbs and cooked—but the name conjures up such memories of pretentious restaurant cooking that I prefer to call it by what it is, not its fantasy name. Use any of the flavored chilled butters on pages 235–237, and make up your own name for the dish if you like.

Bread-crumb coatings need to set before cooking, and when they set in the freezer, there is less likelihood that they will leak during cooking.

*¼ cup flour*

*2 cups fresh bread crumbs*

*2 eggs*

*4 large skinless, boneless chicken breast halves*

*½ cup Chilled Whipped Butter (page 235)*

*3 tablespoons unsalted butter or margarine, melted*

*4 lemon wedges*

SERVES 4

1. Sprinkle the flour in one rimmed plate or pie dish and the crumbs in another. Beat the eggs in a third dish.

2. Lay each chicken breast between two sheets of wax paper or plastic wrap. Using the side of a large chef's knife or the bottom of a heavy skillet, pound the chicken until very thin.

3. Place 2 tablespoons of room-temperature butter sauce on each breast. Fold the short ends over the butter, then fold the long sides over each other. Press the meat together firmly to enclose the stuffing completely.

4. Dust each breast in the flour. Then roll it in the eggs, coating it completely. Finally roll it in the crumbs, patting to make them

adhere. Place the breasts on a tray, and using a brush, dab all over with the melted butter. Freeze for 1 hour, uncovered, before baking. ⊠

**5.** Preheat the oven to 425°F.

**6.** Place the breasts in a baking pan and bake for 20 minutes, turning once.

**7.** Arrange the chicken on plates, garnish with the lemon wedges, and serve immediately.

---

**Chicken Breasts Stuffed with Pâté:** Use a pâté mixture—meat, chicken, or seafood—in place of the butter stuffing. Serve a dab of Herb Butter (page 235) on top of each breast.

---

**Chicken Breasts Stuffed with Mushrooms:** Substitute 2 tablespoons Mushroom Duxelles (page 240) for the butter stuffing, and serve over Mushroom Pasta Sauce (page 196).

---

⊠ To freeze, wrap the breasts individually in plastic wrap, place them in freezer bags and freeze for up to 4 months. To cook, place the frozen breasts directly in a preheated 375°F oven and bake for 40 minutes, turning once.

---

# ROASTED MARINATED CHICKEN THIGHS

This gin marinade for poultry is tasty but it does not predominate, so you can serve the chicken with a variety of condiments such as salsa, chutney, mint jelly, mustard, or olives. The white meat toughens and gets dry when frozen in a marinade, so use white meat for this recipe only if you're going to marinate and cook directly.

(continued)

Roasted Marinated Chicken Thighs   (continued)

18 *chicken thighs*

½ *teaspoon salt, or as desired*

¼ *teaspoon ground white pepper*

1 *cup gin*

¼ *cup olive oil*

1 *cup dry vermouth or white wine*

SERVES 6

**1.** Place the chicken pieces in a mixing bowl or pan, and sprinkle them with the salt and white pepper. Add the gin and olive oil, cover, and refrigerate for 4 hours. ▨

**2.** Preheat the oven to 375°F.

**3.** Remove the chicken pieces from the marinade and pat them dry. Heat the oil in a roasting pan or large ovenproof skillet over medium-high heat. Add the chicken, skin side down, without crowding, and brown on both sides, about 12 minutes total. (You may have to perform this operation in batches.) Remove the pieces as they are browned, and set aside.

**4.** Pour off and discard any grease, and return the chicken, skin side up, to the skillet in one layer. Add the vermouth. Transfer the skillet to the oven, and bake for 30 minutes.

**5.** To serve, arrange the chicken on a platter and scrape any pan juices over the thighs.

**Roasted Chicken Thighs with Green Olive Purée:** While the chicken is cooking, place 2 quartered medium onions and 2 cups of pitted green olives in a food processor and blend until chunky. Place in a medium pot and cook, stirring, for 15 minutes or until the mixture becomes dry. Remove from the heat and stir in 4 tablespoons unsalted butter. To serve, pour the olive purée onto a serving platter and arrange the chicken thighs on top.

**Mustard Chicken:** When the chicken thighs are done, arrange them on a platter. Whisk 3 tablespoons of Dijon mustard and 3 tablespoons of plain yogurt into the juices in the skillet. Scrape this sauce over the thighs and serve.

**Chicken with Mint Jelly:** When the chicken thighs are done, arrange them on a platter. Whisk ¼ cup of mint jelly and 2 tablespoons of white wine vinegar into the juices in the skillet. Scrape this sauce over the thighs and serve.

⊠ To freeze, place all or some of the uncooked chicken, along with a few spoonfuls of the marinade, in a freezer bag or container. Freeze for up to 3 months. Defrost before proceeding with Steps 2–5.

# PEANUT CHICKEN THIGHS

In this variation on Thai saté, you prepare the chicken for freezing by marinating it in beer, soy, and vinegar. Then the peanut butter is added after cooking to flavor and emulsify the sauce.

⅓ *cup soy sauce*

3 *tablespoons rice vinegar*

1 *can (12 ounces) beer*

2 *tablespoons minced garlic*

⅛ *teaspoon cayenne pepper, or as desired*

16 *chicken thighs*

¼ *cup peanut butter*

¾ *cup unsalted peanuts*

1 *large bunch cilantro, long stems trimmed*

SERVES 8

1. Combine the soy sauce, rice vinegar, beer, garlic, and cayenne in a bowl or plastic freezer bag, and add the chicken. Refrigerate, covered, for 1 hour. ⊠

2. Place the chicken and marinade in a Dutch oven or ovenproof casserole, cover, and place in the oven. Turn the oven on to 375°F and bake for 45 minutes. Remove the casserole from the oven.

3. Preheat the broiler.

4. Arrange the chicken in one layer on a broiling pan, and broil for 5 minutes to crisp the skin.

5. Meanwhile, pour the cooking juices into a blender or food processor, add the peanut butter, and blend until smooth.

6. To serve, place the chicken on a serv-

(continued)

Peanut Chicken Thighs (continued)

ing platter and pour the sauce over. Garnish with the peanuts and cilantro.

---

⊠ To freeze, place all or some of the chicken and marinade in freezer bags, squeeze out as much air as possible, and freeze for up to 3 months.

Defrost chicken before proceeding with Steps 2–6; or place the still-frozen chicken in a casserole and bake as directed for 1 hour and 10 minutes.

---

# SAUTÉED MARINATED DRUMSTICKS

It's not a good idea to marinate white meat in this marinade for more than an hour or two because the vinegar toughens it. So if you want to use breasts, marinate and then cook them directly.

**16 chicken drumsticks**

**¼ cup plus 3 tablespoons sherry wine vinegar**

**½ teaspoon salt**

**¼ teaspoon ground white pepper**

**2 tablespoons flavorless cooking oil**

**1 medium onion, finely minced (about ¾ cup)**

**¼ cup Tomato Concassée (page 223), or 1 tablespoon tomato paste**

**⅓ cup All-Purpose Broth (page 222), canned low-sodium chicken broth, or water**

**2 tablespoons unsalted butter**

1. Place the chicken in a large mixing bowl and add ¼ cup vinegar, the salt, and the white pepper. Refrigerate, covered, for 1 hour. ⊠

2. Preheat the oven to 375°F. Remove the chicken from the marinade and pat dry.

3. Heat the oil in an ovenproof skillet over medium-high heat. Add the chicken and onions, reduce the heat to medium, and cook 5 minutes, turning once.

4. Drain off any excess fat and add the tomato concassée, remaining 3 tablespoons vinegar, and broth to the skillet. Cover, transfer the skillet to the oven, and bake for 35 minutes.

5. Transfer the skillet to the stovetop, and arrange the chicken on a serving platter. Add the butter to the skillet and whisk until incorporated.

6. Pour the sauce over the chicken and serve immediately.

SERVES 8

▧ To freeze, place all or some of the chicken and marinade in freezer bags, squeeze out as much air as possible, and freeze for up to 3 months. Defrost before proceeding with Steps 2–6.

# PREPARING TURKEY PAILLARDS FOR FREEZING

Paillards are thin pieces of boneless meat. The gentle pounding breaks the long meat fibers, so when the turkey is frozen, defrosted, and cooked, there is little drip loss or shrinkage.

*1 boneless turkey breast (about 6 pounds), split*
*Salt to taste*
*Ground white pepper to taste*

SERVES 10 TO 12

1. Carefully remove the skin from the turkey. Remove the lozenge-shaped pieces of meat (called the tenderloin) from the underside of the breast halves and set them aside.

2. Place the two breast halves on a cutting board, and cut them against the grain into ½-inch-thick slices. Place each slice between two pieces of plastic wrap or wax paper, and using a mallet or the side of a large chef's knife, flatten each slice until it is ⅜ to ¼ inch thick. Cut the tenderloins crosswise into two pieces each. Lay them on their cut side between two pieces of wax paper, and flatten gently. You should have about 15 slices total.

3. Sprinkle the paillards with salt and white pepper.

4. Place the slices of turkey breast between pieces of freezer paper, and wrap tightly in two layers of plastic wrap; or place them in freezer bags, squeezing out as much air as possible. Seal and freeze for up to 6 months. Defrost paillards in the refrigerator or microwave oven.

# SAUTÉED TURKEY PAILLARDS WITH CRANBERRIES

*4 slices (3 to 4 ounces each) turkey paillard (page 105), frozen or fresh*

*1 tablespoon sugar*

*3 tablespoons red wine vinegar*

*1 tablespoon flavorless cooking oil*

*½ cup frozen or fresh cranberries*

SERVES 2

1. Defrost the paillards if frozen. Pat them dry, and set aside.

2. Combine the sugar and vinegar in a small bowl and set aside.

3. Heat the oil in a medium-size stainless steel or aluminum skillet over medium heat. Add the turkey and cook for 2 minutes on each side. Transfer the turkey to a plate and keep warm in a 250°F oven.

4. Add the sugar/vinegar mixture to the skillet, and cook until it bubbles and turns caramel color, about 3 minutes. Immediately decrease the heat to low and add the cranberries. Cook, stirring, for 5 minutes or until the cranberries soften and burst but do not completely fall apart.

5. Remove the turkey from the oven, and stir any juices that have collected into the skillet. Arrange the paillards on plates, top with a dollop of cranberry garnish, and serve immediately.

# TURKEY PAILLARDS AND PEPPERS

*4 slices (3 to 4 ounces each) turkey paillard (page 105), frozen or fresh*

*3 tablespoons flour*

*1 red bell pepper*

*3 tablespoons olive oil*

*¼ teaspoon ground coriander*

*3 tablespoons plain yogurt*

SERVES 2

1. Defrost the paillards if frozen. Pat them dry and dust lightly with the flour, shaking off the excess. Set them aside on a plate.

2. Halve the pepper from tip to stem. Cut out and discard the stem, core, and seeds. Cut each half into ¼-inch strips and set them aside.

3. Heat the oil in a medium-size skillet over medium heat. Add the turkey and cook for 2 minutes on each side. Transfer the turkey to a plate and keep warm in a 250°F oven.

**4.** Add the peppers and coriander to the skillet and cook, and tossing, for 5 minutes. Then remove the skillet from the heat and stir in the yogurt.

**5.** Arrange the turkey on individual plates, and stir any juices that have collected around them into the sauce. Spoon sauce and peppers over the turkey, and serve.

# TURKEY LOAF

**F**ortunately most ground turkey that we find in the supermarket today is two parts dark to one part white meat—the perfect ratio for achieving good turkey flavor and moist texture. Just make sure it's freshly ground.

½ *cup (1 stick) unsalted butter*

2 *large onions, finely chopped (about 2 cups)*

¼ *cup flour*

1 *cup milk*

1½ *teaspoons salt, or as desired*

1 *teaspoon ground white pepper*

2 *teaspoons chopped fresh thyme leaves, or 1 teaspoon dried*

3 *eggs, beaten*

¼ *cup wheat germ*

3 *pounds fresh ground turkey*

1 *cup dry vermouth*

SERVES 6

**1.** Melt ¼ cup of the butter in a medium-size skillet over medium heat. Add the onions and cook, stirring, for 5 minutes. Sprinkle the flour over the onions and cook, stirring, 1 more minute. Slowly add the milk, stirring. Then add the salt, white pepper, and thyme. Cook about 2 minutes or until the mixture is thick and bubbling. Remove the skillet from the heat and transfer the mixture to a bowl. Stir for a few minutes, let it cool slightly, then refrigerate until chilled, about 20 minutes.

**2.** When the mixture is chilled, add the eggs, wheat germ, and turkey and mix well. ▨

**3.** Place the mixture in a loaf pan. Cover it with aluminum foil, place on the middle rack of the oven, and turn the oven on to 350°F. Bake for 50 minutes.

**4.** Remove the pan from the oven, uncover, and pour any liquid into a small saucepan. Add the vermouth to the saucepan and place it over high heat. Cook until the liquid has reduced by one third, about 10 minutes. Then remove the pan from the heat and whisk in the remaining ¼ cup butter.

(continued)

Turkey Loaf   (continued)

**5.** Invert the loaf onto a serving plate. Cut into inch-thick slices, and arrange them neatly. Drizzle the sauce around the loaf and serve immediately.

---

☒ To freeze, place all or half of the mixture in a freezer bag or container, and freeze for up to 3 months. Defrost turkey loaf before baking.

---

# STEAMING DUCK AND GOOSE FOR FREEZING

This is a great simple technique for defatting large fatty birds. You can steam the birds whole or in pieces; it also works with turkey legs. This method precooks the meat only partially. The result is moist, tender, defatted meat and crispy skin in much less cooking time.

*2 ducklings (4 to 5 pounds each), or 1 goose (8 to 10 pounds)*
*1 tablespoon kosher salt*
*1 teaspoon freshly ground black pepper*

DUCK SERVES 4 TO 6
GOOSE SERVES 6 TO 8

**1.** Remove any giblets from the cavity of the birds and set them aside or freeze for another use. Remove any fat deposits from the cavity, and cut off excess skin around the neck. Rinse the birds under cold running water and pat dry. Sprinkle the cavity with some of the kosher salt and pepper. Sever the wing tips at the first joint and reserve them with the giblets for another use. Tie the legs together at the ankles, and sprinkle the outside of the bird with the remaining salt and pepper.

**2.** If you don't have a steamer, improvise one: Use a roasting rack or create one by placing two small heatproof baking dishes or loaf pans upside down in a larger roasting pan. Fill the steamer with 2 inches of water and place the birds, breast side up, on the rack. Cover tightly with the lid or with aluminum foil, and place over high heat.

When the water boils, reduce the heat to low and steam approximately 15 minutes per pound.

**3.** Remove the steamer from the heat, and transfer the birds to a plate. Let them cool to room temperature, and then wrap tightly in two layers of freezer wrap. Wrap again in freezer paper. Freeze for up to 6 months. Defrost in the refrigerator or microwave oven.

While the birds are cooling, strain the steaming liquid into a container and allow it to cool to room temperature. Then refrigerate until chilled. Remove the fat, discarding any remaining water, and pack it into freezer containers. Freeze for up to 1 year. (Use the fat for frying and sautéing.)

# ROAST DUCKLING OR GOOSE

I once bought two live geese for Christmas dinner. They were slaughtered and hung in a meat cooler for a couple of weeks to develop flavor and become tender. They were by far the worst birds anyone has ever eaten. Frozen geese defrosting in the refrigerator may be less picturesque, but at least I'm assured of a good result!

*2 ducklings (4 to 5 pounds each), or 1 goose (8 to 10 pounds), steamed (page 108), frozen or fresh, with reserved giblets*

*Pan Gravy, Apple Cider Sauce, Green Peppercorn and Raspberry Sauce, or Sweet Spicy Ginger Sauce (recipes follow)*

DUCK SERVES 4 TO 6
GOOSE SERVES 6 TO 8

**1.** Defrost the birds and giblets if frozen. Preheat the oven to 365°F.

**2.** Place the birds on their sides in a roasting pan, and add the giblets, neck, and wings. Place the pan in the oven and cook for 15 minutes. Turn the birds to the other side and cook another 10 minutes. Finally, turn the birds breast side up and cook 12 minutes per pound, basting (another 45 minutes for a 4-pound duck, or 1½ hours for an 8-pound goose).

**3.** Remove the bird from the oven and set it on a platter. Remove any trussing, and serve the bird with one of the sauces.

## PAN GRAVY

**A** simply roasted bird, moistened with a bit of pan gravy, allows for other culinary extravagances. Prepare a variety of vegetable side dishes, some bread stuffing, and sautéed apples for a festive meal.

**3 tablespoons duck or goose fat (page 108)**

**1 medium onion, coarsely chopped (about ¾ cup)**

**Giblets from roasted duck or goose, coarsely chopped**

**2 tablespoons flour**

**½ cup dry red wine**

**1½ cups All-Purpose Broth (page 222) or canned low-sodium chicken broth**

**1.** Melt the fat in a saucepan over medium heat. Add the onions and giblets and cook, stirring, about 5 minutes. Then sprinkle the flour over the onions, and mix to incorporate. Add the wine and broth, and cook until the gravy is thick enough to lightly coat the back of a spoon.

**2.** Pour the gravy through a strainer into a sauceboat, and discard the onions and giblets. Serve with the roasted bird.

1½ CUPS, 4 TO 5 SERVINGS

## APPLE CIDER SAUCE

**T**his tart, astringent sauce lightens the richness of the meat.

**1 green apple**

**1 tablespoon fresh lemon juice**

**⅓ cup cider vinegar**

**2 cups apple cider, preferably unfiltered**

**Giblets from roasted duck or goose, chopped**

**½ cup whipping cream**

**3 tablespoons unsalted butter**

**1.** Peel, core, and finely chop the apple. Place it in a small mixing bowl, toss with the lemon juice, cover, and set aside in the refrigerator.

**2.** Combine the vinegar, cider, and giblets in a small saucepan over medium heat, and bring to a boil. Cook until the liquid has reduced by one third, about 20 minutes. Then add the cream and continue to cook until the sauce is thick enough to coat the back of a spoon, another 10 to 15 minutes. Remove the pan from the heat and whisk in the butter.

**3.** Strain the apples. Strain the sauce into

1½ CUPS, 4 TO 5 SERVINGS

a sauceboat and stir in the apples. Serve with the roasted bird.

# GREEN PEPPERCORN AND RASPBERRY SAUCE

You won't believe how perfect this sauce is until you prepare it. The juxtaposition of spicy peppercorns and fruity, sweet raspberries is a classic with venison and lamb—and tastes equally marvelous with duck or goose.

½ cup dry white wine

¾ cup All-Purpose Broth (page 222) or canned low-sodium chicken broth

2 tablespoons raspberry preserves or raspberry sauce (page 269)

Giblets from roasted duck or goose, coarsely chopped

½ cup whipping cream

1 tablespoon unsalted butter

2 tablespoons green peppercorns in water, drained

1. Combine the wine, broth, preserves, and giblets in a saucepan and bring to a boil over medium heat. Cook until the liquid has reduced by about half, about 15 minutes. Then add the cream and continue to cook until the mixture has reduced enough to coat the back of a spoon, another 10 to 15 minutes.

2. Remove the sauce from the heat and whisk in the butter. Strain it into a sauceboat, and discard the giblets. Stir in the peppercorns, and serve with the roasted bird.

1½ CUPS, 4 TO 5 SERVINGS

# SWEET SPICY GINGER SAUCE

The charm of a gingersnap cookie lies in its sweet and hot quality—like those little cinnamon-flavored red-hot candies. I don't understand why Western cuisines have never used much ginger in their savory cooking. After making this sauce you will wonder why as well.

(continued)

Sweet Spicy Ginger Sauce (continued)

3 tablespoons white wine vinegar

2 cups All-Purpose Broth (page 222) or canned low-sodium chicken broth

Giblets from roasted duck or goose, coarsely chopped

2 ounces crystallized ginger, finely chopped (about ⅓ cup)

½ cup whipping cream

**1.** Combine the vinegar, broth, and giblets in a small saucepan over medium heat and bring to a boil. Cook until the liquid has reduced by about half, about 20 minutes. Add the ginger and cream and continue to cook for another 10 minutes or until the sauce is thick enough to coat the back of a spoon. Remove the pan from the heat, remove the giblets with a slotted spoon, and whisk in the butter.

**2.** Pour the sauce into a sauceboat and serve with the roasted bird.

1½ CUPS, 4 TO 5 SERVINGS

# ROASTED DUCK AND TURNIPS

Turnips taste delicious when they roast along with the duck, bathing in its fatty juices.

1 duckling (4 to 5 pounds), steamed (page 108), with its giblets, frozen or fresh

3 medium turnips, cut into 1-inch cubes, or about 1½ cups frozen diced turnips

1 large onion, finely diced (about 1 cup)

½ teaspoon salt, or as desired

Freshly ground black pepper to taste

½ recipe Pan Gravy (page 110)

**1.** Defrost the duckling and giblets if frozen. Preheat the oven to 375°F.

**2.** Place the duck, breast down, in a roasting pan. Cover and bake for 30 minutes.

**3.** Uncover the pan, turn the bird breast up, and cook another 15 minutes per pound. Thirty minutes before the duck is done, add the turnips, onions, salt, and pepper and toss well, coating the turnips with any duck drippings. Bake, uncovered, another 1¼ hours, tossing the turnips and onions occasionally.

**4.** Meanwhile, prepare the pan gravy.

**5.** Transfer the duck to a serving platter, and surround it with the turnips and onions. Serve immediately, with the gravy on the side.

SERVES 2 TO 3

# BRAISED DUCK WITH CARAWAY, CUMIN, AND CABBAGE

This preparation is an unfamiliar one for many Americans—the accompaniment is savory and aromatic, almost acrid in the way it piques the nose. But it's truly magical. Serve this with small boiled potatoes.

1 *duckling (4 to 5 pounds) steamed (page 108), frozen or fresh*

1 *small head red cabbage*

1 *tablespoon whole cumin seed*

1 *teaspoon whole caraway seed*

½ *teaspoon freshly ground black pepper*

**Salt to taste**

1½ *cups All-Purpose Broth (page 222) or canned low-sodium chicken broth*

SERVES 2 TO 3

**1.** Defrost the duck if frozen.

**2.** Preheat the oven to 350°F.

**3.** Untruss the bird and cut it into 8 serving pieces. Using a small knife, completely remove all remaining meat from the carcass and chop it fine. Set the serving pieces aside on a plate, and place the chopped meat in a mixing bowl.

**4.** Cut the cabbage in half from root to tip, and cut out the core. Lay each half on a work surface, cut side down, and slice as fine as you can from tip to stem. Place the shredded cabbage in the mixing bowl with the chopped meat. Add the cumin, caraway, pepper, and salt. Mix well.

**5.** Make a bed of the cabbage mixture in a roasting pan, and place the duck pieces on top, skin side up. Pour in the broth, cover, and bake for 45 minutes. Then uncover, raise the heat to 375°F, and continue to cook for another 30 minutes or until the skin is crisp.

**6.** Transfer the contents of the roasting pan to a large casserole, and serve immediately.

# BRAISED GOOSE WITH HONEY CARROTS

The colors of the dark golden goose and the pastel orange carrots tell you right away how this dish is going to taste—sweet, but not sugary.

1 *goose (8 to 10 pounds),*
   *steamed (page 108),*
   *frozen or fresh*

4 *cups thinly sliced carrots*

1 *large onion, finely diced*
   *(about 1 cup)*

½ *teaspoon salt, or as*
   *desired*

¼ *teaspoon ground white*
   *pepper*

½ *cup All-Purpose Broth*
   *(page 222) or canned*
   *low-sodium chicken broth*

½ *cup whipping cream*

¼ *cup honey*

SERVES 8

**1.** Defrost the goose if frozen.

**2.** Preheat the oven to 350°F.

**3.** Untruss the cooked bird and cut it into 8 serving pieces. Using a small knife, completely remove all remaining meat from the carcass. Set the meat aside on a plate.

**4.** Combine the carrots, onions, salt, and white pepper in a roasting pan and mix well. Arrange the small bits of meat from the carcass over the vegetables, and place the serving pieces, skin up, on top.

**5.** Combine the broth, cream, and honey. Pour this mixture over the goose, cover, and bake for 30 minutes. Then uncover, raise the heat to 375°F, and cook for another 45 minutes or until the skin is crisp.

**6.** Remove the serving pieces from the pan and keep warm. Transfer the carrot mixture to a 2-quart pot and place it over medium heat. Cook, stirring, for 6 to 8 minutes or until the liquid has thickened.

**7.** To serve, pour the carrot mixture onto a platter and arrange the goose on top.

# MEAT

I find it extremely convenient to have partially prepared meat dishes in the freezer. On short notice, I can defrost and finish them in several ways. The point, as always, is to retrieve high-quality, flavorful, tender meat from the freezer. Cuts of meat that require long cooking to develop their full flavor and tenderness do not suffer when frozen and defrosted—in fact, freezing will actually tenderize them. When liquid freezes, it expands, so as meat freezes and its juices expand, some of the meat fiber is broken in the process, making it more tender. Pot roasts, ribs, shanks, flank steak, London broil, stew meat, leg or shoulder of lamb, and all pork can be successfully frozen. On the other hand, freezing will not improve inferior quality. Don't freeze a chewy steak that should have been tender in the first place, hoping to improve it. The most successfully frozen and defrosted foods are those of the best quality.

When we freeze meats, we want to improve the original product in the process, or at least to do it no damage. Several years ago I would never have suggested that the home cook freeze tender cuts such as prime rib of beef or a sirloin steak. But I've changed my mind, because I've developed a method that maintains the quality of these meats.

If you do choose to buy tender cuts, those that freeze best have been dry-aged, or hung in cold storage with lots of air circulation. Dry-aged meat will change less by being frozen than will non-aged or commercially aged supermarket-type meat.

**PREPARING MEATS FOR THE FREEZER.** Trim the meat and wrap it for the freezer following the directions on page 13, making sure you label and date each package. Meat freezes best when packaged in relatively small (meal-size) quantities and placed in a section of the freezer (preferably the bottom) where air can circulate freely around the package. If you don't have such a space in your freezer, try to create one, moving well-frozen foods to a more crowded section. Other tips:

▪ You can defrost frozen meat, cook it, and refreeze the cooked dish.

- I don't recommend it, but you can refreeze raw meat if it has defrosted in the refrigerator. However, don't keep it for more than a few weeks before cooking it. Bacteria in the meat multiplies even in the freezer and needs to be killed by cooking.
- It is also risky to refreeze ground meat. Bacteria grows on the cut surfaces of meat, so the fewer exposed sides the better. Ground meat by its nature is a mass of cut surfaces.
- If you buy commercially frozen ground meat, don't defrost it until you're ready to use it. If you buy ground meat to freeze or grind it yourself, make sure you freeze it promptly.
- Don't let cooked meat or poultry come in contact with any platter, cutting board, draining board, or other surface previously touched by the meat when it was raw, unless that surface has been washed thoroughly. That goes for utensils and hands, too. Bacteria in the raw product can contaminate the cooked food. When we then freeze this food in our home freezers, we can't kill all the bacteria—we just slow its growth significantly.
- For defrosting cooked or uncooked meat, follow the instructions on page 14. Do not defrost foods on the kitchen counter or in the sink under running water. Don't leave frozen meat to defrost all day in an automatic oven set to cook the meat before you arrive home. Meat is not safe if left above 40°F (in other words, unrefrigerated) for more than 2 hours.

**BRAISING CUTS.** A technique that I find invaluable, especially for entertaining, is to braise certain meats at my leisure, freeze them, then defrost and reheat or place it on a grill to barbecue or smoke. The time-consuming preparation is done ahead, while the final step is done in the presence of your guests. I use this method for ribs (see page 122), but it also works perfectly with chuck roast, brisket, small pot roast, shoulder of lamb, pork and veal roast, and top round—any large or tough piece of meat that you may eventually want to grill. Begin by browning the meat in a skillet or in the oven; then add liquid, cover, and braise in a slow oven for part of the required cooking time. Cool the meat in the braising liquid (it will still be tough). Remove the meat; chill and freeze it. Strain the braising liquid and freeze it separately. For entertaining, simply defrost the meat and braising liquid. Finish the meat by grilling or smoking it, covered, over indirect heat, and reduce the braising liquid to a sauce or glaze.

**ROASTS.** You can enjoy a large roast even if you're a family of only 2 or 4 and freeze the remainder. Retrieve it from the freezer to serve again or use it in a variety of different ways—for hash or sandwiches, in pastas and salads for instance. Here's how it's done: Double-wrap a defrosted cooked roast in microwave plastic wrap. Place on a rack in a casserole. Cover and reheat in a 250°F oven. After it's completely hot, unwrap it. Turn the temperature to

450°F and replace the roast in the oven to crust the outside. This technique works wonders with large cuts such as whole pork loins, veal round roasts, fresh ham, prime rib and whole sirloins.

**PAILLARDS AND CUTLETS.** These small, thin pieces of uncooked meat are versatile and quick to defrost. You can have your butcher slice paillards for you if you don't trust your knife skills. Pound them thin prior to freezing.

# STANDING RIB ROAST

I love prime ribs, but usually not the restaurants that serve them, so I make them at home. I believe in slow cooking for large tender cuts of red meat, and the larger the piece of meat the better it roasts. But many cooks are intimidated by the size of an 8-rib roast, so the recipe is written for one with 4. If you do attempt the full 8-rib size, increase the cooking time by about 12 minutes per pound. Count on a rib feeding 2 people and let your guests fight over the bone.

A meat thermometer should read 110°F, or very rare, when the roast is removed from the oven because it will continue to cook while it sits, eventually reaching an internal temperature of 127°F, a nice rare. If that is too rare for you, add another minute per pound to the cooking time.

1 *standing beef roast (4 ribs, 10 to 11 pounds)*

2 *tablespoons flavorless cooking oil*

*Salt and freshly ground black pepper to taste*

**TO SERVE:**

*Horseradish, mustard, or Caraway, Cabbage, and Potatoes, or Red Wine Sauce, or Onion and Dried Tomato Sauce (optional; recipes follow)*

SERVES 8

1. Preheat the oven to 450°F.

2. Trim the excess fat from the roast, leaving a thickness of only ¼ inch. Heat the oil in a large roasting pan over medium-high heat. When the oil is hot, place the roast, fat side down, in the pan and brown for 5 minutes. Turn the roast on one end and cook another 5 minutes. Turn it on the other end and cook 5 minutes. Remove the roast from the heat and discard the fat. Set the roast on a rack in the pan. Sprinkle with salt and pepper.

3. Place the roast in the oven and immediately reduce the heat to 350°F. Roast approximately 12 minutes per pound for medium-rare, or about 2 hours for a 10-pound roast.

(continued)

Standing Rib Roast   (continued)

**4.** Remove the roast from the pan, and let it stand for 25 minutes before carving.

**5.** Serve the roast with horseradish and mustard, or prepare one of the accompaniments.

---

⊠ To freeze: Do not carve the entire roast if you don't have to. A whole piece of meat will cook more successfully when defrosted than will a few smaller pieces. Place a heavy skillet over high heat and when it is hot, place the remainder of the roast, cut side down, in the pan. Sear it well. Then allow the meat to cool to room temperature. Wrap it in plastic wrap, and then overwrap with freezer paper. Freeze for up to 1 month. Defrost, without unwrapping, in the refrigerator for 24 to 28 hours. Reheat as below, or use to make Pepper Steak (page 121).

To reheat a defrosted cooked rib roast, doublewrap in microwave plastic wrap, and place it on a rack in a casserole. Cover and reheat in a 250°F oven. Cook about 8 to 10 minutes per pound, or until a meat thermometer placed in the thickest part of the roast reads 110°F. Remove the casserole from the oven and raise the temperature to 450°F. Unwrap the roast, replace it in the casserole, and roast, uncovered, for about 15 minutes or until the outside is crisp.

---

# CARAWAY, CABBAGE, AND POTATOES

*3 cups shredded red cabbage*

*1 tablespoon brown sugar*

*1 tablespoon caraway seeds*

*¼ cup red wine vinegar*

*½ cup All-Purpose Broth (page 222) or canned low-sodium chicken broth*

*2 tablespoons unsalted butter*

**1.** Combine the cabbage, brown sugar, caraway, vinegar, and broth in a saucepan and stir well. Cook over medium heat, stirring occasionally, until the cabbage is tender, about 7 minutes. Remove the pan from the heat and stir in the butter.

**2.** Arrange the cabbage on a platter, and place the slices of rib roast on top of the cabbage. Serve immediately.

SERVES 4

## RED WINE SAUCE

1 *cup dry red wine*

1 *cup All-Purpose Broth*
   *(page 222) or canned*
   *low-sodium chicken broth*

3 *tablespoons unsalted butter*

SERVES 4

Discard any excess fat in the roasting pan, and add the wine and stock (or combine the wine and stock in a small saucepan). Bring to a boil and cook, stirring, until the liquid has reduced by about two thirds, 10 to 15 minutes. Remove the pan from the heat and whisk in the butter. Pour the sauce into a sauceboat, and serve it alongside the roast.

## ONION AND DRIED TOMATO SAUCE

2 *onions, finely sliced*

½ *cup dehydrated tomatoes,*
   *chopped*

1 *teaspoon chopped fresh*
   *rosemary, or* ½ *teaspoon*
   *dried*

1 *cup dry white wine*

3 *tablespoons unsalted butter*

SERVES 4

Combine the onions, tomatoes, rosemary, and wine in a small saucepan. Cook, stirring, over high heat until the wine has almost completely evaporated, 8 to 10 minutes. Remove the pan from the heat and whisk in the butter. Pour the sauce into a sauceboat, and serve it alongside the roast.

# ROAST SIRLOIN OF BEEF

**A** whole sirloin strip cooks rather differently from the same piece of meat cut into individual (New York) steaks. I think the roast develops better flavor and certainly better texture when cooked in a large piece. And I also find it economical to buy a large strip and freeze half of it after roasting. Ask your butcher for the entire strip. Have him trim off the "butt end"—it has a gristly vein through part of it—and freeze it for a minute steak or for preparing a quick sauté, stir-fry, or fajitas.

(continued)

Roast Sirloin of Beef   (continued)

1 *beef sirloin strip (about 6 pounds, trimmed weight)*

½ *teaspoon salt*

¼ *cup Worcestershire sauce*

2 *tablespoons finely minced or puréed garlic*

*Freshly ground black pepper to taste*

½ *cup finely minced shallots*

2 *cups robust red wine, such as a California cabernet*

1 *cup red wine vinegar*

6 *tablespoons (¾ stick) unsalted butter*

*Salt to taste*

SERVES 8 TO 10

1. Preheat the oven to 500°F.

2. If the butcher hasn't done so, trim the thick outer layer of fat from the strip, leaving ¼ inch. Using a paring knife, score the remaining fat in a crisscross pattern.

3. Sprinkle the fat side of the strip with the salt, and place the strip, fat side down, in a roasting pan. Mix the Worcestershire sauce and garlic together in a small bowl, and rub this on the meat sides of the steak.

4. Place the strip in the oven and immediately reduce the heat to 325°F. Cook the steak for 20 minutes.

5. Using two tongs or spatulas, turn the steak over without piercing the crust that has formed. Cook another 35 minutes for medium-rare. (Total cooking time is about 9 minutes per pound.)

6. Remove the pan from the oven and transfer the roast to a platter. ⊠ Let it rest for 15 minutes before carving. Pour out any fat in the roasting pan.

7. While the strip is resting, place the roasting pan over medium heat, add the shallots, and cook, stirring, about 2 minutes.

8. Add the wine and vinegar. Continue to cook, stirring, until the liquid has almost evaporated, about 10 minutes. Remove the pan from the heat, and pour in any juices that have collected from the roast. Whisk in the butter. Taste for salt and add as desired.

9. Pour the sauce into a sauceboat, and serve it alongside the sirloin. Carve the meat at the table.

⊠ To freeze, slice off a portion of the roasted strip. Place a heavy skillet over high heat and when it is hot, add the sirloin, cut end down. Sear the meat for 1 minute. Then transfer it to a platter and let it cool completely. Wrap the meat in plastic wrap; then overwrap with freezer paper. Freeze for up to 1 month. Defrost, still wrapped, in the refrigerator.

To reheat the defrosted cooked sirloin, double-wrap in microwave plastic wrap, and place on a rack in a casserole. Cover and reheat in a 250°F oven. Cook about 6 minutes per pound or until a meat thermometer inserted in the thickest part reads 110°F. Remove the pan from the oven and raise the temperature to 500°F. Unwrap the roast, replace it in the pan, and roast, uncovered, for about 5 minutes or until the outside is crisp. Serve with one of the sauces on page 119, or with Caraway, Cabbage, and Potatoes (page 118). Or use to make Pepper Steak (recipe follows).

# PEPPER STEAK

In order for the peppercorns to form a crust, they must be crushed, not ground. Don't think that you are committing gastric suicide when you eat so many large pieces of pepper—it is digestively milder than if you ground the same amount of pepper and spread it on the steak.

1 *piece roasted beef sirloin or prime rib (3 pounds) (pages 117–119), frozen or fresh*

2 *tablespoons whole black peppercorns*

1 *tablespoon flavorless cooking oil*

2 *tablespoons finely minced shallots*

2 *tablespoons Dijon mustard*

1 *cup dry white wine*

¼ *cup brandy*

½ *cup whipping cream*

1 *tablespoon fresh tarragon leaves, or 1 teaspoon dried*

2 *tablespoons unsalted butter*

*Salt to taste*

SERVES 4

1. Defrost the meat if frozen.
2. Preheat the oven to 450°F.
3. Place the peppercorns in a brown paper bag and pound them with the bottom of a heavy skillet or the side of a hammer. Spread the crushed pepper on a plate.
4. Pat the meat dry, and roll it in the peppercorns, pressing them into the meat.
5. Place a heavy ovenproof skillet over high heat, and add the oil. When the oil is smoking hot, add the meat and cook 1 minute on each side.
6. Transfer the skillet to the oven and roast for 12 minutes, turning once.
7. Remove the skillet from the oven, and transfer the meat to a platter; keep warm. Discard any grease in the skillet, and place the skillet over medium heat. Add the shallots, mustard, wine, and brandy. Cook, stirring, to scrape up any brown bits on the bottom of the skillet. If you are using dried tarragon, add it now.
8. Add the cream and cook until the sauce is thick enough to coat the back of a wooden spoon, about 5 minutes.
9. Remove the skillet from the heat, add the fresh tarragon, and whisk in the butter. Add salt to taste.    (continued)

Pepper Steak   (continued)

**10.** To serve, cut the meat into 4 steaks, and arrange them on a platter. Stir any liquid that has escaped from the meat into the sauce, pour the sauce into a sauceboat, and serve.

# BRAISED BEEF SHORT RIBS

Braising is the universal way of cooking ribs. These are delicious with buttered noodles or boiled potatoes—and you can freeze a batch to serve at another time with a variety of sauces.

1 *large onion, finely minced (about 1 cup)*

1 *medium carrot, finely minced (about ½ cup)*

1 *stalk celery, finely sliced (about ½ cup)*

1 *tablespoon minced garlic*

1 *tablespoon Fresh Tomato Paste (page 227) or canned*

6 *pounds beef short ribs*

1½ *teaspoons salt*

1 *teaspoon freshly ground black pepper*

4 *cups All-Purpose Broth (page 222) or canned low-sodium chicken broth*

3 *bay leaves*

1 *sprig fresh thyme, or ½ teaspoon dried*

**TO SERVE**

*Horseradish and mustard*

**1.** Preheat the oven to 350°F.

**2.** Combine the onions, carrots, celery, garlic, and tomato paste in a bowl and mix well. Arrange the mixture in a roasting pan large enough to hold the ribs in a single layer. Lay the ribs on top, bones down, and sprinkle with the salt and pepper. Cover, and bake for 1 hour.

**3.** Remove the roasting pan from the oven. Turn the ribs on their sides, and add the broth, bay leaves, and thyme. Replace the cover and cook for 1 hour more.

**4.** Remove the ribs from the pan and set them aside. Strain and reserve the braising liquid, discarding the vegetables. Carefully remove and discard the fat that has collected on the surface of the liquid. ▨

**5.** Place the ribs in soup bowls, and ladle some broth into each bowl. Pass the mustard and horseradish.

SERVES 8

⊠ To freeze, pour all or part of the braising liquid into a small plastic container, and place it in the refrigerator to cool for 1 hour. When it is cool, discard any additional fat that has congealed on the surface and cover tightly. Wrap the meat in plastic wrap, then place it in freezer bags or containers. (The following three recipes call for half of this recipe.) Freeze the meat and liquid for up to 3 months. Partially defrost in the refrigerator (2 hours per pound) or on the defrost setting of a microwave oven.

# MOCK BARBECUED SHORT RIBS

½ *recipe Braised Beef Short Ribs (page 122), frozen or fresh*

1 *cup rib braising liquid (page 122), frozen or fresh, or All-Purpose Broth (page 222)*

1 *tablespoon brown sugar*

¼ *cup cider vinegar*

2 *tablespoons catsup*

1 *tablespoon powdered mustard*

1 *teaspoon Worcestershire sauce*

¼ *teaspoon ground cloves*

1 *teaspoon chili powder*

¼ *teaspoon cayenne pepper*

SERVES 4

1. Defrost the short ribs and braising liquid if frozen.

2. Preheat the oven to 375°F or light a charcoal grill.

3. Combine the brown sugar and vinegar in a 1-quart saucepan and place over medium heat. Cook until the mixture has reduced and formed a syrup, about 8 minutes. Watch carefully, as the syrup will suddenly darken in color.

4. As soon as this happens, add the braising liquid, then the catsup, mustard, Worcestershire, cloves, chili powder, and cayenne. Cook about 8 minutes, reducing the sauce by half or until thick. Pour half the sauce over the short ribs and mix to coat them well.

5. To cook the ribs in the oven, arrange them in a roasting pan, cover, and place the pan in the oven. Turn the oven on to 350°F. Cook for 30 minutes, basting with the remaining sauce every 10 minutes.

To cook the ribs on the grill, wait until the coals are covered with white ash. Pile the coals on one side of the grill. Place the ribs on the grill so that they are not directly over the coals, and cover the grill. (If your grill does not have a cover, improvise one

(continued)

Mock Barbecued Short Ribs (continued)

out of aluminum foil.) Cook for 30 minutes, basting with the remaining sauce every 10 minutes.

**6.** When the ribs are well heated, transfer them to a platter and serve. Offer any additional barbecue sauce on the side.

# SHORT RIBS WITH TAPENADE SAUCE

½ **recipe Braised Beef Short Ribs (page 122), frozen or fresh**

1 **cup rib braising liquid (page 122), frozen or fresh, or All-Purpose Broth (page 222)**

4 **anchovy fillets, or 1 tablespoon anchovy paste**

¼ **cup pitted Niçoise or Greek black olives**

2 **tablespoons finely minced garlic**

2 **tablespoons olive oil**

¼ **cup capers, drained**

SERVES 4

**1.** Defrost the short ribs and braising liquid if frozen.

**2.** Place the ribs in a skillet large enough to hold them in one layer, and add the braising liquid. Cover, place over high heat, and bring to a boil. Reduce the heat to medium and cook for 10 minutes. Then remove the cover, turn the meat, and cook 10 minutes longer.

**3.** Meanwhile, combine the anchovies, olives, garlic, olive oil, and capers in a blender or mini food processor, and blend to form a chunky paste.

**4.** Transfer the ribs to a platter and keep warm. Add the puréed olive mixture to the liquid in the skillet, and cook until the sauce is thick enough to coat a wooden spoon.

**5.** Nap the ribs with the sauce, and serve.

# SHORT RIBS AND BRAISED LETTUCE WITH HORSERADISH SAUCE

The pleasure of cooked lettuce is often overlooked except by the French. It is delicious when cooked with meat because it takes on all the flavors of the braising liquid.

½ recipe Braised Beef Short
   Ribs (page 122), frozen
   or fresh
1 cup rib braising liquid
   (page 122), frozen or
   fresh, or All-Purpose
   Broth (page 222)
3 tablespoons flavorless
   cooking oil
4 small heads butter lettuce
½ cup dry white wine
¼ cup white or white wine
   vinegar
1 small onion, finely diced
   (about ⅓ cup)
2 tablespoons grated
   horseradish (preferably
   fresh)
8 small new potatoes
½ cup sour cream

SERVES 4

1. Defrost the ribs and braising liquid if frozen.

2. Heat the oil in a large skillet over medium heat and add the lettuce heads. Cook until the edges are golden, about 5 minutes. Then turn and cook on the other side until golden, another 5 minutes.

3. Transfer the lettuce to a medium roasting pan and add the wine, vinegar, onions, and horseradish. Arrange the ribs and potatoes among the lettuces, and add the braising liquid. Cover, place in the oven, and turn the oven on to 375°F. Bake for 35 minutes.

4. Transfer the lettuce, potatoes, and ribs to a serving platter and keep warm.

5. Strain the contents of the roasting pan into a saucepan, and place it over high heat. Cook until the liquid has reduced by one third and started to thicken slightly, 5 to 7 minutes. Remove the pan from the heat and whisk in the sour cream. Pour the sauce into a sauceboat, and serve with the meat and vegetables.

# PAN-GRILLED FLANK STEAK

Flank steaks and skirt steaks are "striated" muscles—you could say stringy. They are not extremely tender, but they are not tough the way a piece of chuck is. To be tender they must be cut against the grain. Cooked rare or stewed for a long time, these are enormously flavorful cuts. So don't assume that because a particular cut is not buttery tender, it is not good. These steaks make a great grill item and are really the best cut to use for dishes such as fajitas, chili, and open-faced sandwiches. And for freezing they can't be beat. Because of their grain, uncooked flank and skirt steaks succumb less to drip loss than do more finely grained, tender cuts of meat.

(continued)

Pan-Grilled Flank Steak (continued)

1 *flank or skirt steak (2 pounds)*

5 *large cloves garlic, sliced crossways in ¼-inch slivers*

1 *tablespoon flavorless cooking oil*

*Freshly ground black pepper to taste*

¼ *teaspoon salt, or as desired*

1 *medium onion, finely minced (about ¾ cup)*

½ *cup dry white wine*

3 *tablespoons white wine vinegar*

½ *teaspoon Angostura bitters*

3 *tablespoons Dijon mustard*

3 *tablespoons unsalted butter*

SERVES 4

**1.** Using a small paring knife, cut small slits in the steak. Stuff the slices of garlic into the slits.

**2.** Heat the oil in a cast-iron or heavy aluminum skillet over high heat. When it is nearly smoking, add the steak and give it a few turns of the peppermill. Cook 3 minutes. Then turn the steak, sprinkle it with the salt and additional pepper, and add the onions. Reduce the heat to medium and cook 3 minutes for medium rare, another minute for medium. (If you prefer your steak more well done, cover the pan and cook about 3 to 5 minutes, depending on the thickness, for medium-well.)

**3.** Transfer the steak and onions to a platter and keep warm. Discard any fat that has collected in the skillet, and add the wine, vinegar, bitters, and mustard. Cook, stirring to dissolve the mustard and scrape up any residue that has collected in the pan, for about 1 minute. When the mixture starts to thicken, remove it from the heat and whisk in the butter.

**4.** Transfer the steak to a cutting board, and pour any juices that accumulated into the sauce.

**5.** Cut the steak, against the grain, into thin diagonal slices. Arrange them on a serving platter, and offer the sauce separately. ▨

▨ To freeze, wrap slices of steak in freezer paper and place in a freezer bag or container. Freeze for up to 3 months. Defrost in the refrigerator or microwave oven.

# FLANK STEAK ROULADES

Begin this recipe at least 6 hours before cooking, or up to a day in advance, to blend the flavors. Or you can prepare and freeze the roulades and cook them directly from the freezer.

1 *flank steak (1¼ to 1½ pounds)*

2 *tablespoons finely minced garlic*

*Small pinch of ground cloves*

¼ *teaspoon ground coriander*

½ *teaspoon salt*

¼ *teaspoon freshly ground black pepper*

¼ *cup flavorless cooking oil*

1 *medium onion, coarsely chopped (about ¾ cup)*

1 *pound fresh spinach, washed*

6 *ounces ground beef*

6 *ounces bacon, coarsely chopped*

1 *egg*

1 *bunch parsley, coarsely chopped*

1 *cup All-Purpose Broth (page 222) or canned low-sodium chicken broth*

1 *pound mushrooms, thinly sliced.*

2 *tablespoons unsalted butter*

SERVES 3 TO 4

1. Lay the flank steak on a cutting board and using a very sharp knife, carefully split the steak horizontally—like a cake layer. (If you don't trust your knife skills, a butcher will usually be happy to do this for you. Ask him to "butterfly" it into two pieces.) Place each piece between two sheets of wax paper, and flatten them slightly by pounding with a mallet or the flat side of a large chef's knife.

2. Rub both sides of the steaks with the garlic. Stir together the cloves, coriander, salt, and pepper. Sprinkle this mixture over the steaks. Cover with wax paper and place in the refrigerator.

3. Heat 2 tablespoons of the oil in a small skillet over medium heat. Add the onions and cook, stirring, 2 minutes to soften. Then add the spinach and cook until completely wilted, about 5 minutes. Transfer the spinach mixture to a colander, and press it against the sides to extract as much liquid as possible. Coarsely chop the spinach.

4. Combine the ground beef, bacon, egg, and parsley in a food processor and purée until smooth. Transfer the purée to a mixing bowl, add the spinach mixture, and mix well.

5. Remove the steaks from the refrigerator and lay them flat on a work surface. Divide the meat/spinach mixture between the two steaks, and spread it over them evenly. Roll each steak up jelly roll–style, against the grain, and tuck in the ends so the roll is even. Tie the rolls with string. ▨

6. Preheat the oven to 350°F.

7. Heat the remaining 2 tablespoons oil in an ovenproof skillet over medium heat. Add the roulades and brown on all sides, 5

(continued)

Flank Steak Roulades   (continued)

to 7 minutes. Pour off the fat and add the broth. Cover, transfer to the oven, and bake for 1¼ hours.

**8.** Remove the skillet from the oven and transfer the roulades to a platter; keep warm. Skim the fat off the liquids in the skillet. Place the skillet over medium heat, add the mushrooms, and cook for 6 to 8 minutes. Remove it from the heat and whisk in the butter.

**9.** Remove the string and slice the roulades into 1-inch serving pieces. Pour the mushrooms and sauce onto a large serving platter and arrange the slices of steak on top of the mushrooms. Serve immediately.

---

To freeze, wrap the roulades in a double thickness of plastic wrap, then overwrap with freezer paper. Freeze for up to 3 months. To finish, unwrap and follow Steps 6 through 9, increasing the cooking time to 1¾ hours.

---

# MEAT LOAF

This meat loaf may be flavored like a pâté, but it is still just a meat loaf. It even passes the meat loaf test of making great cold sandwiches. Instead of the traditional bread crumbs and eggs, I use a dry mushroom purée—called duxelles—as a binder, both for the flavor and because it freezes better. This meat loaf won't get soggy if it is frozen and defrosted.

2 slices crustless white bread, or 1 cup fresh bread crumbs, or ½ cup dry crumbs

2 tins (4 ounces each) goose liver pâté

2 sprigs fresh thyme, leaves only, or 1 teaspoon dried

1 teaspoon salt

½ teaspoon freshly ground black pepper

½ teaspoon ground coriander

1 pound mushrooms

1 large onion, finely minced (about 1 cup)

1 tablespoon minced garlic

2 tablespoons unsalted butter or flavorless cooking oil

2 eggs, beaten

2 pounds ground beef round or sirloin

**TO SERVE**

1 tablespoon unsalted butter

2 tablespoons flour

2 cups All-Purpose Broth (page 222) or canned low-sodium chicken broth

½ cup dry white wine

SERVES 8

**1.** Place the bread in a dry food processor bowl, and process into crumbs. Add the pâté, thyme, salt, pepper, and coriander; purée until smooth. Transfer the mixture to a large mixing bowl.

**2.** Place the mushrooms, onions, and garlic in the food processor, and purée.

**3.** Melt 2 tablespoons of the butter in a large skillet over medium heat. Add the mushroom purée and cook, stirring occasionally, for 20 minutes or until the mixture has begun to dry out.

**4.** Add the purée to the mixing bowl and mix it with the crumbs. Add the eggs and ground beef, and mix thoroughly.

**5.** Divide the mixture between two 1-quart loaf pans. Cover them tightly with aluminum foil. Place the loaf pans in a roasting pan (to catch any juices that may bubble over during cooking), and place it in the oven. Turn the oven on to 350°F, and cook for 1 hour.

**6.** Remove the meat loaves from the oven, and pressing down on the foil with a large spatula, pour any liquids that have collected in the loaf pans into a bowl. You should have about 1 cup. Skim the surface and discard the fat. ▨

**7.** Melt the remaining 1 tablespoon butter in a small saucepan over low heat, add the flour, and cook 1 minute. Add the meat loaf juices, broth, and wine. Cook the sauce about 5 minutes.

**8.** Slice the meat loaf and arrange it on a platter. Serve the sauce separately.

▨ To freeze: While the meat loaf is still warm, place a 2-pound weight on the foil (supermarket cans work fine). Refrigerate for 1 hour. When the loaf is cool, remove the weight and foil, and wrap the loaf in a double layer of plastic wrap. Seal it in a freezer bag, and freeze for up to 3 months. Place pan juice in a freezer bag or container and freeze for up to 3 months. Defrost loaf and juices and finish sauce before reheating.

# POT-ROASTED VEAL

If your pot is large enough, you can start two roasts. Partially cook one of them (for an hour) and freeze it for up to 3 months. Defrost and finish it on a charcoal grill, or cook from frozen in a pot.

¼ cup olive oil

1 tablespoon chopped shallots

1 tablespoon fresh rosemary leaves, or 1 teaspoon dried

1 teaspoon salt

½ teaspoon freshly ground black pepper

1 veal round roast (5 pounds)

¼ cup fresh lemon juice

½ cup white wine

2 tablespoons unsalted butter

SERVES 6

1. Mix 3 tablespoons of the oil, the shallots, half the rosemary, and the salt and pepper together. Rub this over all the surfaces of the veal. Cover and refrigerate for at least 4 hours, or overnight.

2. Heat the remaining 1 tablespoon oil in a Dutch oven or flameproof casserole over medium-high heat. Add the veal and sear on all sides until browned, about 15 minutes. Use a pair of large spoons or tongs to turn the meat so you don't pierce it.

3. Drain excess fat from the casserole, and add the lemon juice and wine. Add the remaining rosemary. Cover, reduce the heat to low, and cook for 2 hours or until tender. (1 hour if cooking partially for the freezer). ▨ Check periodically; if the casserole is dry, add a tablespoon or two of water.

4. Transfer the roast to a carving board, and let it rest for 15 minutes before slicing. Swirl the butter into the cooking juices in the casserole.

5. Cut the roast into ¼-inch slices and arrange them on a platter. Strain the sauce over the meat, and serve immediately.

▨ Allow the partially cooked meat to cool to room temperature. Wrap in plastic wrap, then overwrap with freezer paper. Freeze for up to 3 months.

Defrost the meat and finish by slow-cooking on a charcoal grill for 1 to 1½ hours. Or place the still-frozen roast in a Dutch oven and follow Steps 3 and 4, but increase the cooking time to 2¾ hours. Check the pot carefully during the last hour of cooking.

# ROAST BRISKET OF VEAL

Soak the garbanzo beans overnight before preparing this recipe.

2 cups dried garbanzo beans

2 veal briskets (about 1¾ pounds each)

½ teaspoon salt

Freshly ground black pepper to taste

2 tablespoons flavorless cooking oil

1 large onion, finely chopped (about 1 cup)

1 carrot, finely chopped (about ½ cup)

1 stalk celery, finely sliced (about ½ cup)

1 cup dry white wine

2 cups All-Purpose Broth (page 222) or canned low-sodium chicken broth

¼ cup finely minced garlic

6 plum tomatoes, peeled, seeded, and chopped

SERVES 6 TO 8

1. Soak the garbanzo beans in water for 10 hours to soften before cooking.

2. Preheat the oven to 350°F.

3. Sprinkle the veal on both sides with the salt and pepper. Heat the oil in a flame-proof casserole or Dutch oven over medium heat. Add the veal and cook about 6 minutes on each side, until dark golden brown.

4. Remove the briskets and set them aside. Discard any fat that has collected in the casserole, and add the onions. Reduce the heat to low and cook for 3 minutes. Add the carrots and celery and cook, stirring occasionally, another 5 minutes.

5. Return the briskets to the casserole, raise the heat to high, and add the wine, broth, and garlic. Cover and bring to a boil. Drain the beans, and add them along with the tomatoes. Transfer the casserole to the oven and bake, covered, for 2 hours or until the beans are very tender. Check occasionally to see that the mixture is moist; if the beans have absorbed too much liquid, add a little water or broth. ▨

6. Remove the casserole from the oven and place the meat on a cutting board. Slice it against the grain into ½-inch pieces. Scoop the beans onto a serving platter and arrange the sliced meat on top. Serve immediately.

▨ To freeze, place the garbanzos in a freezer bag or container, and freeze for up to 6 months. Place the meat in a freezer bag, pressing it flat to remove as much air as possible, and freeze for up to 3 months. To reheat, rewrap defrosted brisket in two layers of microwave plastic wrap and place on a rack in a casserole. Cover and cook in a 250°F oven for 20 minutes. Unwrap, add beans, re-cover and return to a 375°F oven for 15 minutes.

# BRAISED VEAL SHANKS

Shanks contain delicious meat surrounding cross-sections of marrow bone. They have incredible flavor, but the texture of the meat is what makes them special for me—the finely fibered meat is lubricated by the layer of connective tissue, and they melt together as they cook.

Veal shanks should braise in liquid for a long time—until they are falling apart and tender.

16 *center-cut veal shanks*
*(10 to 12 ounces each)*

*Salt and freshly ground*
*black pepper to taste*

*4 to 6 tablespoons olive oil*

*1 large onion, coarsely*
*chopped (about 1 cup)*

*1 medium carrot, coarsely*
*chopped (about ¾ cup)*

*2 stalks celery, coarsely*
*chopped (about 1 cup)*

*3 cups All-Purpose Broth*
*(page 222) or canned*
*low-sodium chicken broth*

*3 tablespoons finely minced*
*garlic*

*3 bay leaves*

*2 sprigs fresh thyme, or*
*¼ teaspoon dried*

*1 lemon, cut in half*

SERVES 8 TO 10

**1.** Preheat the oven to 375°F.

**2.** Pat the veal shanks dry and sprinkle them with salt and pepper. Heat the oil in a large roasting pan, Dutch oven, or oven-proof skillet over medium heat. Add the shanks and brown well on both sides, about 5 minutes per side. Do not crowd the pan or the shanks will not brown; do this in batches if necessary. Remove the shanks from the pan as they brown and set them aside.

**3.** Pour off and discard any fat in the pan. Return the pan to low heat and add the onions, carrots, and celery. Cook, stirring occasionally, about 5 minutes or until the vegetables have softened.

**4.** Add the broth, garlic, bay leaves, thyme, and lemon halves. Return the shanks to the pan. (It is all right to overlap the shanks when you arrange them in the pan.) Raise the heat to high and bring to a boil. Then cover the pan and immediately transfer it to the oven. Bake for 1 to 1½ hours or until the shanks are tender. ▨

**5.** Remove the pan from the oven, and transfer the shanks to a plate. Remove as much fat as possible from the surface of the braising liquid. Serve the shanks in individual soup bowls, and strain the liquid into the bowls. (When you are handling the shanks, take care not to disturb the delicious marrow in the bones.)

⊠ To freeze, strain all or some of the braising liquid into a freezer container and let it cool to room temperature; then refrigerate until chilled. Discard any fat that has collected on the surface, cover, and freeze for up to 3 months. Place all or some of the shanks in the refrigerator to cool, uncovered. Then place them in freezer bags, seal, and freeze for up to 3 months.

To serve, defrost, then reheat separately, covered, for 25 minutes in a 375°F oven, or proceed with one of the following two recipes; each calls for ¼ of this recipe.

# BRAISED VEAL SHANKS WITH TOMATO

¼ *recipe Braised Veal Shanks (4 shanks; page 132), frozen or fresh*

1 *cup braising liquid (page 132), frozen or fresh*

½ *cup Tomato Concassée (page 223), or drained, seeded, chopped canned tomatoes*

1 *tablespoon chopped fresh oregano leaves, or 1 teaspoon dried*

SERVES 4

**1.** Defrost the veal shanks and braising liquid if frozen.

**2.** Place the shanks in a roasting pan, cover, and place in the oven. Turn the oven on to 375°F, and bake for 25 minutes.

**3.** Meanwhile, combine the braising liquid and tomato concassée in a medium saucepan and bring to a boil over high heat. If you are using dried oregano, add it now.

**4.** Uncover the shanks and add the tomato broth. Cook, uncovered, another 20 minutes.

**5.** Remove the pan from the oven, arrange the shanks on a platter, and sprinkle them with the fresh oregano. Pour the sauce into a pitcher and serve it on the side.

# BRAISED VEAL SHANKS WITH CREAMED MUSHROOMS

Traditionally shanks are not served with creamy sauces because the meat and marrow are so rich by themselves. Serve this variation with mashed potatoes or risotto.

¼ *recipe Braised Veal Shanks (4 shanks; page 132), frozen or fresh*

1 *cup braising liquid (page 132), frozen or fresh*

¼ *cup whipping cream*

1 *cup Mushroom Duxelles (page 240), or ¾ pound puréed uncooked mushrooms*

1 *tablespoon chopped fresh thyme leaves, or 1 teaspoon dried*

1. Defrost the veal shanks and braising liquid if frozen.

2. Place the shanks in a roasting pan, cover, and place in the oven. Turn the oven on to 375°F, and bake for 20 minutes.

3. Meanwhile, combine the braising liquid, cream, mushrooms, and thyme in a medium saucepan. Bring to a boil over high heat and cook for 1 minute.

4. Uncover the shanks and ladle the sauce over them. Cook, uncovered, another 20 minutes.

5. Remove the pan from the oven, arrange the shanks on a platter, and nap them with the sauce. Serve immediately.

SERVES 4

# LEG OF LAMB WITH ONION AND RICE PURÉE

When meat roasts, the outside cooks quickly and forms a flavorful crust that helps retain the juices. The very center—the bone—takes the longest time to heat up and begin to cook, so we have a more well done outer part and a rarer center. When the bone finally does heat to the point of cooking, it exudes a wonderful flavor. It really is true that the meat nearest the bone is the tastiest. So cook a whole leg of lamb, even if you won't need it all for one meal.

In this recipe, the roast is cooked in a covered pan with onions and rice. The rice absorbs the moisture from the onions, and the roast still forms its crust.

1 *leg of lamb (about 6 pounds)*

5 *cloves garlic, cut into ¼-inch slivers*

2 *tablespoons flavorless cooking oil*

5 *large onions, finely sliced (about 6½ cups)*

1 *cup rice*

½ *tablespoon chopped fresh thyme leaves, or 1 teaspoon dried*

½ *tablespoon salt, as desired*

**Ground white pepper to taste**

½ *cup water*

¼ *cup whipping cream*

SERVES 8

**1.** Trim excess fat from the leg of lamb, leaving only a thin layer. Using a small knife, cut slits in the meat and stuff the garlic slivers into them.

**2.** Preheat the oven to 350°F.

**3.** Heat the oil in a roasting pan over high heat. Sear the lamb well on all sides for about 10 minutes. Remove the lamb to a plate, and drain the oil from the pan.

**4.** Add the onions, rice, and thyme to the pan. Sprinkle the lamb with the salt and white pepper, and place it, fat side down, in the pan. Tightly cover the pan and place it in the oven. Cook for 1 hour.

**5.** Turn the lamb fat side up and add the water. Stir the onion/rice mixture, replace the cover, and roast another 30 minutes for medium-rare (approximately 15 minutes per pound total roasting time).

**6.** Remove the pan from the oven and place the lamb on a cutting board. Transfer the onion/rice mixture to a food processor, add the cream, and process until fairly smooth. ▨

**7.** Serve the onion/rice purée in a vegetable dish. Let the lamb rest for 15 minutes before carving.

▨ To freeze the lamb, remove any remaining meat from the long bone; when you have reached the joint, twist to remove the bone and discard it. Place the sliced meat (you may have both slices and large pieces) in a freezer bag and press out as much air as possible. Seal and freeze for up to 3 months. Place the onion/rice purée in a freezer bag or container, seal, and freeze for up to 6 months.

Defrost packages of cooked meat in the refrigerator or microwave oven. Reheat the meat, uncovered, in a 375°F oven, and the purée, covered, over low heat. Or use in any of the improvised dishes on pages 177–220.

If you're reheating a large piece, double-wrap in microwave plastic wrap, place on a rack in a covered casserole, and heat in a 250°F oven (8 minutes per pound). Remove from the oven, unwrap, and heat in an uncovered casserole in a 450°F oven 5 minutes longer.

# RACK OF LAMB WITH GINGER AND MINT

Mint is classic with lamb because it seems to make the lamb taste less "fatty." But you don't want to serve a cliché, so I've added ginger—which is often paired with mint in Southeast Asian cooking.

*2 racks of lamb with bone
  (2 to 2½ pounds total
  weight)*

*1½ tablespoons finely minced
  fresh ginger, or 2
  teaspoons powdered*

*Salt and freshly ground
  black pepper to taste*

*1 tablespoon flavorless
  cooking oil*

*1 cup All-Purpose Broth
  (page 222) or canned
  low-sodium chicken broth*

*¼ cup cider vinegar*

*2 tablespoons unsalted butter*

*2 tablespoon finely chopped
  fresh mint leaves*

SERVES 4

1. Trim excess fat from the racks, leaving a layer ¼ inch thick. Mix the ginger, salt, and pepper; season the meat with the mixture. Cover and refrigerate 1 hour.

2. Preheat the oven to 400°F.

3. Heat the oil over high heat in a roasting pan just large enough to hold the racks. Place the lamb fat side down in the pan, and brown for about 5 minutes. Then turn the racks fat side up and transfer the pan to the oven. Roast 15 to 18 minutes for medium-rare, 18 to 20 minutes for medium, or about 22 minutes for medium-well.

4. When the meat is cooked as desired, transfer the lamb to a plate; keep warm. Place the pan over medium heat and cook to concentrate any meat juices that are mixed with the fat in the pan. Discard the fat.

5. Add the broth and vinegar to the pan, and cook over medium heat until the liquid has reduced by two thirds and begun to thicken. Remove the pan from the heat, whisk in the butter, and add the mint.

6. Place the lamb on a cutting board, and pour any juices that have collected on the plate into the sauce. Cut the racks into chops and arrange them on a serving platter. Serve the sauce in a sauceboat. ▨

▨ To freeze leftover lamb chops, place them between layers of freezer paper and seal in a freezer bag. Freeze for up to 3 months.

Use the defrosted chops in salads, pastas, or sandwiches. Whip leftover sauce with 2 tablespoons room-temperature unsalted butter and serve as a flavored butter accompaniment to grilled meat.

# BRAISED LAMB SHANKS

Lamb shanks are small—about 12 ounces total weight, one third of which is bone. I love to serve them because the bone makes a handle that invites picking up—they make me think of tavern dinners in merry olde England—at least the Hollywood version—with people carousing, singing, ripping pieces of meat off whole roasted birds. Lamb shanks allow us better table manners, but they're still hearty. And of course, the meat is divine, especially when braised.

Make two or more batches of shanks at the same time and put one in the freezer. I've even thrown them straight from the freezer onto a slow-cooking fire.

2 tablespoons olive oil

4 lamb shanks (about 12 ounces each)

1 large onion, coarsely chopped (about 1 cup)

2 large carrots, coarsely chopped (about 2 cups)

2 stalks celery, coarsely chopped (about 1 cup)

1 tablespoon finely minced garlic

1½ cups dry red wine

1 cup water

1 lemon, cut in half

½ tablespoon salt

½ teaspoon freshly ground black pepper

SERVES 4

1. Preheat the oven to 325°F.

2. Heat the olive oil over medium heat in a heavy roasting pan or Dutch oven large enough to hold the shanks in one layer. Add the shanks and cook 10 minutes on each side.

3. Pour off all but 2 tablespoons fat. Add the onions, carrots, and celery, and cook 5 minutes. Then add the garlic, wine, water, lemon halves, salt, and pepper. Cover, and transfer the pan to the oven. Cook for 1½ hours or until the meat is tender, turning the lamb every 30 minutes and checking to ensure that the liquid has not evaporated. If the pan gets dry, add another cup of water.

4. When they are tender, remove the shanks from the sauce. Strain the sauce through a fine-mesh sieve and discard the vegetables and lemon. Skim and discard the fat from the surface of the braising liquid.

5. Arrange the shanks on a platter, and serve the braising liquid on the side. ▨

⊠ To freeze, strain all or some of the braising liquid into a freezer container and let it cool to room temperature. Then refrigerate it until chilled. Discard any fat that has collected on the surface, cover, and freeze for up to 3 months. Place the shanks in the refrigerator to cool, uncovered. Then seal them in freezer bags and freeze for up to 3 months.

Partially defrost the meat (3 hours per shank) and braising liquid and reheat in a 375°F oven, or finish as one of the following two variations.

# BRAISED LAMB SHANKS WITH DRIED FRUITS

This is a very May-December combination—fresh meat and dried fruits. And it tastes unbelievably delicious. The fruits sop up the flavors of the lamb sauce and the tart yogurt finish sparks the ensemble without adding fat.

1 *recipe Braised Lamb Shanks (page 137), frozen or fresh*

1 *cup braising liquid (page 137), frozen or fresh, All-Purpose Broth (page 222), or low-sodium chicken broth*

1 *cup dry white wine*

8 *pieces dried apricots*

8 *pieces dried apples*

½ *cup plain yogurt*

SERVES 4

1. Defrost the lamb shanks and braising liquid if frozen.

2. Preheat the oven to 375°F.

3. Combine the braising liquid and wine in a Dutch oven. Add the dried fruit and the shanks. Cover tightly and bake until the meat is heated through, about 45 minutes.

4. When the shanks are hot, transfer them to a serving platter. Whisk the yogurt into the dried fruit mixture, and pour the sauce over the shanks.

# LAMB SHANKS WITH RASPBERRY PRESERVES AND GREEN PEPPERCORNS

This is a fancy way of presenting a humble cut of meat—a lamb shank in venison's clothing.

1 *recipe Braised Lamb Shanks (page 137), frozen or fresh*

1 *cup braising liquid (page 137), frozen or fresh, All-Purpose Broth (page 222), or low-sodium chicken broth*

2 *tablespoons raspberry preserves*

3 *tablespoons green peppercorns packed in water, drained*

½ *cup whipping cream*

2 *tablespoons unsalted butter*

1. Defrost the lamb shanks and braising liquid if frozen.

2. Preheat the oven to 375°F.

3. Combine the braising liquid, preserves, peppercorns, and cream in a medium roasting pan or Dutch oven. Cook over medium heat, stirring, for 5 minutes.

4. Add the shanks, cover, and transfer the pan to the oven. Cook until the meat is heated through, about 45 minutes.

5. Remove the pan from the oven and place the shanks on a serving platter. Quickly boil down the sauce until it is thick enough to coat a spoon. Remove the pan from the heat and whisk in the butter. Pour the sauce over the shanks and serve immediately.

SERVES 4

# BRAISED PORK LOIN

The pork loin contains the chops, and I like to cook the whole loin on the bone because the resulting individual chops are more tender when cooked this way. You also get better-quality meat when you buy the whole loin—it's leaner and meatier. So buy a pork loin, braise it, and then cut it into chops for the meal at hand. Freeze the remainder in one piece—it will provide even better chops after you've cooked it a second time. Ask your butcher to remove the chine bone so that you can easily cut the loin into chops. (continued)

Braised Pork Loin  (continued)

1 *tablespoon salt*

**Freshly ground black pepper
to taste**

1 *tablespoon fresh thyme
leaves, or 1 teaspoon
dried*

1 *tablespoon finely minced
garlic*

1 *teaspoon ground coriander*

3 *tablespoons olive oil*

1 *pork loin, chine bone
removed, containing 11
or 12 chops (6 to 7
pounds)*

1 *large onion, coarsely
chopped, (about 1 cup)*

2 *stalks celery, coarsely
sliced (about 1 cup)*

2 *tablespoons flour*

2 *cup All-Purpose Broth
(page 222) or canned
low-sodium chicken broth*

SERVES 8

**1.** Combine the salt, pepper, thyme, garlic, coriander, and oil in a blender or food processor, and blend to form a paste. Place the pork on a work surface, and rub the surface with the paste. Refrigerate the meat, covered, for 2 hours, or up to 8.

**2.** Preheat the oven to 400°F.

**3.** Place the pork on a rack in a roasting pan, and put it in the oven. Immediately reduce the heat to 350°F, and roast for 1 hour. As the roast cooks, occasionally remove any excess fat with a basting bulb.

**4.** Add the onions and celery, and roast for 1 more hour. Continue to remove excess fat as necessary. The meat is done when a meat thermometer reads 165° to 170°F in the thickest part of the roast. The juices should run barely pink when the meat is pierced with a knife (the roast will continue to cook while it rests outside of the oven).

**5.** Remove the roasting pan from the oven and raise the heat to 425°F. Transfer the roast to a plate and let it rest for 30 minutes before carving.

**6.** Add the flour to the vegetables in the roasting pan, mix well, and return the pan to the oven. Cook for 15 minutes.

**7.** Transfer the roasting pan to the stovetop, place it over medium heat, and add the broth and any juices that have escaped from the pork. Cook, stirring, until the gravy has thickened, about 3 minutes. ▨

**8.** To serve, cut the loin into individual chops and arrange them on a platter. Strain the gravy into a sauceboat, and serve it on the side.

▨ To freeze, slice off as many individual chops as you will be serving immediately, and reserve the remainder of the roast in one piece. Allow the roast to cool to room temperature, and then refrigerate it until chilled. Wrap it tightly in microwave plastic wrap, then in freezer paper. Seal, and freeze for up to 3 months. Pour the gravy into a plastic container, seal, and freeze for up to 3 months. Defrost roast and gravy in the refrigerator or microwave oven.

Reheat the roast, still wrapped in microwave plastic wrap, in a 250°F oven for 45 minutes. Remove from the oven and increase the oven temperature to 425°F. Unwrap the meat and return it to the oven. Heat for 5 minutes to crisp the surface. Can be served whole, in chops, or as one of the following three variations; each calls for half of this recipe.

# PORK AND BEANS

Meats that are enjoyed very well cooked need not be defrosted prior to cooking, especially in a dish like pork and beans when the beans themselves require such long cooking.

**2 cups dried kidney beans**

**1 tablespoon powdered mustard**

**¼ teaspoon ground cloves**

**2 tablespoons tomato paste**

**1 tablespoon brown sugar**

**¼ cup unsulphured molasses**

**3 cups water**

**1 cup pork gravy (page 139), All-Purpose Broth (page 222), or canned low-sodium chicken broth**

**1 piece Braised Pork Loin (3 to 4 chops; page 139), frozen or fresh**

**1 teaspoon salt**

**6 tablespoons chopped fresh parsley**

1. The night before, place the beans in a bowl, cover with 2 inches of cold water, and refrigerate overnight or up to 12 hours.

2. Drain and rinse the beans, and place them in a 3-quart ovenproof casserole or Dutch oven. Add the mustard, cloves, tomato paste, brown sugar, molasses, water, and gravy. Mix well, and bury the pork roast in the mixture.

3. Cover the casserole. Turn the oven to 300°F and bake for 3 hours. Check the casserole every 45 minutes, and if the beans are drying out, add ½ cup of water. When the beans are soft, remove the casserole from the oven and transfer the pork to a platter. Add the salt and parsley to the beans and mix well.

4. Transfer the beans to a large serving dish. Cut the roast into 4 chops, arrange them on top of the beans, and serve immediately.

SERVES 4

# BROILED SOY PORK CHOPS

Cooked chops soak up the salty soy mixture and don't dry out when they are reheated under a broiler—a trick that Chinese cooks know. If you prefer, a charcoal grill also cooks the chops nicely and adds a smokey flavor to the meat.

1 *piece Braised Pork Loin (3 to 4 chops; page 139), frozen or fresh*

¼ *cup soy sauce*

2 *tablespoons dry sherry*

2 *tablespoons rice vinegar*

1 *tablespoon finely minced garlic*

¼ *teaspoon cayenne pepper*

2 *tablespoons finely minced fresh ginger, or 1 teaspoon powdered*

2 *tablespoons dark sesame oil*

1 *tablespoon unsalted butter*

2 *tablespoons chopped cilantro*

SERVES 4

1. Defrost the pork roast if frozen and cut it into chops.

2. Combine all the remaining ingredients except the butter and cilantro in a bowl or plastic bag. Mix well. Then add the chops, cover, and refrigerate to marinate for 4 hours or up to 10.

3. Preheat the broiler.

4. Arrange the chops in a single layer in a small roasting pan, and pour the soy mixture over them. Broil for 5 minutes. Then turn the chops and broil for another 5 minutes.

5. Remove the roasting pan from the broiler and transfer the chops to a platter. If the soy marinade is completely dried up, add a little water to dissolve it slightly, and then whisk in the butter. Spoon this sauce over the chops, garnish with the cilantro, and serve.

# CORN-BREADED PORK CHOPS
# WITH MADEIRA APPLES

**S**ometimes it's a good idea to give an added outer crust to defrosted meats that you're recooking.

1 *piece Braised Pork Loin (3 to 4 chops; page 139), frozen or fresh*

¼ *cup yellow cornmeal*

3 *tablespoons grated Parmesan or Romano cheese*

4 *Granny Smith apples*

*Juice of 1 lemon*

3 *tablespoons unsalted butter*

½ *cup All-Purpose Broth (page 222) or canned low-sodium chicken broth*

1 *cup Madeira*

SERVES 4

**1.** Defrost the pork loin if frozen. Cut it into chops, and set them aside.

**2.** Mix the cornmeal and cheese together on a plate, and dust the chops with the mixture, pressing so that it adheres. Set aside on a plate.

**3.** Peel and core the apples, and cut each one into 4 wedges. Place them in a bowl, sprinkle with the lemon juice, and set aside.

**4.** Melt the butter in a medium-size skillet over medium heat, and add the pork chops. Cook for 5 minutes. Then turn the chops over and cook another 5 to 10 minutes. Remove them from the skillet and keep warm.

**5.** Add the apples, broth, and Madeira to the skillet, raise the heat to high, and cook about 10 minutes or until the liquids concentrate and the apples start to compote.

**6.** To serve, arrange a bed of apples on a platter, and arrange the chops on top.

# FRESH HAM WITH CRACKLINGS

**T**oo often we forget about hams that have not been cured and smoked—a good roast leg of pork. The leg contains fairly compact meat—lean, compact muscles with good fat between them and a nice outer covering—which give a superior result when roasted.

It's too large a cut to cook for most family dinners, except for festive gatherings when you want to present a bountiful table. But the leftover roasted meat in the freezer is a bonanza to the meal planner.

When you purchase a whole fresh pork leg, insist that the butcher leave the skin on. It acts as a kind of natural basting bag and becomes a crisp treat called crackling.

(continued)

Fresh Ham with Cracklings   (continued)

1 *bone-in fresh ham (12 to 15 pounds), skin intact*

¼ *cup ground coriander*

¼ *teaspoon ground allspice*

2 *tablespoons freshly ground black pepper*

¼ *cup finely minced garlic*

1 *tablespoon salt*

1 *cup white wine*

1 *cup All-Purpose Broth (page 222) or canned low-sodium chicken broth*

2 *tablespoons whole-grain mustard*

2 *tablespoons grated fresh horseradish or prepared horseradish*

SERVES 12 TO 16

**1.** One to 3 days before serving, rinse the ham under cold water and pat it dry. Place it on a work surface, and using a sharp knife, score the skin in a crisscross pattern, making cuts about 1 inch apart and ¼ inch deep.

**2.** In a small bowl combine the coriander, allspice, pepper, garlic, and salt. Rub the surface of the ham with the spice mixture. Cover and refrigerate the ham overnight, or as long as 3 days.

**3.** Preheat the oven to 400°F.

**4.** Place the ham, fat side down, on a rack in a large roasting pan and bake for 20 minutes. Then reduce the heat to 350°F and continue to roast for 1½ hours. Turn the ham right side up and roast another 1½ hours or until a meat thermometer in the center of the ham reads 170°F. (Total roasting time is approximately 20 minutes per pound.) Transfer the pork to a serving platter and let it rest for 20 minutes (it will continue to cook while resting).

**5.** Remove the rack from the pan, pour off and discard all grease in the pan, and place the pan over medium heat. Add the wine and cook for 5 minutes, stirring to scrape up the brown bits on the bottom of the pan.

**6.** Add the broth, mustard, and horseradish, and cook until the liquid has reduced to form a thin gravy. ⊠

**7.** To serve, pour the sauce into a sauceboat. Remove the crackling (skin) from the pork and cut it into pieces. Cut the ham in half from the thigh to the ankle, then cut it into ½-inch-thick slices. Arrange the meat on a platter, decorate it with squares of crackling, and pass the gravy.

⊠ To freeze, remove the pork from the bone in large pieces, trying to respect the natural separation of muscle in the leg (the separations are marked by a thin layer of fat or connective tissue; the meat separates easily if you make little cuts with the tip of a sharp knife while pulling the pieces apart). You will end up with some nice roast-like larger pieces; wrap them in plastic wrap, then overwrap with freezer paper. The outer muscle of the leg is a flatter, more striated piece of meat—cut it into 1-inch pieces. Add any smaller scraps that you've trimmed off, and freeze in a freezer bag. Try to keep as much crispy crackling intact as possible. Discard the bone. Freeze the meat for up to 3 months. Defrost in the refrigerator or microwave oven. Larger pieces of the ham can be used to make Braised Caraway Pork with Brussels Sprouts (below); and odds and ends are perfect for the Carnitas (page 146).

# BRAISED CARAWAY PORK WITH BRUSSELS SPROUTS

Use a single, large piece of pork for this dish, and serve it thinly sliced as you would a pot roast. Caraway seed and Brussels sprouts make this hearty fall or winter fare.

1½ to 2 pounds cooked fresh ham (page 143), frozen or fresh

1 pound Brussels sprouts

2 tablespoons flavorless cooking oil

2 large onions, finely sliced (about 4 cups)

½ tablespoon caraway seeds

1 cup All-Purpose Broth (page 222) or canned low-sodium chicken stock

1 teaspoon salt, or as desired

2 tablespoons unsalted butter

SERVES 3 TO 4

1. Defrost the ham if frozen.
2. Preheat the oven to 375°F.
3. Trim and discard the outer leaves from the sprouts. Cut an X in the root tip of each one, and set them aside.
4. Heat the oil in a small roasting pan or Dutch oven over medium heat. Add the onions and cook, stirring, for 5 minutes. Then add the caraway seeds, broth, and salt. Bring to a boil, add the pork, cover, and transfer the pan to the oven. Bake for 15 minutes. Add the Brussels sprouts and cook another 20 minutes, covered.
5. Transfer the pan to the stovetop and remove the pork to a cutting surface. Place the pan over high heat and cook until the liquid has reduced to form a sauce, 5 minutes. Remove the pan from the heat and whisk in the butter.
6. Arrange the sauce and vegetables on a platter. Slice the pork into ½-inch-thick pieces, lay them on top, and serve.

# CARNITAS WITH SOFT TACOS

**D**on't bother to defrost the meat for this marvelous dish of shredded pork using the incidental scraps from the fresh ham on page 143, or if you prefer to recook a whole piece, cube it first. Serve these carnitas with cooked black beans and Pico de Gallo (page 226).

*2½ to 3 pounds cooked fresh ham (page 143), frozen or fresh*

*Salt and freshly ground black pepper to taste*

*1 medium onion, finely chopped*

*2 tablespoons finely minced garlic*

*1 tablespoon chili powder*

*1 teaspoon ground cumin*

*½ teaspoon cayenne pepper*

*½ teaspoon unsweetened cocoa powder*

*2 cups milk*

*12 medium corn tortillas*

*½ cup sour cream*

*2 hothouse tomatoes, sliced*

*2 avocados, peeled, pitted, and sliced*

SERVES 8

**1.** Defrost the pork if frozen and cut it into 2-inch pieces.

**2.** Sprinkle the pork with salt and pepper. Place it in a roasting pan or Dutch oven with the onion, garlic, chili, cumin, cayenne, and cocoa. Cover the pan and place it in the oven. Turn the oven on to 375°F, and cook for 1½ hours.

**3.** Add the milk, cover, and cook for 1 hour. Uncover and cook another 30 minutes, or until the meat is falling apart and the milk is reduced and curdled.

**4.** Remove the pan from the oven and transfer the meat to a cutting board. Scrape the residue in the pan into a bowl. Using two forks, shred the meat, discarding any gristle and pieces of fat. Add the meat to the bowl and keep warm. ▨

**5.** To serve, heat the tortillas by placing them directly over a medium flame if you have a gas range, or under a broiler, for about 30 seconds on each side. Arrange the sour cream, tomatoes, and avocadoes on a condiment tray or platter, and serve on the side. Let your guests fill their tortillas with meat and condiments as they like.

▨ To freeze, chill the meat, uncovered, in the refrigerator. Then place it in plastic containers or freezer bags, and freeze for up to 6 months. To serve, defrost, then reheat, covered, in a 350°F oven.

# BOILED TONGUE

If tongue makes you think of the salty red meat that comes in deli sandwiches, think again. Fresh tongue is delicately flavored, has a smooth texture, and fits with many flavors and garnishes. However you serve it, all tongue preparations begin with braising, so think about boiling two and putting one in the freezer to use in either of the following two variations. Mustard is the traditional accompaniment.

1 *fresh beef tongue (about 4 pounds)*

1 *onion, cut in half*

1 *carrot, cut into chunks*

1 *stalk celery, cut into 4 pieces*

2 *whole cloves*

1 *whole medium head garlic*

1 *teaspoon whole black peppercorns*

2 *tablespoons salt, or as desired*

6 *bay leaves*

SERVES 6

**1.** Combine all the ingredients in a large pot and cover generously with cold water. Cover the pot, place it over high heat, and bring to a boil. Then reduce the heat to low and simmer gently for 3 hours. Check the pot periodically to make sure the tongue is completely submerged; add more water if necessary.

**2.** Remove the tongue from the pot and let it cool until you can handle it comfortably. Discard the water and vegetables.

**3.** Make a shallow incision down the top of the tongue, and carefully peel the outer layer off the entire tongue. Trim any cartilage or vein from the base.

**4.** To serve, slice the tongue thin, starting at the tip. ⊠

⊠ To freeze, wrap the whole or sliced tongue in plastic wrap, then overwrap with freezer paper. Freeze for up to 3 months. Defrost in the refrigerator or microwave oven.

# HONEY-MUSTARD BAKED TONGUE

The honey-mustard combination glazes the tongue beautifully, and as you can guess, makes us think of more creamy-textured ham.

(continued)

Honey-Mustard Baked Tongue   (continued)

½ cup honey

¼ cup balsamic vinegar

2 tablespoons powdered
    mustard

¼ teaspoon ground cloves

1 cup All-Purpose Broth
    (page 222) or canned
    low-sodium chicken broth

1 boiled tongue (page 147)

SERVES 6

1. Combine the honey, vinegar, mustard, cloves, and broth in a Dutch oven. Lay the tongue in the liquid and cover the pot. Cook in a 350°F oven for 30 minutes on each side. (For frozen tongue, increase the cooking time to 45 minutes on each side.)

2. Transfer the pot to the top of the stove and place over medium heat. Remove the cover and cook, basting the tongue, until the juices have reduced and become syrupy, another 15 to 20 minutes.

3. To serve, transfer the tongue to a cutting board and slice it thin, beginning at the tip. Arrange the slices on a platter and spoon a small amount of sauce over them. Serve the remaining sauce in a sauceboat.

# BRAISED TONGUE WITH BACON, CAPERS, AND TOMATOES

Two salty ingredients—bacon and capers—give the impression of cured tongue without the chemical additives. Serve with mashed potatoes.

½ pound bacon, cut into ½-
    inch pieces

6 plum tomatoes, peeled,
    seeded, and chopped, or 1
    can (17 ounces) plum
    tomatoes, drained and
    chopped

¼ cup capers, drained

1 cup dry white wine

1 boiled tongue (page 147)

2 tablespoons whole-grain
    mustard

SERVES 6

1. Place a 2-quart flameproof casserole or Dutch oven over medium heat, and add the bacon. Cook, stirring occasionally, 5 minutes.

2. Add the tomatoes, capers, wine, and tongue. Cover the casserole, transfer it to the oven, and turn the oven on to 350°F. Cook for 1 hour, 2 hours if it is still frozen.

3. Remove the casserole from the oven and transfer the tongue to a carving board. Starting at the tip, thinly slice the tongue. Arrange the slices on a platter.

4. Stir the mustard into the braising liquid, and pour the sauce over the tongue.

# BRAISED SWEETBREADS

**N**early all recipes for sweetbreads ask the cook to blanch them, clean them, and finally cook them. The finished product has none of the character of sweetbreads—they become a bland vehicle for a sauce and a garnish. Sweetbreads have a delicate flavor and texture that should be respected. Instead, sear the sweetbreads and then braise them.

**3 pounds calf's sweetbreads**

**¼ teaspoon ground mace**

**½ teaspoon salt**

**¼ teaspoon freshly ground black pepper**

**3 tablespoons flour**

**¼ cup flavorless cooking oil**

**2 tablespoons finely minced shallots**

**1 cup dry white wine**

**1 cup All-Purpose Broth (page 222) or canned low-sodium chicken broth**

**½ cup whipping cream**

**1 tablespoon unsalted butter**

**6 to 8 lemon slices**

SERVES 6 TO 8

1. Preheat the oven to 375°F.
2. Pat the sweetbreads dry. Peel and discard the most obvious membranes without breaking up the sweetbreads.
3. Mix the mace, salt, and pepper with the flour. Dust the sweetbreads with the mixture, shaking off the excess.
4. Heat the oil in a heavy ovenproof skillet over medium heat. Add the sweetbreads and cook until they are a deep honey on both sides, about 5 to 6 minutes per side. Do not crowd the pan or they will not brown; do this in batches if necessary.
5. Pour off any remaining oil in the skillet, and add the shallots, wine, and broth. Bring to a boil. Then transfer the skillet to the oven and cook, uncovered, 25 to 30 minutes, turning once.
6. Remove the skillet from the oven and using a slotted spoon, transfer the sweetbreads to a platter; keep warm. Add the cream to the cooking juices, and quickly boil the liquid until it forms a sauce, about 10 minutes. Remove it from the heat and whisk in the butter.
7. Strain the sauce into a sauceboat, and decorate the sweetbreads with the lemon slices. Serve immediately. ▨

▨ To freeze, let all or part of the sweetbreads cool to room temperature; then place them in a freezer bag or container, seal, and freeze for up to 6 months. (The following three recipes call for half of this recipe.) Defrost in the refrigerator or microwave oven.

# SWEETBREADS WITH WALNUTS AND SHERRY

This is a home adaptation of restaurant cooking—the sauce is elegantly smooth and the flavor is subtly nutty. Walnuts add a crunchy contrast to the creamy sweetbreads.

½ recipe Braised
    Sweetbreads (page 149),
    frozen or fresh
½ cup dry sherry
½ cup All-Purpose Broth
    (page 222) or canned
    low-sodium chicken broth
½ cup whipping cream
¼ cup walnut halves

SERVES 3 TO 4

1. Defrost the sweetbreads if frozen.
2. Place a medium-size skillet over medium heat and add the sherry. Cook 1 minute to burn off the alcohol. Then add the broth and cream and bring to a boil.
3. Add the sweetbreads and walnuts and cook for 10 minutes, turning once. If the liquid becomes too thick, add a little more broth, cover, and continue cooking.
4. Remove the skillet from the heat, and using a slotted spoon, transfer the sweetbreads and walnuts to serving platter.
5. Strain the sauce over the sweetbreads, and serve immediately.

# PAN-FRIED CRISPY SWEETBREADS

In my family, sweetbreads were considered restaurant fare; they were always served in sauce. At my first restaurant job, one of the waiters described his grandmother's method for preparing sweetbreads for the family. Now I make them all the time. I love serving a pile of these crunchy delights with just a squeeze of lemon to complement them.

These are excellent as an appetizer—in which case you'll be able to serve eight people. When I offer these crisp nuggets as hors d'oeuvres at cocktail parties, someone invariably compliments me on serving the best fried oysters in the world! And they are delicious—garlicky, salty, and cheesy.

½ *recipe Braised Sweetbreads (page 149), frozen or fresh*

1 *teaspoon finely minced garlic*

6 *tablespoons grated Parmesan or Romano cheese*

6 *tablespoons flour*

½ *teaspoon salt*

½ *teaspoon freshly ground black pepper*

*Flavorless cooking oil*

8 *lemon wedges*

SERVES 4

1. Defrost the sweetbreads if frozen and cut them into 1-inch pieces.

2. Preheat the oven to 250°F.

3. Combine the garlic, cheese, flour, salt, and pepper in a small bowl and mix well. Toss the sweetbreads in the mixture and coat the pieces well.

4. Place a medium-size skillet or saucepan over medium heat and add 1 inch of oil. The oil is hot enough when a droplet of water jumps across the surface and disappears.

5. Cook the sweetbreads in the hot oil until golden brown, 6 to 7 minutes. Do not crowd the pan or the sweetbreads will not become crispy or brown; you may have to perform this operation in batches. Remove the pieces as they are done, drain them on paper towels, and keep warm on a plate in the oven.

6. When all the sweetbreads are fried, arrange them on a platter, surround with the lemon wedges, and serve.

# GRILLED SWEETBREADS

**A** couple of years ago I took my Trumps staff to a winery so we could see the winemaking process and tour the cellars. Afterward they prepared a giant barbecue for us in the fields. The sweetbreads were better than any I had ever eaten, and I began toying with different glazes to flavor them while they grilled. The one that has become the favorite is both salty and sweet, with a surprising hint of anise and clove that adds to the smokey flavor of the grill.

1 *teaspoon wasabe powder or powdered mustard*

4 *tablespoons soy sauce*

2 *tablespoons Pernod (optional)*

2 *tablespoons honey*

**Pinch of ground clove**

8 *lemon wedges*

½ *recipe Braised Sweetbreads (page 149), frozen or fresh*

SERVES 4

**1.** The night before you are going to serve the sweetbreads, combine all the ingredients except the sweetbreads and lemon wedges in a bowl or plastic bag and mix well. Place the sweetbreads in the marinade, cover or seal, and refrigerate overnight. (If they're frozen, you can let them defrost in the marinade.)

**2.** Light a charcoal grill or preheat a broiler. Place the sweetbreads on the grill or under the broiler, and cook 10 minutes on each side.

**3.** Arrange the sweetbreads on a platter, surround with the lemon wedges, and serve immediately.

# VEGETABLES AND RICE

I really don't believe in using valuable freezer space for vegetables. These days supermarkets carry a fresh array of almost every vegetable you could want, and many commercially frozen items are as good as or better than what we can process at home. If you have a carefully tended garden and want to preserve its bounty, however, that's another story. Use the guidelines under "Blanching" in the Freezer Dictionary to prepare vegetables for freezing.

And to give yourself a "leg up" on time-consuming vegetable dishes by doing some or most of the work beforehand, the freezer is the ideal tool. Here are a few delightful vegetable dishes that you might enjoy more often if you can just pull them from your freezer.

## PREPARING ASPARAGUS FOR FREEZING

Asparagus is never in season long enough for me to get bored with it. Freezing can extend the season, but only for a few weeks' time; if left too long in the freezer, enzymes cause it to acquire a slightly bitter taste. Asparagus freezes best when uncooked. Surprisingly, the expansion of water in the stalks when you freeze them makes defrosted asparagus seem blanched, so if you want to serve chilled asparagus vinaigrette as a starter, simply defrost, gently squeeze the stalks to rid them of excess water and serve. Asparagus from the freezer cooks best from its frozen state.

To prepare asparagus for the freezer, remove and discard the woody ends and soak stalks in salted water for 10 minutes. Place them on a cookie sheet in the freezer and open-freeze for 30 minutes. Pack into freezer bags or double-wrap with plastic wrap. Freeze for up to 8 weeks.

# ASPARAGUS WITH BALSAMICO BUTTER

This is the simplest of recipes, and it works beautifully with many other vegetables as well—broccoli or cauliflower, diced eggplant, okra, carrots or onions.

1 *pound asparagus, frozen (page 153) or fresh*

2 *tablespoons unsalted butter*

3 *tablespoons finely minced shallots or onions*

2 *tablespoons balsamic vinegar*

SERVES 4

1. Combine the butter, shallots, and asparagus in a medium-size nonreactive saucepan and place over medium heat. Cook, tossing the asparagus in the butter, until the asparagus is heated through, about 5 minutes for fresh, 6 minutes for frozen.

2. Remove the pan from the heat and transfer the asparagus to a serving platter. Stir the vinegar into the butter sauce, pour over the asparagus, and serve immediately.

# ASPARAGUS PURÉE

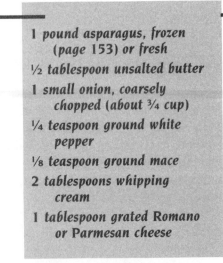

1 *pound asparagus, frozen (page 153) or fresh*

½ *tablespoon unsalted butter*

1 *small onion, coarsely chopped (about ¾ cup)*

¼ *teaspoon ground white pepper*

⅛ *teaspoon ground mace*

2 *tablespoons whipping cream*

1 *tablespoon grated Romano or Parmesan cheese*

SERVES 4

1. Cut off the tips, chop them coarsely, and set them aside. Coarsely chop the stalks and place them in the bowl of a food processor.

2. Melt the butter in a skillet over medium heat. Add the onions, white pepper, and mace. Cook, stirring, for about 7 minutes or until the onions are soft and translucent. Add the onions and butter to the asparagus stalks, and purée until smooth.

3. Return the asparagus purée to the skillet and add the chopped tips. Cover, and place over medium heat until hot, 7 to 10 minutes. Serve immediately.

# SAUTÉED GREEN BEANS
# WITH MUSHROOMS AND PINE NUTS

Freshly picked green beans—whether French haricots verts, Chinese long beans, or common string beans—freeze well: simply blanch them briefly, drop them into an ice-water bath to keep them crisp and vibrantly colored, then drain and freeze.

I love the combination of crunchy green beans, creamy mushrooms, and soft pine nuts. Vegetable side dishes should not interfere with the main dish, but that does not mean they have to be plain and boring.

*1 pound fresh green beans*

*4 quarts water*

*2 tablespoons kosher salt*

*½ pound mushrooms*

*2 tablespoons olive oil*

*1 tablespoon unsalted butter*

*3 tablespoons pine nuts*

*1 teaspoon chopped fresh tarragon leaves, or ¼ teaspoon dried*

SERVES 5 TO 6

1. Snap both ends off the beans and pull off any strings. Cut large beans into 2-inch pieces. Don't cut smaller haricots verts.

2. Fill a mixing bowl with 4 cups of cold water and add 1 tray of ice cubes. Set aside.

3. Combine the 4 quarts water and the kosher salt in a large saucepan and bring to a boil over high heat. Add the beans, bring the water back to a boil, and cook, uncovered, until the beans are barely tender, about 2 to 4 minutes, depending on the size and age of the beans. This is only a preliminary preparation, so do not overcook the beans.

4. Drain the beans and drop them immediately into the ice water. Stir until cool, then drain. Spread the beans on towels and pat dry. ▨

5. Thinly slice the mushrooms and set them aside on a plate.

6. Heat the oil and butter in a medium-size skillet over medium heat, and add the pine nuts and mushrooms. If you are using dried tarragon, add it now. Cook, stirring, about 5 minutes. Add the green beans and fresh tarragon and cook until the beans are hot, about 3 minutes longer. Transfer to a serving platter and serve immediately.

(continued)

⌧ To freeze plain blanched beans, prepare through Step 4. Place all or some of the beans in plastic bags, seal, and freeze for up to 6 months.

Beans should be cooked from the frozen. To serve, place the plastic bags directly into gently simmering water and cook for 8 minutes; or open the bag and reheat in a microwave oven.

# PREPARING BROCCOLI FOR FREEZING

Most people eat broccoli florets and only the tender upper stems of the vegetable. I also love the crunch of the large, woody stems. You have to peel them in order to get to the good part, but it's more than worth the extra effort.

I prepare broccoli for either freezing or cooking by blanching it first.

*4 pounds broccoli*

*2 quarts water*

*1 tablespoon kosher salt*

6 CUPS (SERVES 8)

1. Cut the flower tops off the broccoli and set them aside. Using a small knife or vegetable peeler, remove and discard the tough outer layer from the stalks, exposing the light green interior. Slice the stalks ⅛ inch thick, and set them aside.

2. Combine the water and salt in a large saucepan and bring to a boil over high heat. Add the broccoli florets and stems. When the water returns to the boil, cook another 2 minutes.

3. Remove the pan from the heat and drain the broccoli. Rinse the broccoli under cold running water until it is cool. Spread it out on absorbent towels to dry.

4. Divide the broccoli among freezer bags, and freeze for up to 6 months. (The following two recipes call for half of this recipe.)

To defrost, hold the bags of broccoli under cold running water; or defrost in the microwave oven.

# SAUTÉED BROCCOLI

3 cups (½ recipe) prepared
   *broccoli (page 156),*
   *frozen or fresh*
2 tablespoons olive oil
1 tablespoon finely minced
   *garlic*
1 tablespoon Pernod

**1.** Defrost the broccoli if frozen.

**2.** Heat the olive oil in a medium-size skillet over medium heat. Add the garlic and broccoli and cook, stirring, about 7 minutes, or until the broccoli is well heated. Add the Pernod and cook 1 minute more.

**3.** Pour into a serving dish and serve immediately.

SERVES 4

# CURRIED BROCCOLI

**Y**ogurt, often served as a condiment to cool hot, spicy Indian curries, is also the preferred ingredient in low-fat cream sauces.

3 cups (½ recipe) prepared
   *broccoli (page 156),*
   *frozen or fresh*
2 tablespoons olive oil
1 teaspoon finely chopped
   *fresh dill, or ½ teaspoon*
   *dried*
1 teaspoon curry powder
2 tablespoons plain yogurt

**1.** Defrost the broccoli if frozen.

**2.** Heat the oil in a medium-size skillet over medium heat. Add the broccoli and cook, stirring, 5 minutes. Then add the dill and curry, and cook, stirring, another 2 minutes.

**3.** Remove the skillet from the heat and stir in the yogurt.

**4.** Transfer the mixture to a serving dish, and serve immediately.

SERVES 4

# PREPARING BRUSSELS SPROUTS FOR FREEZING

I generally prefer vegetables slightly undercooked, but the flavor of Brussels sprouts does not develop if they are not tender. Of course you don't want to cook them until they are gray-green and mushy. Cooking the sprouts in water until the pan is dry lets us freeze them successfully—the flavor stays in the sprouts. This technique, which rids a vegetable of excess water and concentrates its flavor, works with onions, leeks, celery, and endive.

**4 pounds Brussels sprouts
(about 6 cups)**

**1 teaspoon salt**

**3 tablespoons olive oil**

SERVES 8

1. Using a small knife, cut off and discard the stem tip of the sprouts. Remove and discard the outer leaves, and cut an X in the base of each sprout.

2. Combine the sprouts, salt, and oil in a 12-inch skillet. Add cold water until the sprouts are submerged barely halfway, cover, and place over high heat.

3. Bring the water to a boil, and then cook for 2 minutes. Remove the cover and continue to cook, stirring occasionally, until the water has completely evaporated, 12 to 15 minutes.

4. Remove the skillet from the heat, pour the sprouts into a serving bowl, and serve.
⊠

⊠ To freeze, allow some or all of the Brussels sprouts to cool to room temperature. Then place them in freezer bags or containers, seal, and freeze for up to 6 months.

Cook from frozen, or partially defrost and use in one of the following variations.

# GLAZED BRUSSELS SPROUTS

The traditional way of glazing vegetables uses water, sugar, and butter, and it's mostly a cosmetic addition to the dish. Shiny vegetables or dark golden ones are the two results. I prefer to sacrifice a little visual perfection for better flavor, so I glaze mine with chicken stock.

*1 tablespoon unsalted butter*

*2 cups prepared Brussels sprouts (page 157), frozen or fresh*

*½ cup All-Purpose Broth (page 222) or canned low-sodium chicken broth*

*1 teaspoon sugar*

SERVES 4

1. Partially defrost the Brussels sprouts if frozen.
2. Combine the butter, sprouts, broth, and sugar in a skillet and place over medium-high heat. Cook until the broth has evaporated, 7 to 8 minutes. Then cook another 1 or 2 minutes to brown the sprouts lightly.
3. Transfer to a serving bowl and serve immediately.

# GRATINÉED BRUSSELS SPROUTS

Serve this flavorful casserole with a simple entrée. Things become muddled when there are too many flavors or sauces on a single plate.

*4 cups prepared Brussels sprouts (page 157), frozen or fresh*

*2 tablespoons unsalted butter*

*1 tablespoon flour*

*½ cup beer*

*½ cup grated Gruyère or Swiss cheese*

SERVES 6

1. Partially defrost the Brussels sprouts if frozen.
2. Preheat the oven to 350°F.
3. Cut the sprouts in half from tip to stem, and place them in a 9 × 11-inch baking dish.
4. Melt the butter in a small saucepan over medium heat. Add the flour and mix thoroughly to form a paste; cook 1 minute. Then stir in the beer and cook until the mixture has thickened, 1 minute. Spoon the thickened beer over the sprouts, add the cheese, and mix well.
5. Bake until the mixture is bubbling hot, about 35 minutes. Serve immediately.

# PREPARING CABBAGE FOR FREEZING

Very often recipes ask for cabbage to be degorged prior to cooking—salted and left to sit while water is drawn out of the leaves. The freezer accomplishes this without salt, allowing you to have shredded cabbage on hand, ready for cooking or using in salads. Save the outer leaves for stuffed cabbage (pages 242–243).

**2 tablespoons kosher salt**
**¼ cup white vinegar**
**1 medium head red or green cabbage (about 3 pounds)**

16 CUPS (SERVES 12)

1. Fill a 3-quart pot three-quarters full with water, and add the salt and vinegar. Cover, place over high heat, and bring to a boil.

2. Meanwhile, using a small knife, remove and discard the center core of the cabbage.

3. Place the cabbage in the boiling water, cover, and cook for 5 minutes. Then remove the cabbage and hold it under cold running water until it is cool enough to handle.

4. Carefully remove the outer leaves from the head without tearing them. You should be able to remove about 8 leaves before the interior ones start tearing. Set them aside for another use.

5. Cut the remaining cabbage in half from tip to stem. Then lay it flat on a work surface and cut it into ⅛-inch-thick shreds.

6. Place the shredded cabbage in 2-cup plastic bags or containers. Seal, and freeze for up to 6 months. Defrost at room temperature or in a microwave oven.

# COLE SLAW

What can I say about cole slaw? Everyone has their favorite and I wouldn't presume to be a judge. But I do know that I like mine only slightly crunchy—some might say I like it too soggy—and I find that the freezer is the ideal tool for achieving this texture.

4 cups frozen shredded
    cabbage (page 160)
3 tablespoons cider vinegar
1 teaspoon sugar
1 teaspoon celery seeds
½ teaspoon ground white
    pepper
1 teaspoon Dijon mustard
1 teaspoon sour cream

**1.** Defrost the cabbage and press out any excess liquid.

**2.** Place the vinegar in a mixing bowl and dissolve the sugar in it. Add the celery seeds, white pepper, mustard, and sour cream; mix well. Add the cabbage, stir well, cover, and refrigerate for at least 1 hour before serving. ▨

SERVES 4

▨ To freeze, place all or some of the cole slaw in a freezer bag or container, and seal. Freeze for up to 2 months. Defrost at room temperature or in the microwave oven. Serve chilled.

# SAUTÉED CABBAGE

**E**ven though you shouldn't be able to detect it, vinegar is an important addition to any cabbage recipe.

2 cups frozen shredded
    cabbage (page 160)
1 tablespoon flavorless
    cooking oil
2 tablespoons red or white
    wine vinegar
2 tablespoons water
⅛ teaspoon ground caraway
    seeds
⅛ teaspoon ground black
    pepper

**1.** Defrost the cabbage and press out any excess liquid.

**2.** Heat the oil in a medium-size skillet over medium heat. Add the cabbage, vinegar, water, caraway, and pepper. Cover and cook for 5 minutes.

**3.** Remove the cover and continue to cook, stirring, another 7 minutes or until the cabbage is soft. Remove the skillet from the heat, transfer the cabbage to a serving dish, and serve immediately.

SERVES 3 TO 4

# CREAMED CUCUMBERS AND TOMATOES

Too many people think of cucumbers as something to use only in a salad. But they make a delicious hot vegetable, as you'll find out when you prepare this dish.

3 *medium cucumbers*

1 *tablespoon kosher salt*

1 *tablespoon olive oil*

1 *cup Tomato Concassée (page 223) or drained, seeded canned tomatoes*

*Freshly ground black pepper to taste*

2 *tablespoons chopped fresh basil leaves, or 1 teaspoon dried*

¼ *cup whipping cream*

SERVES 5 TO 6

1. Peel the cucumbers. Halve them lengthwise, and scoop out and discard the seeds. Cut the halves into ¼-inch-thick crescent-shape slices. You should have about 3½ cups. Place the cucumbers in a colander, mix with the salt, and place over a plate or in the sink to catch the draining liquid. Let drain for 30 minutes.

2. Rinse the cucumbers under cold running water; then squeeze handfuls of them to eliminate excess water. Place the drained cucumbers in a bowl.

3. Heat the oil in a medium-size saucepan over medium heat. Add the cucumbers and tomato concassée, and give the mixture a few turns of the peppermill. Stir in the basil and cream. Raise the heat to high and cook, stirring occasionally, until the cream has reduced and the mixture has thickened, about 5 minutes.

4. Remove the pan from the heat, pour the creamed cucumbers into a serving dish, and serve immediately. ▨

▨ To freeze, allow some or all of the mixture to cool to room temperature. Then place it in a freezer bag or container, seal, and freeze for up to 4 months.

# PREPARING EGGPLANT FOR FREEZING

Eggplant soaks up lots of cooking oil if it's not degorged before cooking. Ridding eggplant of its water not only lets us cook with less oil; it enables us to freeze the eggplant slices and have a ready ingredient for a vegetable side dish or entrée.

**2 medium eggplants (about ¾ pound each)**
**¼ cup kosher salt**
**½ cup olive oil**

SERVES 6 TO 8

**1.** Remove and discard the stem end of the eggplants. Cut the eggplants lengthwise into ⅜-inch-thick slices, discarding the two side pieces that are mostly skin. Sprinkle the salt over the eggplant, and arrange the slices in layers in a colander. Place the colander over a plate or in the sink, and let drain for 1 hour.

**2.** Rinse the eggplant under cold water and pat it dry with kitchen towels, pressing out more liquid.

**3.** Heat 2 tablespoons of the oil in a large skillet over medium heat. When the oil is almost smoking, add the eggplant slices and cook about 1 minute on each side. Transfer the slices to a baking sheet lined with paper towels as they are done, and repeat until all the eggplant has been sautéed, adding more oil as necessary. Allow the eggplant to cool.

**4.** Wrap the slices in layers between sheets of plastic wrap or freezer paper and then seal in a freezer bag. Freeze for up to 6 months. Defrost in the refrigerator or microwave oven.

# ZUCCHINI-STUFFED EGGPLANT

Zucchini and eggplant often show up in the same dish—ratatouille being the most common—because they are often grown together and ripen in late summer. They also happen to taste delicious together. Make these little roulades to serve as a side dish to a poultry entrée or as a vegetarian main course.

(continued)

Zucchini-Stuffed Eggplant (continued)

8 *large slices prepared*
  *eggplant (page 163),*
  *fresh or frozen*

1 *large zucchini (about ½*
  *pound)*

1 *tablespoon unsalted butter*

1 *teaspoon salt, or as desired*

*Freshly ground black pepper*
  *to taste*

¼ *cup whipping cream*

2 *tablespoons fresh lemon*
  *juice*

SERVES 4

1. Defrost the eggplant if frozen.
2. Preheat the oven to 350°F.
3. Trim and discard the zucchini stem. Shred the zucchini with the fine blade of a food processor or hand grater, and set aside. You should have about 2 cups.
4. Melt the butter in a medium-size skillet over medium heat, and add the zucchini, salt, and pepper. Cook, stirring, for 5 minutes or until well wilted. Add the cream and lemon juice, and cook until the mixture has become dry, about 5 minutes. Remove the skillet from the heat.
5. Place dollops of zucchini on the slices of eggplant, and roll them up tightly. Stand the rolls upright in a baking dish, press down lightly, and bake for 15 minutes.
6. Arrange the eggplant on a warm platter, and serve immediately.

# GRATINÉED EGGPLANT

My favorite childhood food, eggplant parmigiana, is a whole meal, or at least a first course. This gratin is a scaled-down version (it's missing the tomato sauce) that can accompany many grilled or roasted meats, fish, and poultry.

12 *slices prepared eggplant*
   *(page 163), frozen or*
   *fresh*

2 *tablespoons unsalted butter*

2 *tablespoons flour*

⅓ *cup milk*

¾ *cup grated Swiss or*
   *Gruyère cheese*

SERVES 3 TO 4

1. Defrost the eggplant if frozen.
2. Preheat the oven to 375°F.
3. Melt the butter in a small saucepan over low heat. Add the flour, mix well to form a paste, and cook for 1 minute. Add the milk and cook, stirring, until the mixture has thickened and is bubbling, about 5 minutes. Remove the pan from the heat and set aside.
4. Line the bottom of a lightly oiled 8-inch square or round casserole with 3 or 4 slices of eggplant. Spread some sauce over

the eggplant and sprinkle with some of the cheese. Repeat until everything is used up, finishing with sauce and cheese.

**5.** Bake until the sauce is bubbling and the top is golden, about 25 minutes. Serve immediately.

---

**Eggplant Parmigiana:** Substitute a mixture of mozzarella and Parmesan cheese for the Swiss cheese, and pour 1 cup of Fresh Tomato Sauce (page 226) over the layers before baking.

# MARINATED EGGPLANT

Offer this dish chilled or at room temperature as an accompaniment for grilled rabbit, chicken, veal, shrimp, or lobster. Or serve it as a starter, perhaps adding a slice of mozzarella or goat cheese. It also makes a great dip for chips.

12 *slices prepared eggplant (page 163), frozen or fresh*

¼ *cup olive oil*

¼ *cup dry white wine*

¼ *cup white wine vinegar*

2 *tablespoons finely minced shallots or onions*

1 *tablespoon finely minced garlic*

6 *anchovy fillets, chopped*

**1.** Defrost the eggplant if frozen, and arrange the slices in a serving dish or on a rimmed platter.

**2.** Combine the oil, wine, vinegar, shallots, and garlic in a small saucepan and bring to a boil over high heat. Remove the pan from the heat, stir in the anchovies, and pour the hot marinade over the eggplant. Cover and let sit at room temperature for 15 minutes before serving, or refrigerate for at least 2 hours to serve chilled.

SERVES 3 TO 4

# EGGPLANT CAVIAR

The thousands of little eggplant seeds in this dish give it its name. It's an old standby in New York dairy restaurants. Serve it as a dip or a vegetable accompaniment. You can add many things to this purée, such as roasted peppers, peeled and seeded tomatoes, olives, or anchovies.

**2 medium eggplants (about ¾ pound each)**

**¼ cup olive oil**

**2 tablespoons minced garlic**

**½ teaspoon salt, or as desired**

SERVES 4

**1.** Prick the eggplant in a couple of places with a fork. Place it in a baking dish, put the dish in the oven, and turn the oven on to 425°F. Bake for 35 minutes, turning once.

**2.** When the eggplant is shriveled and the skin looks burnt, remove the baking dish from the oven and transfer the eggplant to a work surface. Let it cool for 10 minutes to make handling easier. Then cut a slit down one side of the eggplant. Scoop out all the seeds and flesh, and place in a work bowl. Discard the skin.

**3.** Combine the olive oil and garlic in a small saucepan over medium heat, and cook until the garlic stops bubbling, about 3 minutes. Pour the garlic oil over the eggplant, and using a two forks, mash the eggplant until no large chunks remain. Add the salt and mix well.

**4.** Transfer the mixture to a serving bowl and serve hot; or chill, covered, in the refrigerator before serving. ▨

▨ To freeze, place all or some of the cooled Eggplant Caviar in a freezer bag or container. Seal, and freeze for up to 6 months. Defrost before reheating, or serve chilled.

# BRAISED BELGIAN ENDIVE

**B**elgian endive is a winter vegetable that's grown in darkness from specially prepared roots. It's always expensive, and in the summer it can be very difficult to find. Endive is one of my very favorite vegetables—either cooked or in salad.

8 *medium heads Belgian endive (about 1½ pounds total)*

3 *tablespoons unsalted butter*

2 *tablespoons flavorless cooking oil*

½ *cup All-Purpose Broth (page 222), canned low-sodium chicken broth, or water*

½ *teaspoon salt*

SERVES 4

**1.** Cut each endive in half lengthwise, and set them aside.

**2.** Heat the butter and oil in a large skillet over medium heat. Add the endive in one layer, and cook until the outer leaves are nicely browned, about 7 minutes. Turn and brown the other side, about 4 minutes. (Do this in two batches if necessary.)

**3.** Add the broth, sprinkle with the salt, and cook until the liquid has evaporated, about 10 minutes. Transfer the endive to a serving platter, and serve immediately. ▨

**Braised Lettuce:** Substitute whole heads of Bibb or Boston lettuce for the endive.

▨ To freeze, allow the endive to cool to room temperature. Then seal in a freezer bag or container, and freeze for up to 4 months.

Reheat in a covered casserole in a 325°F oven for 25 minutes or in a microwave oven.

# ONION AND RICE PURÉE

**T**his is an adaptation of a French dish called a *soubise*. Don't be fooled by the scant amount of liquid in the recipe—the rice soaks up moisture from the onions. Rice takes on a nutty flavor when cooked this way, and the onions become sweetly caramelized. Serve this as an accompaniment to meat or poultry in sauce.

(continued)

Onion and Rice Purée (continued)

**2 tablespoons unsalted butter**

**½ cup long-grain rice**

**6 medium onions, thinly
sliced (12 cups)**

**½ cup All-Purpose Broth
(page 222), canned low-
sodium chicken broth, or
water**

**¼ teaspoon ground nutmeg**

**½ teaspoon salt, or as
desired**

**½ teaspoon ground white
pepper**

**½ cup whipping cream**

1. Preheat the oven to 325°F.
2. Melt the butter in a flameproof casserole or Dutch oven over low heat. Add the rice and cook 1 minute, mixing to coat the grains with the butter.
3. Remove the casserole from the heat, and stir in the onions, broth, nutmeg, salt, and white pepper. Cover tightly, transfer to the oven, and bake for 1 hour.
4. Transfer the mixture to a food processor, add the cream, and coarsely purée using the pulse button.
5. Return the purée to the casserole, cover, and reheat in the oven before serving. ☒

SERVES 6

☒ To freeze, place purée in a freezer bag and squeeze out as much air as possible. Seal, and freeze for up to 6 months.

Defrost and reheat by placing the bag in a pot of gently boiling water for 10 minutes or in the microwave oven.

# PICKLED ONIONS AND MUSHROOMS

Raw mushrooms don't freeze well because they change texture, but cooked marinated mushrooms freeze nicely (cooking the mushrooms briefly allows them to soak up the pickling flavors before freezing). Serve these pickled vegetables as a first course, use them in a salad, or toss them with chilled macaroni and mayonnaise and take them on a picnic.

1 *pound pearl onions*

2 *pounds button mushrooms*

⅔ *cup white wine vinegar*

1 *cup dry white wine*

1 *teaspoon ground coriander*

½ *teaspoon celery seeds*

½ *teaspoon salt, or as desired*

*Freshly ground black pepper to taste*

2 *tablespoons finely chopped parsley*

¼ *cup plain yogurt*

¼ *cup olive oil*

8 *medium leaves Romaine lettuce*

SERVES 6 TO 8

**1.** Place the onions in a bowl, cover with lukewarm water, and set aside for 1 hour. When the skins have softened, peel the onions from tip to root, and cut a small X in the root tip of each one. Set the onions aside.

**2.** Wash the mushrooms and trim off the stems. (You can use the stems for making duxelles, page 240.) Set the mushroom caps aside on a plate.

**3.** Combine the vinegar, wine, coriander, celery seeds, salt, and pepper in a saucepan. Place it over high heat, cover, and bring to a boil. Then add the onions, reduce the heat to low, and cook, covered, for 3 minutes. Add the mushrooms and cook 1 minute. Remove the pan from the heat and pour the contents into a bowl.

**4.** Let the mushrooms and onions cool to room temperature in the cooking liquid, about 30 minutes. Strain the liquid into a small saucepan and place the mushrooms and onions, covered, in the refrigerator. Place the saucepan over medium heat and reduce the cooking liquid by half, 4 to 5 minutes. Remove the pan from the heat and spoon the reduction over the mushrooms and onions.

**5.** Place the mushrooms and onions in a bowl, add the parsley, yogurt, and oil, and mix well. Place a lettuce leaf on each plate, and mound mushrooms, onions, and sauce on top. ▨

**Pickled Onions and Okra:** Substitute small whole okra for the mushrooms, or even cauliflower florets. Cook them the same way as you would mushrooms.

▨ To freeze, place all or part of the mixture in a freezer bag, squeeze out as much air as possible, and seal. Freeze for up to 6 months. Defrost in the refrigerator or microwave oven.

# PAPPA AL POMIDORI

This bread and tomato stew is unbelievably delicious—and perfect for freezing. Serve as a first course, or spoon it over fish fillets, shrimp, or chicken breasts and then broil them.

Pappa al Pomidori should be thick and a little oily. If it's too thick, however, add a little extra water, All-Purpose Broth (page 222), or liquid from a tin of canned tomatoes.

½ *cup olive oil*

2 *medium onions, finely diced (about 1½ cups)*

8 *cloves garlic, finely sliced*

¼ *medium loaf stale French or Italian bread (baguette), sliced (about 3 ounces)*

4 *cups Tomato Concassée (page 223), or drained chopped, seeded canned tomatoes (liquid reserved)*

3 *tablespoons fresh marjoram leaves, or 2 teaspoons dried*

1 *teaspoon salt*

½ *teaspoon ground white pepper*

½ *cup dry white wine*

1 *cup water or liquid from canned tomatoes*

*Grated Parmesan or Romano cheese*

**1.** In a medium skillet over low heat, combine the olive oil, onions, and garlic. Cook, stirring occasionally, for 5 minutes, until the onions are soft and translucent.

**2.** Roughly crumble the bread into ¼-inch pieces, and add it to the skillet. Cook, stirring, for 1 minute.

**3.** Add the tomatoes, marjoram, salt, white pepper, wine, and water. Cover and cook, stirring occasionally, for 25 minutes.

**4.** Serve the stew in soup bowls, and pass the grated cheese. ▨

**Pappa al Melanzane:** Substitute ½-inch cubes of peeled eggplant for the tomato.

**Tomato Pudding:** Add 2 beaten eggs to 1 cup of stew and bake in a preheated 375°F oven until set, about 20 minutes. Serve as a vegetable side dish or on a bed of arugula as a starter.

SERVES 4

▨ To freeze, cool the stew to room temperature. Then place it in a freezer bag or a tightly covered container, and freeze for up to 6 months. Defrost in the refrigerator or microwave oven.

# SHELLFISH POMIDORI

¼ *recipe (1 cup) Pappa al*
    *Pomidori (page 170),*
    *frozen or fresh*
½ *cup dry white wine*
4 *pounds clams or mussels,*
    *scrubbed*

SERVES 4 TO 5

**1.** Defrost Pappa al Pomidori if frozen.

**2.** Combine all the ingredients in a large pot, cover, and place over medium heat. Cook until the shells have opened, 10 minutes for clams, 5 minutes for mussels. (Discard any that do not open.)

**3.** Ladle into soup bowls and serve immediately.

# ROASTED PEPPERS

Like Joseph's robe, peppers come in a rainbow of colors. Red, yellow, and orange peppers are sweeter than green. Purple ones taste like green, and their deeply blushed skins turn green when cooked. Peppers are wonderful in puréed sauces, or as a good side vegetable. Roast and peel them and the freezer won't bother their flavor or texture.

4 *medium peppers*
2 *tablespoons olive oil*
1 *tablespoons freshly*
    *squeezed lemon juice*
*Salt and pepper to taste*

SERVES 4

**1.** If you have a gas range, place peppers directly over the flame and cook until peppers are completely blackened. If you have an electric range, preheat broiler. Cook peppers, turning so that skins blacken completely. Place immediately in a paper bag, close the top and let rest 5 minutes. Wash peppers under cold running water, rubbing until all blackened skin is removed. Slice peppers in half from tip to stem and remove and discard stem and seeds. ▩

**2.** Heat the oil in a small pan over medium heat, add the peppers and lemon juice, cover and cook until well heated. Arrange peppers on 4 plates, alternating different colored halves, and serve. (continued)

Roasted Peppers   (continued)

▨ To freeze roasted peppers, place in a plastic container or freezer bag, label, and place in the freezer for up to 6 months.

# PUMPKIN GRATIN

**P**repare this simple casserole as accompaniment to roasted veal, pork, chicken, or turkey, or turn it into a vegetarian main course by adding a cup of peeled seeded tomatoes to the mixture and flavoring it with a little garlic and oregano.

*1½ pounds fresh pumpkin*

*1 large onion, finely chopped (about 1 cup)*

*½ teaspoon salt, or as desired*

*¼ teaspoon ground white pepper*

*2 tablespoons unsalted butter, melted*

*2 eggs*

*¾ cup milk*

*¾ cup farmer's, hoop, or ricotta cheese*

SERVES 6

**1.** Using a paring knife or vegetable peeler, peel and discard the outer skin of the pumpkin. Cut the pumpkin flesh into ¼-inch-thick slices and place them in a mixing bowl. Add the onions, salt, white pepper, and melted butter, and toss well.

**2.** Pour the pumpkin mixture into a greased 9-inch round or square baking dish, cover with foil, and place in the oven. Turn the oven on to 375°F, and bake for 30 minutes.

**3.** Meanwhile, beat the eggs, milk, and cheese together in a bowl until smooth.

**4.** Remove the baking dish from the oven, and pour the cheese mixture over the pumpkin. Bake, uncovered, another 20 minutes. The gratin is done when it is golden brown. ▨

▨ To freeze, allow the gratin to cool to room temperature. Seal in plastic wrap, then overwrap with freezer paper. Freeze for up to 3 months.

Reheat leftover gratin in a 325°F oven for 25 minutes or in a microwave oven.

# PREPARING RUTABAGAS OR TURNIPS FOR FREEZING

For many people, these root vegetables became unfashionable during what I call the foodie era—when people began trying to cook restaurant food at home. Well, happily foodies have returned to their senses and have rediscovered the charms of these healthy, delicious, old-fashioned friends.

You can prepare parsnips by this method also; cut them into 2-inch pieces before cooking.

1½ *pounds rutabagas or*
   *turnips*
1 *teaspoon salt*

SERVES 6

1. Peel and discard the skins. Remove and discard the top and the root tip. Cut the rutabagas in half crosswise, and cut each half into quarters.

2. Place the rutabagas in a 2-quart saucepan, cover with cold water, and add the salt. Cover the pan, place it over high heat, and bring to a boil. Immediately drain the rutabagas.

3. Allow the rutabagas to cool to room temperature. Then place them in 2-cup freezer bags or containers, seal, and freeze for up to 4 months.

# ROASTED RUTABAGAS

The perfect way to prepare this recipe is to add the rutabagas (or parsnips or turnips) directly to the pan when you are roasting chicken or meat. (Allow 35 minutes cooking time and toss occasionally to coat the vegetable with the fat from the roast.) Of course you can roast them separately—as described here—to serve as an accompaniment to sauced poultry, meats, or fish.

(continued)

Roasted Rutabagas   (continued)

1½ cups prepared rutabagas,
  (page 173), frozen or
  fresh
1 tablespoon flavorless
  cooking oil
½ teaspoon salt, or as
  desired
¼ teaspoon ground white
  pepper

**1.** Combine the frozen or fresh rutabagas with the remaining ingredients in a medium roasting pan, and toss well to coat with the oil. Place the pan, uncovered, on the middle rack of the oven, turn the oven on to 375°F, and cook for 35 minutes, stirring occasionally.

**2.** Transfer the rutabagas to a serving dish, and serve immediately.

SERVES 3

# TURNIP AND APPLE PURÉE

Mash these two ingredients together and you have a new hybrid flavor—it's hard to know where one leaves off and the other begins. This is a perfect side dish for poultry (especially duck) and white meats. It also cooks up a fine soup—add about an equal volume of stock or milk to any leftover purée and you'll get the picture.

1½ cups prepared turnips
  (page 173), frozen or
  fresh
2 Granny Smith apples,
  peeled, cored, and
  coarsely chopped
1 large onion, coarsely
  chopped (about 1 cup)
1 tablespoon unsalted butter
½ teaspoon salt, or as
  desired
¼ teaspoon ground white
  pepper

**1.** Preheat the oven to 350°F.

**2.** Combine the frozen or fresh turnips with the remaining ingredients in a baking dish and toss well. Cover, and bake for 35 minutes.

**3.** Transfer the mixture to a food processor, and purée until smooth. Spoon the purée into a serving dish, and serve immediately.

SERVES 3

# RICE PILAF

There are two basic varieties of rice. The rounder grains such as Arborio are used mostly in "wet" dishes such as paella and risotto. The long grains—basmati and patna are the best—are used to make dry dishes such as pilaf. The rice is tossed with oil, then cooked with liquid until the grains are soft and the liquid is completely absorbed.

2¼ cups All-Purpose Broth (page 222) or water

3 tablespoons flavorless cooking oil

2 medium onions, finely minced (about 1½ cups)

1½ cups long-grain rice

1 teaspoon salt, or as desired

½ teaspoon ground white pepper

SERVES 8

1. Preheat the oven to 350°F.
2. Bring broth to a boil in a saucepan.
3. Meanwhile, heat the oil in a flame-proof casserole over low heat. Add the onions and cook, stirring occasionally, for 5 minutes. Then add the rice, and stir to coat it with the oil. Add the boiling broth, sprinkle with the salt and white pepper, and cover tightly. Transfer the casserole to the oven and cook without disturbing for 25 minutes.
4. Remove the casserole from the oven, scoop the rice into a serving dish (if necessary), and serve piping hot. ▨

▨ To freeze, allow some or all of the rice to cool to room temperature. (The following recipe calls for half of this recipe.) Then place it in freezer bags or containers, seal, and freeze for up to 6 months. Reheat frozen rice, covered, in a 350°F oven or in the microwave oven.

# VEGETABLE FRIED RICE

**F**ried rice should always be made with cooked rice and is best when the rice was cooked at least a day in advance. You can also use frozen cooked rice without defrosting it first. In addition to the vegetables listed in the recipe, add cooked or uncooked items from your freezer. Chicken, shrimp, pork, beef or lamb, fried egg, tofu, or just more vegetables can turn this into a one-dish meal.

1 tablespoon flavorless
    cooking oil

2 tablespoons sesame oil

¼ cup fresh or frozen peas

¼ cup finely diced red bell
    pepper

½ cup soybean or mung bean
    sprouts

½ cup broccoli florets

½ recipe (2 cups) Rice Pilaf
    (page 175), or other
    leftover cooked rice

3 tablespoons soy sauce

**1.** Place a large skillet over medium heat. Add both oils and the peas, bell pepper, sprouts, and broccoli. Cook, stirring, for 1 minute.

**2.** Add the cooked rice, cover, and cook, stirring occasionally, for 10 minutes.

**3.** Toss the rice with the soy sauce, scoop it into a serving dish, and serve immediately.

SERVES 4 TO 5

# LIGHT MEALS FROM LEFTOVERS

I f there's one thing I hope you learn from this book it is the joy of improvising from the freezer. Some of you will find it a source of creative fulfillment to be able to retrieve wonderful components you've already cooked and—one, two, three—make something delightful and entirely different from the original. For cooks lured more by efficiency than by art, improvising can be something like compiling a Dagwood sandwich: Let's see, we can use this and this and how about some of that . . . a mix-and-match operation.

Your improvisation may be a chicken and tomato omelette, using the tomatoes you froze during the season last summer and the chicken you roasted for that picnic in the country. It could be a lasagna layered with filling you made for veal chops, moistened with some of the tomato concassée you made with your crop of home-grown tomatoes. Maybe it will be crab hash and poached eggs, or an Asian-inspired stir-fry cooking everything together quickly in a wok.

The freezer allows us to store, at home, all the materials needed to create a dish on the spur of the moment. Instead of going to the cupboard for a can of tuna, a package of noodles, and a can of mushroom soup, you can use your own handmade ingredients. Furthermore, the menu will always hold a surprise, depending on what your freezer holds.

After becoming acquainted with these recipes, you will see the contents of your freezer change. You may have always given the last piece of roast beef to the puppy, but now you'll save it because a 2-ounce piece of meat can be the crux of a salad, pasta dish, pressed sandwich, or frittata.

Often I find that I like an improvisation better than the original dish. In my mind a recipe in this section should really read like this: The Saturday before preparing this hash, prepare a sirloin roast and eat most of it, leaving only the ends. Follow the directions for freezing and defrosting, and proceed with the completion of the hash recipe. Oh, how annoying to have to eat a whole roast sirloin so that we can prepare a favorite recipe from the ends!

The recipes in this chapter are based on using frozen leftovers, but of course you can make all of them with fresh ingredients as well.

## CROQUETTES

People love croquettes, whether they are served as cocktail food or as moist sautéed patties that replace a hamburger on a bun. Make them from meat, fish, poultry, or vegetables bound together with either eggs, bread crumbs, potatoes, or flour. Choose one of the warm or chilled butters (pages 234–239) or accompany them with mayonnaise. They are best served immediately out of the frying pan, so don't attempt them as an entrée for a large crowd unless you can have a few pans cooking at the same time.

## FISH CROQUETTES

This recipe can serve as a model for croquettes made of cooked meat as well—finely chopped or shredded pork, veal, or beef.

3 tablespoons unsalted butter

½ small onion, finely minced (about ¼ cup)

½ stalk celery, finely diced (about 2 tablespoons)

3 tablespoons flour

⅓ cup milk

¼ teaspoon ground nutmeg

½ cup dry bread crumbs

1 pound frozen cooked fish, defrosted

1 tablespoon finely chopped fresh parsley

1 tablespoon chopped chives

1 teaspoon salt, or as desired

¼ teaspoon cayenne pepper, or as desired

Flavorless cooking oil

24 CROQUETTES
(SERVES 4 AS AN ENTRÉE,
12 AS HORS D'OEUVRES)

1. Melt the butter in a small skillet over medium heat. Add the onions and celery and cook, stirring occasionally, for 5 minutes or until soft. Add the flour, stirring to form a paste. Add the milk and nutmeg and cook another minute or so, until the mixture has thickened.

2. Meanwhile, place the bread crumbs on a plate.

3. Transfer the mixture to a mixing bowl and add the fish, parsley, chives, salt, and cayenne. Using two forks, mash the fish into the mixture. When it is well blended, form the mixture into 3-inch-wide patties. Dredge them in the crumbs, patting to make sure the crumbs adhere. Set the croquettes aside on a plate. ▨

4. Fill a medium-size cast-iron or other heavy skillet with 1½ inches of oil, and place it over medium heat. Heat the oil to frying temperature: 350°F. When the oil is hot enough, a droplet of water will dance across the surface and evaporate. Lower the croquettes into the hot oil and fry them—in batches if necessary, to avoid crowding the skillet—until golden brown, about 3 minutes. Using a slotted spoon, remove them from the oil and drain on paper towels.

5. Arrange on a platter and serve.

▨ To freeze the croquettes, cooked or uncooked, place on a lightly oiled cookie sheet and place it in the freezer. When the croquettes are frozen, transfer them to freezer bags or containers.

To serve frozen uncooked croquettes, do not defrost; simply add 5 minutes to the cooking time in Step 4. To serve frozen cooked croquettes, place on a cookie sheet and bake in a preheated 375°F oven for 20 minutes.

# VEGETABLE AND CHEESE CROQUETTES

Use this recipe as a model for making croquettes out of either cooked vegetables or cooked poultry.

2 medium potatoes, baked

2 tablespoons unsalted butter

2 cups finely diced frozen cooked green vegetables, defrosted: any combination of green beans, broccoli, Brussels sprouts, spinach, asparagus, and zucchini

⅓ cup grated Parmesan or Romano cheese

1 cup grated Swiss cheese

4 egg yolks

½ teaspoon salt, or as desired

½ teaspoon ground white pepper

¾ cup fine dry bread crumbs

Flavorless frying oil

24 CROQUETTES
(SERVES 4 AS AN ENTRÉE OR
12 AS HORS D'OEUVRES)

1. Cut the baked potatoes in half and scoop the pulp into a mixing bowl. Mash the potatoes with a fork until smooth.

2. Melt the butter in a small skillet over medium heat. Add the vegetables and cook, stirring often, until they seem dry, 3 to 7 minutes. (Boiled vegetables contain more moisture than sautéed ones and will take a little longer to dry out.) Spoon the vegetables into the mixing bowl and mix with the potato. Let the mixture cool, uncovered, to room temperature. Then add both cheeses, egg yolks, salt, and white pepper. Mix well.

3. Place the bread crumbs on a plate. Form the mixture into 3-inch-wide patties and dredge them in the crumbs, patting to make sure the crumbs adhere. Set the croquettes aside on a plate. ▨

4. Fill a medium-size cast-iron or other heavy skillet with 1½ inches of oil and place it over medium heat. Heat the oil to 350°F. When the oil is hot enough, a droplet of water will dance across the surface and evaporate.

5. Without crowding the skillet, carefully lower the croquettes into the hot oil and fry, in batches, until golden brown, about 5 minutes. Using a slotted spoon, remove the croquettes from the oil as they are done, and drain on paper towels.

6. Arrange the croquettes on a platter and serve immediately.

▨ Place the croquettes, cooked or uncooked, on a lightly oiled cookie sheet and place it in the freezer. When the croquettes are frozen, transfer them to freezer bags or containers.

To serve frozen uncooked croquettes, do not defrost; simply add 5 minutes to the cooking time in Step 4. To serve frozen cooked croquettes, place on a cookie sheet and bake in a preheated 375°F oven for 20 minutes.

## PANCAKES

Whether they are savory or sweet, stuffed, rolled, or stacked, pancakes appear in all cuisines. They can be a thin skin for a filling—a blintze or a crepe, for example—or a leavened cake that soaks up a sauce or syrup, such as griddle cakes. Take one of the recipes below and experiment with other puréed ingredients or with other grains. Serve pancakes as a starter or main course by combining them with a sauce, or serve them plain as a side dish.

# BEAN PANCAKES

All cooked beans—whole, puréed, or made into soup—can be turned into batter and cooked as pancakes. It's really quite simple: Make a batter using a cooked bean base—milk moistens, flour adds body, eggs bind the mixture, and baking powder makes them rise. The proportions given here for flour, milk, and eggs will most likely need some fine tuning, depending on the kind of bean used. Whole beans will need more batter than puréed beans. And a cooked bean that doesn't blend with the batter—garbanzo beans, for instance—will need to be mashed a bit. Puréed beans might need a tablespoon more of flour to hold them together. Bean soups might need an additional egg and a spoonful more flour to give the batter elasticity. Fuss a little and you will surely succeed. Make a small test pancake in your skillet. If it falls apart, add more egg. If it is too thin, add more flour. If it is too thick, add a little milk. If it sticks to the pan, more flour and a little melted butter should solve the problem. (continued)

Bean Pancakes (continued)

¼ *cup leftover cooked beans or ½ cup bean soup (page 34), defrosted if frozen*

1 *egg*

⅓ *cup flour*

½ *teaspoon baking powder*

¼ *to ⅓ cup milk*

2 *tablespoons unsalted butter, melted*

16 SMALL PANCAKES
(SERVES 8 AS A SIDE DISH)

1. Preheat the oven to 250°F.

2. Place the beans in a mixing bowl, add the egg, and mix well. If the beans are whole, mash them lightly with a fork or pulse in a food processor to break them up a little. Stir in the flour until incorporated, and add the baking powder. Stir in the milk and 1 tablespoon of the butter. The mixture should have the consistency of a thick sauce and be able to coat a wooden spoon.

3. Place a nonstick or heavy iron skillet over medium heat, and add ½ teaspoon butter. Spoon 2 tablespoons of batter per pancake into the skillet, and cook until bubbles rise to the surface and break, 1 to 2 minutes. Using a spatula, flip the pancakes and cook another 2 minutes. Remove the pancakes from the skillet and keep them warm on a covered plate in the oven. Repeat until all the pancakes are cooked, adding just enough butter to keep the pancakes from sticking to the pan. ▨

▨ To freeze, place pancakes between layers of freezer paper, seal in freezer bags, and freeze for up to 2 months.

To serve, remove the pancakes from their package while still frozen, and place them on a nonstick cookie sheet. Cook under a hot broiler for about 1 minute on each side, or bake in a 375°F oven until hot.

# VEGETABLE PANCAKES

These pancakes depend on cooked vegetables for their flavor. Chopped vegetables give a coarse texture to a pancake and need to be bound with only an egg and the smallest amount of flour.

Almost any combination of vegetables can be used to make these pancakes. Some of my favorites are celery and spinach, carrots and peas, broccoli and carrots. Vegetables that I use alone are Brussels sprouts, parsnips, turnips, and rutabagas.

**2 tablespoons unsalted butter**

**½ medium onion, finely minced (about ¾ cup)**

**2 cups chopped leftover cooked vegetables, defrosted if frozen**

**2 eggs, beaten**

**2 tablespoons flour**

**⅛ teaspoon ground white pepper**

**Salt to taste**

**TO SERVE**

**Sour cream**

16 PANCAKES (SERVES 4)

1. Preheat the oven to 250°F.
2. Melt 2 teaspoons of the butter in a small saucepan over medium heat. Add the onions and cook, stirring, for 2 minutes.
3. Scrape the onions and butter into a mixing bowl. Add the vegetables, eggs, flour, white pepper, and salt. Mix well.
4. Place a nonstick or heavy iron skillet over medium heat, and add ½ teaspoon butter. Spoon tablespoon-size dollops of batter into the skillet, and cook until the surface of the pancakes begins to look dry, about 3 minutes. Using a spatula, flip the pancakes and cook another 1 to 2 minutes. Remove the pancakes from the skillet and keep them warm on a covered plate in the oven. Repeat until all the batter is cooked. ▨
5. To serve, arrange the pancakes on a platter, and serve the sour cream on the side.

▨ To freeze, place the pancakes between layers of freezer paper, wrap tightly in freezer bags, and freeze for up to 2 months.

To serve, remove the pancakes from their package while still frozen, and place them on a lightly buttered cookie sheet. Cook under a hot broiler for about 1 minute on each side, or bake in a 375°F oven until hot.

# HASH

Hashed meat, especially corned beef, is a traditional dish commonly categorized as "mystery meat" by generations of school kids and other cafeteria habitués. I prepare mine with uncooked potatoes to create a dish that is more pleasing to the eye and more interesting in its combination of textures.

Hash cooks easiest in a nonstick frying pan, but any well-seasoned heavy skillet will do. And don't feel obliged to serve it with eggs for breakfast. The

(continued)

Hash (continued)

various hashes that follow make elegant luncheon fare and are especially welcome choices on a buffet. Try adding defrosted cooked meats, fish, poultry, or vegetables—whatever your freezer has to offer.

# HASHED POTATOES AND ONIONS

Uncooked potatoes don't freeze well, but hash is so easy and quick to make that it would take longer to defrost the potatoes than to cook them from scratch anyway. Cooked hash does freeze and reheat well.

8 tablespoons (1 stick)
  unsalted butter

2 stalks celery, finely diced
  (about 1 cup)

1 large onion, finely diced
  (about 1 cup)

2 tablespoons flour

¼ cup milk

2 medium potatoes
  (about 1 pound total)

½ teaspoon salt

Freshly ground black pepper
  to taste

4 to 6 poached eggs
  (optional)

SERVES 2 TO 3

1. Preheat the oven to 250°F.

2. Melt 2 tablespoons of the butter in a small saucepan over medium heat. Add the celery and onions, and cook, stirring often, for 5 minutes. Sprinkle the vegetables with the flour and cook, stirring constantly, 1 minute longer. Then add the milk (the mixture will immediately thicken). Cook for 1 minute and remove from the heat. Transfer the mixture to a mixing bowl to cool.

3. Wash the potatoes but don't peel them. Shred them on the shredding blade of a food processor, or coarsely grate them by hand. Add the potatoes to the vegetables and mix well.

4. Melt 1 teaspoon butter in a 6-inch nonstick skillet over medium heat. Add ¾ to 1 cup of the hash mixture, forming a patty about 2 inches thick. Cook, without stirring or moving the hash, for 3 minutes. Flip the patty, turn the heat to low, and cook another 5 minutes. Repeat with the remaining mixture, adding more butter to the skillet as needed. As each hash patty is done, transfer it to the oven and keep warm. ▨

5. To serve the hash, place 2 poached eggs on each serving. Or accompany the hash with a flavored butter (pages 235–237) or Fresh Tomato Sauce (page 226).

**Meat or Fish Hash:** Add 1 cup of finely diced cooked meat, poultry, or seafood—such as steak, corned beef, pastrami, smoked or unsmoked turkey or chicken, crab, or smoked trout or salmon—to the potatoes. (Serves 3 to 4.)

**Vegetable Hash:** For an interesting side dish, add 2 cups of diced cooked vegetables such as asparagus, broccoli, or spinach. (Serves 3 to 4.)

▨ To freeze, place individual hash patties between layers of plastic wrap, then seal in a freezer container. Freeze up to 6 months.

To serve, place the frozen hash patties on an ungreased baking sheet and bake in a preheated 375°F oven for 20 minutes.

## SOUFFLÉS

Soufflés intimidate most cooks who have never made one, but they're really only inventions for using up little bits of cooked ingredients and presenting them in an exciting way. What so intrigues cooks and guests alike is their temporary nature. They're ready and ruined in an instant, so a great fuss is usually made over them—even by jaded gourmets. And the extra kitchen personnel that their preparation demands in restaurants make them expensive. Nevertheless a soufflé is merely a thickened ingredient folded together with stiffly beaten egg whites. When baked, the whites rise to a precarious height—only to fall minutes after being taken out of the oven. The pleasure of watching something so delicate be destroyed so instantly ranks as one of the great, if perverse, dining pleasures.

By adding a finely diced cooked ingredient to a thick bechamel base, you can improvise endless combinations of flavors for soufflés. Use the model below, and add your own defrosted ingredients from the freezer.

(continued)

Soufflés  (continued)

A recipe for a 6-cup soufflé consists of four steps:

1. Make a thick bechamel sauce and add 4 egg yolks. 2. Add ¾ cup flavor ingredient. 3. Fold in 5 stiffly beaten egg whites. 4. Bake until puffed and golden.

# BASIC SOUFFLÉ

## BECHAMEL SAUCE

**3 tablespoons unsalted butter**

**3 tablespoons flour**

**1 cup milk or leftover**
**puréed soup**

**4 egg yolks**

**1 teaspoon salt**

**½ teaspoon ground white**
**pepper**

## FLAVOR INGREDIENTS

**¾ cup cheese or cooked meat,**
**fish, poultry, or**
**vegetables, finely diced**

## STIFF WHITES

**5 egg whites**

**½ teaspoon cream of tartar**

SERVES 4 AS AN APPETIZER,
2 AS AN ENTRÉE

**1.** Preheat the oven to 425°F. Butter a 6-cup soufflé mold and set it aside.

**2.** Melt the butter in a small skillet over medium heat. Sprinkle in the flour and mix well. Immediately add the milk in a slow, steady stream, stirring, and cook until the mixture boils and thickens, about 3 minutes.

**3.** Transfer the mixture to a mixing bowl, add the yolks, and mix well. Stir in the salt and white pepper. Add the cheese or other flavor ingredient, and set the mixture aside.

**4.** Combine the egg whites and the cream of tartar in a mixing bowl (preferably copper), and beat until stiff peaks form. (Beat slowly at first and increase your speed when the whites begin to get frothy.)

**5.** Mix about one fourth of the stiff whites into the soufflé base. Pour the remainder of the whites on top of the mixture, and very gently fold the two together.

**6.** Pour the mixture into the buttered mold and place it on the middle rack of the oven. Immediately reduce the heat to 350°F, and bake for 35 minutes, until the soufflé has risen above the rim of the mold and has a dark golden top.

**7.** Serve the soufflé immediately.

# SHRIMP AND SCALLION SOUFFLÉ

The crust of this soufflé should be light golden. You can substitute other seafood such as crab or lobster, and add creamy-textured green vegetables such as asparagus or okra.

3 tablespoons unsalted butter or a flavored butter (pages 235–237)

8 medium scallions, cut into thin rounds (about 1 cup)

10 ounces frozen or fresh cooked or uncooked shrimp, diced (about 1¼ cups)

¼ teaspoon cayenne pepper

½ teaspoon curry powder

3 tablespoons flour

¼ cup dry white wine

¾ cup milk

4 egg yolks

5 egg whites

½ teaspoon cream of tartar

½ teaspoon salt

SERVES 4 AS AN APPETIZER, 2 AS AN ENTRÉE

1. Defrost shrimp if frozen.
2. Preheat the oven to 425°F. Butter a 6-cup soufflé mold and set it aside.
3. Melt the butter in a small saucepan over medium heat. Add the scallions, shrimp, cayenne, and curry, and cook, stirring, for 1 minute. Sprinkle the flour over the shrimp and mix well. Immediately add the wine and then the milk in a slow, steady stream, stirring. Cook until the mixture boils and thickens, about 3 minutes. Transfer the mixture to a mixing bowl. Add the yolks, mix well, and set aside.
4. Place the egg whites in a mixing bowl (preferably copper), and add the cream of tartar and the salt. Beat until stiff peaks form. (Beat slowly at first and increase your speed when the whites begin to get frothy.)
5. Mix about one fourth of the stiff whites into the shrimp mixture. Pour the remainder of the whites on top of the mixture, and gently fold the two together.
6. Pour the mixture into the buttered mold and place it on the middle rack of the oven. Immediately reduce the heat to 350°F, and bake for 35 to 40 minutes, or until the soufflé has risen above the rim and has a golden crust.
7. Serve the soufflé immediately.

**Crab and Asparagus Soufflé:** Substitute chopped cooked asparagus for the scallions, and lump crabmeat for the shrimp.

## SALADS

Just as a bed of noodles defines a pasta dish, so a bed of lettuce defines a salad. But a salad is not necessarily a plate of dressed iceberg lettuce. Instead of having the food groups—starch, vegetable, and protein—served as a main event with two accompaniments, they can be combined in a salad, their flavors united by the dressing.

Many foods freeze nicely but are not special enough to present on their own. Sometimes this is because they are in unattractive pieces, other times it's because they seem a bit dry. The solution is to cut them up, cook them with a flavorful oil, add vinegar to complete the warm dressing, and serve them as a salad meal. The juxtaposition of chilled and warm ingredients and the flavor of the dressing will add interest to your "freezer salad."

# WARM CHICKEN AND POTATO SALAD

This is not the beloved potato salad that we all know from deli counters, but it's no less delicious. It captures all the charm of a picnic potato salad, but it's meant as a main dish for lunch or a light dinner.

2 cups diced chicken, frozen or fresh, cooked or uncooked

1 egg

3 tablespoons whole-grain mustard

¼ cup whipping cream

1 tablespoon chopped fresh tarragon leaves, or 1 teaspoon dried

3 tablespoons olive oil

1½ pounds medium potatoes

¼ cup white wine vinegar

2 tablespoons olive oil

1 bunch watercress

1 head butter lettuce

SERVES 4

1. Defrost the chicken if frozen.
2. Combine the egg and the mustard in a large mixing bowl, mix well, and set aside. Place the cream and dried tarragon (if you are using it) in a small saucepan and bring to a boil over medium heat. Remove the pan from the heat and whisk the hot cream into the mustard/yolk mixture. If you are using fresh tarragon, add it now. Slowly whisk in the 3 tablespoons oil. Set the dressing aside.
3. Cut the unpeeled potatoes into 1-inch pieces. Place them in a saucepan, cover with water, and cook over high heat until the potatoes are soft, about 12 minutes. Drain the potatoes, place them in a mixing bowl, and pour the vinegar over them. Cover and let sit for 5 minutes.
4. Meanwhile, heat the 2 tablespoons oil in a medium-size skillet over medium heat. Add the chicken, cover, and cook about 5 minutes (a few minutes longer for un-

cooked chicken). Pour the chicken into the bowl with the dressing, add the potatoes and vinegar, and mix well.

**5.** Remove and discard any tough watercress stems and discolored leaves, and place the trimmed sprigs in the salad bowl. Remove and discard any dark green outer leaves and the root tip of the butter lettuce. Add the remaining leaves to the salad bowl. Toss the ingredients well, and serve immediately.

# SALMON SALAD WITH WARM TARTAR VINAIGRETTE

This salad dressing is a version of tartar sauce, diluted with vinegar and oil.

1½ *pounds salmon, frozen or fresh, cooked or uncooked*

2 *small heads Romaine lettuce*

1 *bunch watercress*

½ *cup olive oil*

1 *medium red onion, finely diced (about ½ cup)*

4 *anchovy fillets, finely chopped*

2 *tablespoons capers, drained and finely chopped*

1 *tablespoon grated horseradish, fresh or prepared*

½ *cup dry white wine*

1 *tablespoon Dijon mustard*

½ *cup red wine vinegar*

SERVES 4

**1.** Defrost the salmon in the refrigerator if frozen.

**2.** Remove and discard any skin and bones from the salmon. Flake the flesh and set it aside. (If the salmon is uncooked, slice the flesh into small strips about ½ inch wide.)

**3.** Remove and discard the dark outer leaves of the lettuce. Cut the light green leaves into 1-inch crosswise pieces. Rinse, dry, and arrange on salad plates. Trim and discard the large stems and any yellow leaves from the watercress. Rinse and dry the tender sprigs, and arrange with the Romaine.

**4.** Heat the oil in a large skillet over medium-high heat. Add the onions, anchovies, capers, horseradish, and wine. Cook, stirring, about 2 minutes. Dissolve the mustard in the pan, add the vinegar and salmon, and continue to cook, stirring, until the salmon is warm (or raw salmon is cooked).

**5.** Remove the skillet from the heat, and using a slotted spoon, arrange the salmon on top of the lettuce. Pour the warm dressing over the salad, and serve immediately.

# FISH FRY CHIFFONADE SALAD

"Fish-fry special—all the shrimp you can eat." As a child I was intrigued by that Howard Johnson's come-on because I figured I could eat at least two dozen shrimp myself. Today, a fish-fry salad intrigues people looking for a lighter way to resurrect a memory!

8 *large shrimp, frozen or fresh, cooked or uncooked*

8 *large sea scallops (page 86), frozen or fresh, cooked or uncooked*

8 *pieces (2 ounces each) assorted uncooked fish, frozen or fresh, cooked or uncooked*

3 *tablespoons capers, drained*

2 *tablespoons Dijon mustard*

2 *tablespoons chopped fresh dill, or 1 tablespoon dried*

1 *egg, separated*

1/3 *cup white wine vinegar*

2/3 *cup flavorless salad oil*

3/4 *cup flour*

1/2 *teaspoon salt*

1/4 *teaspoon ground white pepper*

2/3 *cup beer*

1 *medium head iceberg lettuce*

2 *tomatoes, quartered*

*Flavorless cooking oil*

SERVES 4

1. Defrost the shrimp, scallops, and fish if frozen. If you are using pieces of frozen breaded fish (page 89), do not defrost them. Peel and devein the shrimp.

2. Combine the capers, mustard, dill, egg yolk, and vinegar in a blender or food processor and blend for 1 minute. Slowly add the oil, blending continuously, until emulsified. Transfer the dressing to a small bowl and set aside.

3. To make the batter, combine the egg white, flour, salt, white pepper, and beer in a blender or food processor and blend until smooth. Transfer to a medium-size bowl and set aside.

4. Remove any damaged or discolored outer leaves from the lettuce, and cut the head in half from root to tip. Place the cut sides down on a work surface, and cut the lettuce into 1/4-inch shreds. Place the shredded lettuce in a mixing bowl, add the tomatoes, and toss with 1/4 cup of the dressing. Arrange mounds of the lettuce mixture on individual plates, and set aside.

5. Fill a deep saucepan with 2 inches of oil and place over medium heat. When the oil is hot enough, a droplet of water will dance across the surface and evaporate.

6. When the oil is hot, dip pieces of shrimp, scallops, and unbreaded fish into the batter, letting the excess run off. Carefully drop the seafood into the oil and fry for 4 minutes. Do not fry more than 6 pieces at a time or the oil temperature will drop, causing the seafood to steam and become soggy.

If you are using breaded fish, place the

pieces directly into the hot oil from the freezer, and fry for about 7 minutes.

As the pieces of seafood are finished, use a slotted spoon to remove them from the fryer, and drain on paper towels.

**7.** Arrange 2 shrimp, 2 scallops, and 1 piece of fish on top of each mound of salad; drizzle remaining dressing over the top.

# LAMB, GARBANZO, AND BLUE CHEESE SALAD

**Y**ou can use cooked or uncooked lamb for this salad—whichever you have in the freezer.The quick sautéeing won't tenderize a tougher cut such as uncooked shoulder or stew meat, but you can use stewed lamb without its sauce.

1 *pound lamb, frozen or fresh, cooked or uncooked*

1 *cup leftover cooked garbanzo beans, frozen or fresh*

2 *heads Belgian endive*

1 *cup (tightly packed) lamb's lettuce or Boston lettuce*

¼ *pound blue cheese, such as Stilton, Roquefort, Gorgonzola, or Maytag, crumbled*

3 *tablespoons olive oil*

½ *pound pancetta or bacon, cut into ¼-inch pieces*

1 *teaspoon finely minced garlic*

¼ *cup balsamic vinegar*

**1.** Defrost the lamb if frozen and cut it into thin narrow strips. Defrost the garbanzo beans if frozen.

**2.** Trim and discard the root end of the endives. Cut each endive head into ½-inch-thick rounds, and place them in a mixing bowl. Trim and discard any lettuce root tips, and add the lettuce to the bowl. Toss in the garbanzo beans and blue cheese, mix thoroughly, and mound on individual plates.

**3.** Place a medium-size skillet over medium heat and add the oil and pancetta. If you are using uncooked lamb, add it now. Cook, stirring, about 3 minutes. Then add the garlic, vinegar, and cooked lamb if you are using it, and cook for 1 minute.

**4.** Remove the skillet from the heat, and using a slotted spoon, arrange the pancetta and lamb on the salads. Drizzle the dressing over the salads, and serve immediately.

SERVES 4

# STEAK CAESAR SALAD

**V**egetarian additions to this salad could be diced tomato or cooked beans, or you could top the salad with a dollop of cooked Eggplant Caviar (page 166) or Mushroom Duxelles (page 240).

*1 pound leftover cooked steak, frozen or fresh*

*5 slices white bread*

*2 tablespoons unsalted butter*

*¾ cup olive oil*

*1 egg*

*1 tablespoon minced garlic*

*¼ teaspoon ground white pepper*

*12 anchovy fillets*

*½ teaspoon Worcestershire sauce*

*3 tablespoons grated Parmesan or Romano cheese*

*3 tablespoons red wine vinegar*

*¼ cup fresh lemon juice*

*1 head Romaine lettuce*

SERVES 4 AS A MAIN COURSE,
2 AS AN ENTRÉE

**1.** Defrost the steak if frozen. Slice into ¼-inch strips.

**2.** Preheat the oven to 375°F.

**3.** To make the croutons, remove and discard the crust from the bread. Cut the slices into ½-inch pieces and place them in a bowl. Place a small saucepan over medium heat, and add the butter and ¼ cup of the oil. Cook until the butter has melted. Drizzle this mixture over the bread and toss well. Arrange the bread in one layer on a rimmed cookie sheet or in a shallow roasting pan, and bake, stirring occasionally, until the bread dries out and turns golden brown, about 10 to 12 minutes. Remove the croutons from the oven and place them in a large salad bowl.

**4.** To make the Caesar dressing, bring some water to a boil in a small saucepan over high heat. Add the egg and cook exactly 2 minutes. Then remove the egg and break it into a blender or food processor, scraping out any congealed white. Add the garlic, white pepper, 4 of the anchovies, Worcestershire, and cheese. Blend for 30 seconds. With the motor running, add the remaining ½ cup oil in a slow, steady stream. The dressing will begin to look like a mayonnaise. Add the vinegar and lemon juice, and blend until incorporated. Transfer the dressing to a bowl and set aside. ▨

**5.** To assemble the salad, remove and discard the outer leaves of the lettuce. Cut the head crosswise into 1-inch pieces and add them to the croutons in the salad bowl. Add the steak and the dressing and toss.

**6.** Mound the salad on chilled plates. Garnish each salad with 2 crisscrossed anchovies, and serve.

⊠ Caesar dressing can be frozen for up to 3 months in a plastic container. To reconstitute, defrost the dressing, scrape it into a bowl, and stir in a few tablespoons of hot tap water until emulsified.

# TORTILLA SALAD

Any choice of cooked meat or poultry—veal, lamb, turkey, chicken, duck—is appropriate in this salad. Cooked fish is not very appealing in combination with the other ingredients, but shrimp, lobster, and crab hold their own.

1 *pound leftover cooked flank steak, frozen or fresh*

1 *cup leftover cooked black beans, frozen or fresh*

1 *bunch cilantro*

1 *fresh jalapeño pepper*

¼ *cup fresh lemon or lime juice*

⅓ *cup flavorless salad oil*

½ *teaspoon salt*

¼ *cup sour cream*

2 *heads butter lettuce*

2 *medium ripe tomatoes*

1 *medium red onion, finely chopped (about ½ cup)*

¼ *pound Sonoma or Monterey Jack or Cheddar cheese, grated (about 1 cup)*

2 *cups corn tortilla chips*

SERVES 4

1. Defrost the steak and the black beans if frozen.

2. Remove and discard the long stems from the cilantro and place the leafy sprigs in a blender or food processor. Remove and discard the stem from the jalapeño pepper; cut the pepper in half and remove and discard the seeds. Coarsely chop the pepper and add it to the blender. Add the lemon juice, oil, and salt, and blend until smooth. Then add the sour cream and blend quickly, just until incorporated. Transfer the dressing to a salad bowl and set aside. ⊠

3. Remove and discard any damaged outer lettuce leaves, and cut out and discard the center core. Tear the leaves into large pieces and place them in the salad bowl. Remove and discard the stems from the tomatoes. Cut the tomatoes in half and squeeze out the seeds. Dice the flesh into ½-inch pieces, and add to the salad bowl. Slice the steak diagonally against the grain into thin, narrow pieces and add them to the salad bowl. Add the beans, red onion, cheese, and tortilla chips. Toss all the ingredients together with the dressing, mound on individual plates, and serve immediately.

(continued)

Tortilla Salad   (continued)

⊠ The dressing can be frozen for up to 3 months in a plastic container. Before using, place the defrosted dressing in a blender and blend at high speed for 1 minute.

## FRITTATAS

A *frittata* is the Italian version of an omelette. It makes a good light meal—for lunch or a late supper. A proper frittata cooks slowly over very low heat so that it is firm but not dry. The top and bottom should not be allowed to brown—that indicates that it has cooked too quickly and too intensely.

Frittatas offer a delicious way to use up odds and ends from the freezer, and you'll be happily surprised when you see how far you can stretch a small amount of food. Meats and poultry, vegetables, fish, cheese . . . all find their way into frittatas.

## BASIC FRITTATA

9 eggs
2 tablespoons finely chopped
    fresh parsley
¼ cup grated Parmesan or
    Romano cheese
2 tablespoons olive oil
1 large onion, finely minced
    (about 1 cup)

SERVES 3

1. Preheat the oven to 325°F.
2. Beat the eggs in a bowl until the yolks and whites are blended. Add the parsley and cheese, mix well, and set aside.
3. Heat the oil in a 9-inch ovenproof skillet over medium heat. Add the onions and cook, stirring occasionally, for 3 minutes.
4. Pour in the egg mixture, cover the skillet with a lid or aluminum foil, and place it on the middle rack of the oven. Bake for 15 to 20 minutes or until the frittata is puffy.
5. Remove the skillet from the oven and run a knife around the edges to loosen the frittata. Slide the frittata onto a warm platter and serve immediately.

**Other Frittatas:** When you sauté the onions in olive oil, add 1½ cups of some other defrosted cooked ingredients from your freezer, diced into pieces no larger than ½ inch. Some suggestions:

- Artichoke hearts and ham
- Shrimp, tomatoes, and basil
- Asparagus, potatoes, garlic, and Swiss cheese
- Eggplant, zucchini, and tomatoes
- Roasted peppers and anchovies
- Smoked salmon and scallions
- Spinach and celery
- Avocado, tomatoes, and steak
- Potatoes and pesto

# POACHED EGGS, PEPPERS, AND ANCHOVIES

Although we usually reserve eggs for breakfast, beginning a meal with an egg dish is soothing—and when combined with roasted peppers, you won't think of morning.

*8 roasted pepper halves
   (page 171)*

*3 tablespoons olive oil*

*2 tablespoons white vinegar*

*8 room-temperature eggs*

*8 anchovy fillets*

*1 tablespoons freshly
   squeezed lemon juice*

SERVES 4

1. Defrost peppers if frozen.
2. Place peppers in a small skillet, drizzle with 2 tablespoons olive oil, and place over medium heat. Cook, tossing, until warm, about 5 minutes. Remove from the heat and arrange peppers on 4 plates.
3. Meanwhile, fill a pot with 3 inches of water, add the vinegar, and bring to a boil over high heat. Lower heat to medium. Carefully break the eggs into the water and cook about 4 minutes.
4. When the eggs are cooked, remove them from the water using a slotted spoon and arrange on the peppers. Place 2 anchovy fillets on each egg and drizzle with oil and lemon juice. Serve immediately.

## PASTA

I'm not going to offer recipes for classic pasta dishes here—you probably already have plenty of them anyway. Instead, these recipes illustrate how useful pasta can be as a way of combining miscellaneous vegetables and meats with a sauce for a delicious meal.

Pasta is more shape and texture than it is flavor. All sizes and shapes of pasta are vehicles for other ingredients. We love pasta for that texture and for the feeling of well-being it gives us. And since nutritionists tell us that it's healthier to eat more complex carbohydrates and less fat and protein, pasta dishes are good for us too.

Once you've tried some of the following recipes, you'll realize that you can vary them endlessly, according to what's available in your freezer. There are only a couple of things to remember. First, lighter sauces go on thinner strands of pasta—such as angel hair and spaghettini. Larger shapes and strands—fettucine, linguini, spaghetti, bucatini—can take a rich, heavy sauce that coats them well.

Second, do not overcook the pasta. You want to retain its texture. Unless you are preparing a chilled pasta salad, don't rinse it under cold water after cooking it. Simply toss the noodles with a little butter or olive oil, and then toss them with the sauce.

# PASTA WITH MUSHROOM SAUCE

Use macaroni shapes such as elbows, fusilli, macaroni, bow-ties, or shells, or flat strands such as fettucine, linguine, or pappardelle. This is also great with gnocchi (page 202). If you want, dice up to 1 pound cooked or uncooked lobster, shrimp, chicken, or turkey and add it to the sauce when you add the fresh mushrooms.

Use any fresh and dried mushrooms. Cultivated, chanterelle, shiitake, and oyster mushrooms are the most common fresh ones. Cèpes and morels are usually dried or frozen. Or mix varieties if several kinds are available.

¼ *pound dried mushrooms*

3 *cups warm water*

¾ *pound fresh mushrooms or*
  ¾ *cup Mushroom*
  *Duxelles (page* 240)

3 *cups warm water*

4 *quarts cold water*

1 *tablespoon plus* ½
  *teaspoon salt*

2 *tablespoons unsalted butter*

1 *tablespoon finely minced*
  *garlic*

1 *tablespoon finely minced*
  *shallots or onions*

¼ *cup dry sherry or* Madeira

½ *cup whipping cream*

12 *ounces fresh pasta, or* 8
  *ounces dried*

SERVES 4

**1.** Reconstitute the dried mushrooms: Place the mushrooms in a bowl, cover with the warm water, and soak for at least 2 hours or as long as 8.

**2.** When the mushrooms are soft, drain them, pouring the soaking liquid through a double layer of cheesecloth or a clean kitchen towel to remove any sand. You should have about 1½ cups reconstituted mushrooms. Squeeze the mushrooms over the strainer to extract as much water as possible. Reserve 1 cup of this liquid. (Pour the remaining mushroom water into a freezer container, seal, and freeze for up to 1 year. Can be used instead of water for making All-Purpose Broth.)

**3.** Rinse the fresh mushrooms and pat them dry. Slice chanterelles and cultivated mushrooms; trim and discard the stems of shiitake mushrooms; trim and discard the root tips of oyster mushrooms.

**4.** Bring the cold water and 1 tablespoon of the salt to a boil over high heat.

**5.** Meanwhile, melt the butter in a medium-size skillet over medium heat. Add the reconstituted dried mushrooms, garlic, shallots, and remaining ½ teaspoon salt. Cook, stirring, for 10 minutes. Add the fresh mushrooms or duxelles, cover, and continue to cook another 10 minutes.

**6.** Uncover, add the reserved mushroom water and the sherry. Raise the heat to high and cook until the liquid has reduced by about two thirds, about 15 minutes. Then add the cream and cook until the sauce is thick enough to coat a spoon. Remove the skillet from the heat and keep warm. ▨

**7.** Add the pasta to the boiling water, cook as desired, and drain. Toss with the mushroom sauce. Place on a platter or in a large bowl, and serve immediately.

(continued)

⊠ To freeze extra sauce, fill a plastic freezer bag three-quarters full with mushrooms and sauce, and squeeze out as much air as possible. Seal and freeze for up to 3 months.

To reheat, place the bag (still frozen) in simmering water and cook until defrosted, about 7 to 8 minutes.

# PASTA WITH DUCK RILLETTES AND STILTON

This sauce suits hollow shapes such as elbow macaroni, rigatoni, and bucatini, or wide strands such as fettucine or pappardelle.

1 *pound Duck Rillettes (page 210) or uncooked boneless duck meat, frozen or fresh*

4 *quarts cold water*

1 *tablespoon salt*

¼ *cup Fresh Tomato Sauce (page 226)*

½ *cup All-Purpose Broth (page 222), canned low-sodium chicken stock, or water*

½ *cup whipping cream*

6 *tablespoons walnut oil*

6 *ounces Stilton cheese*

12 *ounces fresh pasta, or 8 ounces dried*

1. Defrost the duck and the tomato sauce if frozen.

2. Bring the cold water and salt to a boil over high heat.

3. Meanwhile, shred or cut the duck into ½-inch pieces and set aside.

4. Combine the tomato sauce, broth, cream, and 3 tablespoons of the walnut oil in a skillet over medium heat. Cover, quickly bring to a boil, and add the duck. If you are using uncooked meat, cover and cook 10 minutes. If you are using cooked meat, do not cover.

5. Cook, uncovered, until the liquid begins to thicken, about 3 minutes. Stir in the cheese, and remove the skillet from the heat; keep warm.

6. Add the pasta to the boiling water, and cook as desired. Drain, and toss with the remaining 3 tablespoons walnut oil. Mound the pasta on a platter or in a large

SERVES 4

bowl, spoon the duck and sauce over it, and serve immediately.

**Meat and Blue Cheese Sauce:** Substitute another blue-veined cheese such as Gorgonzola, Roquefort, or Maytag, and pair it with steak or lamb.

**Creamy Cheese and Meat Sauce:** Substitute a runny cheese such as Brie or Camembert, and pair it with chicken, turkey, pork, or veal.

# PASTA WITH TEQUILA SHRIMP

For this sauce use thin pasta strands such as angel hair or spaghettini, or small shapes such as pastina, orzo, riso, or bow-ties. This is also a good accompaniment for gnocchi (page 202).

16 jumbo shrimp, frozen or fresh, cooked or uncooked

4 quarts cold water

1 tablespoon salt

2 tablespoons olive oil

¼ cup tequila

¼ cup All-Purpose Broth (page 222) or canned low-sodium chicken broth

3 tablespoons unsalted butter

1 tablespoon chopped fresh parsley or cilantro

12 ounces fresh pasta, or 8 ounces dry

1. Defrost the shrimp if frozen. Peel and devein them, leaving the tail shell intact.

2. Bring the cold water and salt to a boil over high heat.

3. Meanwhile, heat the oil in a skillet over high heat. Add the shrimp and cook, tossing or stirring, 4 minutes for uncooked, 2 minutes for cooked shrimp. Reduce the heat to medium, add the tequila and broth, and cook another 2 minutes. Then remove the skillet from the heat and whisk in the butter and the parsley.

4. Add the pasta to the boiling water, cook as desired, and drain. Toss with the shrimp, place on a platter or in a large bowl, and serve immediately.

SERVES 4

# PASTA WITH CHICKEN, BROCCOLI, AND PESTO

For this dish use pasta shapes—elbows, bow-ties, or shells—or medium to thick strands; or prepare gnocchi (page 202).

You can improvise similar dishes using fish or another poultry, and select another green vegetable such as green beans or zucchini. Cut the meat into ½-inch pieces and the vegetables into tablespoon-size pieces. The vegetables will overcook if they're too small.

1 *pound boneless cooked chicken, frozen or fresh*

1 *cup prepared broccoli florets, frozen or fresh*

½ *cup Basil Pesto (page 231), frozen or fresh*

4 *quarts cold water*

1 *tablespoon salt*

¼ *cup milk*

¼ *cup All-Purpose Broth (page 222), canned low-sodium chicken stock, or water*

6 *tablespoons olive oil*

2 *tablespoons grated Parmesan cheese*

12 *ounces fresh pasta, or 8 ounces dried*

SERVES 4

1. Defrost the chicken, broccoli, and pesto if frozen.

2. Bring the cold water and salt to a boil over high heat.

3. Meanwhile, shred or cut the chicken into ½-inch pieces; you should have about 2 cups. Set aside. Cut the broccoli florets into tablespoon-size pieces, and set aside with the chicken.

4. Combine the milk, broth, and 3 tablespoons of the oil in a skillet over medium heat. Cover, quickly bring to a boil, and add the broccoli and chicken. Cook for 1 minute.

5. Add the pesto and continue to cook, stirring, another 3 minutes, or until the sauce begins to thicken. Then add the cheese, remove the skillet from the heat, and keep warm. ▨

6. Cook the pasta in the boiling water, and drain well. Toss with the remaining 3 tablespoons oil, and place on a serving platter or in a large serving bowl. Spoon the chicken, broccoli, and sauce over the top, and serve immediately.

▨ To freeze, fill a plastic freezer bag three quarters full with chicken, vegetables, and sauce, and squeeze out as much air as possible. Seal and freeze for up to 3 months.

To reheat, place the bag (still frozen) in simmering water and cook until defrosted, about 7 to 8 minutes.

# BAKED PASTA WITH SPINACH AND CHEESE

Macaroni and cheese is one of those dishes that everyone loves—or loves to hate. It's just as delicious with gnocchi as with macaroni. You can bake an assembled casserole directly from the freezer in a 350°F oven for 1 hour.

4 quarts cold water

1 tablespoon salt

8 ounces shells or elbow pasta; or 1 recipe fresh or frozen gnocchi (page 202) (do not defrost)

2 bunches fresh spinach (about 6½ cups), or 1½ cups cooked, defrosted if necessary

4 tablespoons olive oil

½ small onion, finely diced (¼ cup)

½ cup whipping cream

¼ cup Parmesan or Romano cheese

¼ pound Swiss cheese, grated (about 1 cup)

SERVES 4

1. Bring the water and salt to a boil over high heat. Add the pasta and cook until tender but still firm; drain and set aside.

2. If you are using uncooked spinach, discard the stems and rinse the leaves. If you are using cooked spinach, place it in a colander or strainer, and press out as much moisture as you can.

3. Heat 2 tablespoons of the oil in a medium-size skillet over medium heat. Add fresh spinach in batches and cook until wilted, 1 to 2 minutes. As each batch is done, transfer to a colander to drain. When all the fresh spinach is cooked, place it on a cutting surface and coarsely chop. Arrange the spinach in a medium baking dish and set aside.

4. Combine the remaining 2 tablespoons olive oil and the onions in a small skillet over medium heat. Cook, stirring, until the onions are soft, about 5 minutes. Then add the cream and Parmesan, and boil until reduced to a sauce, 5 minutes. Remove from the heat and set aside.

5. Arrange the pasta or gnocchi on the bed of spinach. Spoon the cream sauce over, and sprinkle with the Swiss cheese.

6. Place the baking dish in the oven. Bake at 375°F until bubbling, about 15 minutes. Serve immediately.

**Gnocchi Casserole:** Arrange 1 cup diced chicken, fish, or shellfish, cooked or uncooked, with the gnocchi on the bed of spinach before baking.

# GNOCCHI

Gnocchi are Italian potato dumplings. They can be made with leftover mashed potatoes or with freshly cooked potatoes. Remember that the amount of butter and milk in the potatoes will determine the exact amount of flour you need. Work potatoes and flour together until the mixture is smooth and only slightly sticky.

Gnocchi can also be served in soup or as a side dish to meat or poultry. Serve them tossed with some good olive oil, with Fresh Tomato Sauce (page 226), or with a pesto (page 231). Combine them with other ingredients (diced chicken, seafood) and serve for lunch, as an appetizer, or a light supper. Or substitute gnocchi for one of the pastas on pages 196–201.

*3 pounds boiling potatoes, or*
  *5 ½ cups mashed*
  *potatoes*
*5 egg yolks*
*⅛ teaspoon ground nutmeg*
*1 teaspoon salt, or as desired*
*Ground white pepper to taste*
*¾ to 1 cup flour*
*⅓ cup olive oil*

SERVES 6

1. If you are using uncooked potatoes, boil them, unpeeled, in a large pot of salted water until soft; drain. Or cook them in a microwave oven according to manufacturer's directions, or bake in a conventional oven. When they are cool enough to handle, peel the potatoes and process them though a food mill or potato ricer while still warm. (Do not use a blender or food processor for this because it excites the gluten in the potato and makes a sticky mess.)

If you are using leftover mashed potatoes, defrost if frozen, place them in a small saucepan and heat them until they are warm.

2. Transfer the potatoes to a mixing bowl, add the yolks, and mix thoroughly. Add the nutmeg, salt, white pepper, and ¾ cup of flour. Knead together until the dough is slightly sticky, adding the remaining flour bit by bit if necessary.

3. Lightly dust a work surface with flour. Form the dough into sausage-like rolls about the thickness of your thumb. Cut them into rounds about 1 inch long. Using a fork, flatten the pieces so that the tines leave an imprint in the gnocchi. Keep a glass of water nearby and dip the fork into it as you work. ▨

4. Meanwhile, fill a 3-quart pot with salted water and bring to a boil. Reduce the

heat to a gentle boil. Drop the gnocchi into the boiling water, about 16 at a time. They will sink to the bottom but will rise to the surface after a minute or so. Continue to cook for another 15 seconds after they rise. Then immediately transfer them to a colander, using a slotted spoon. Sprinkle them with a little olive oil, stir gently, and transfer to a heated platter. Continue until all the gnocchi are cooked.

**5.** Serve the gnocchi ungarnished, or use as an ingredient in another dish.

---

▧ Arrange a single layer of gnocchi on a cookie sheet and place it in the freezer. When they are frozen, pack the gnocchi into freezer bags, seal, and freeze for up to 3 months.

Cook frozen uncooked gnocchi without defrosting. Toss them in a little olive oil, place in a baking dish, cover tightly, and bake at 350° for 15 to 20 minutes. Cooked gnocchi will keep for 5 days in the refrigerator.

---

# LASAGNA

**M**ost people are accustomed to parboiling lasagna noodles before assembling and baking the casserole, but I find that it's really not necessary: the freezing process has the same effect. Not only do you achieve a better texture, but the noodles themselves have a more pronounced flavor because they absorb moisture from the other ingredients. An uncooked lasagna—made with either fresh or dried uncooked noodles—freezes better than a fully cooked one and can be baked without defrosting.

(continued)

Lasagna (continued)

4 cups pasta filling
    (pages 244–247)

2 cups Fresh Tomato Sauce
    (page 226)

5 cups milk

½ cup (1 stick) unsalted
    butter

½ cup flour

1 cup grated Parmesan
    cheese

⅓ cup olive oil

24 fresh or dried lasagna
    noodles

1 cup whipping cream

SERVES 8

1. Defrost the filling and the tomato sauce if frozen.

2. Place the milk in a small saucepan over high heat. As soon as it begins to foam and come to the boil, remove it from the heat and set aside.

3. Meanwhile, melt the butter in a 1-quart saucepan over medium heat. Stir in the flour and cook 1 minute. Then slowly pour the hot milk over the mixture and cook, stirring, until it thickens, about 2 minutes. Remove the saucepan from the heat and stir in the Parmesan cheese.

4. Oil the bottoms of two 4-inch-deep 7-by 11-inch freezer-to-oven baking dishes or foil pans. Spread ¼ cup of the cream sauce in each dish. Place 3 noodles in a single layer in each dish. Place 1 cup of filling on the noodles, and use a rubber spatula to spread it evenly. Place 1 cup of cream sauce on the filling and spread it evenly. Repeat until you have 3 layers of sauce, noodles, and filling. Top with a layer of noodles. ▨

5. Combine the cream and tomato sauce in a small bowl, and pour evenly over the lasagna. Cover tightly with aluminum foil and place on the middle rack of the oven. Turn the oven on to 350°F, and bake for 1 hour.

6. Remove the foil and serve the lasagna directly from the baking dish.

▨ To freeze one or both lasagnas, completely wrap the baking dish in a double layer of plastic wrap. Freeze for up to 3 months.

To cook a frozen lasagna, unwrap the dish, cover it with aluminum foil, and place it on the middle rack of the oven. Turn the oven on to 350°F, and bake for 30 minutes. Meanwhile, combine the cream and tomato sauce. Pour the sauce over the lasagna, replace the foil, and continue to bake another 60 to 70 minutes.

## SANDWICHES

People love food that comes in its own package—egg rolls, crèpes, burritos, and of course, sandwiches. Bread lends form to a sandwich, providing a convenient carrying case for other ingredients such as ham and cheese, peanut butter and jelly, or chicken or tuna salad. Sandwiches make for more friendly, informal eating because so often they are spur-of-the-moment improvisations. With a little effort and imagination, they can become the stuff of epicures. And that doesn't mean that a good sandwich has to include rare or expensive ingredients.

# MONTE CRISTO SANDWICHES

One of the greatest treats of my childhood was a tuna salad sandwich that my mother cooked like French toast. I didn't know it, but this was like a Monte Cristo: make a sandwich, soak it in beaten eggs, and cook it in butter. You can use your favorite salad—chicken, turkey, corned beef, ham, shrimp, crab, or fish—for the filling, or thin slices of cheese and cooked meat. Almost any sandwich is a potential candidate for "Cristoization," even peanut butter and jelly. Don't forget the pickles and potato chips.

*2 cups leftover cooked fish, shellfish, chicken, turkey, ham, or corned beef, frozen or fresh*

*6 tablespoons mayonnaise*

*7 eggs*

*½ cup milk*

*8 slices whole-wheat sandwich bread*

*8 thin slices Swiss cheese*

*3 tablespoons unsalted butter*

SERVES 4

1. Defrost the meat or seafood if frozen.
2. Flake the fish or finely dice the shellfish or meat, and combine it with the mayonnaise in a bowl. Mix together and set aside.
3. Beat the eggs and milk together in another bowl, and set aside.
4. Lay 4 slices of the bread on a work surface. Place a slice of cheese on each slice of bread, and spread each with ½ cup of the mayonnaise mixture. Add a second slice of cheese, close the sandwich with a second slice of bread, and press the sandwiches firmly with the palm of your hand.
5. Place a sandwich in the egg and milk

(continued)

Monte Cristo Sandwiches   (continued)

mixture and leave it for about 3 minutes. Then turn the sandwich over and let it soak for another 3 minutes. Transfer the sandwich to a plate, and repeat until all the sandwiches have been soaked.

**6.** Preheat the oven to 250°F.

**7.** Melt half the butter over medium heat in a skillet that is large enough to hold 2 sandwiches without crowding. When the foam subsides, place 2 sandwiches in the skillet, cover, and cook for 5 minutes. Then remove the cover, carefully turn the sandwiches and cook, uncovered, another 5 minutes. The sandwiches should be a nice golden color. Transfer the sandwiches to a platter and keep warm in the oven. Add the remaining butter and repeat with the remaining 2 sandwiches.

**8.** Cut each sandwich in half diagonally and arrange them on a platter so that the corners overlap. Serve immediately.

# PRESSED SANDWICH

**S**ecretly, most of us love to play with our food, which is why sandwiches are so much fun. One of the best sandwich ideas is what is called a Cuban sandwich in New York. It's usually made of cheap cold cuts— bologna, salami, turkey breast—and cheese and tomatoes. An enormous pile of these ingredients goes on a large roll, which is then cooked on a griddle with a weighted lid. The ingredients are compressed and the roll soaks up butter and becomes a little crispy. I like the idea so much that I make it with good ingredients, using cooked meat or poultry combined with a tasty cheese. Most people don't own a griddle with a lid, but an improvised one achieves the same result.

I make this sandwich at Trumps using cooked chicken and Brie cheese, but I've also tried it at home with cooked turkey, steak, veal, and meat loaf. And don't be afraid to use other cheeses, such as Swiss, Cheddar, Gouda, or mozzarella.

½ pound leftover cooked diced or sliced chicken, frozen or fresh

2 long loaves French or Italian bread

8 slices bacon

¼ cup olive oil

1 medium onion, peeled and thinly sliced

4 thin slices (½ pound) Brie cheese

SERVES 4

1. Defrost the meat if frozen.

2. Cut the ends off the bread and cut each loaf in half, making 4 short loaves. Using a knife or your hands, remove the center of the bread. (Save it for bread crumbs.) Set the hollow loaves aside.

3. Arrange the bacon in a large skillet and place over medium heat. Cook, turning once, until crisp, about 7 minutes. Remove the bacon and drain it on paper towels. Discard the fat in the skillet.

4. Replace the skillet on the stove, and add 2 tablespoons of the oil and the onions. Cover, and cook over medium heat until the onions are soft, about 7 minutes. Uncover, raise the heat to high, and cook, stirring often, until the onions begin to dry out and turn a light golden color, another 10 minutes. Remove the skillet from the heat, transfer the onions to a bowl, and set aside.

5. Preheat the oven to 250°F.

6. Stuff a slice of cheese and a slice of bacon in each bread half. Using the handle of a large wooden spoon, stuff in the chicken and onions.

7. Choose a skillet or roasting pan large enough to hold the 4 sandwiches, and use a flat cover that is smaller than the pan. (A pie dish will work.)

8. Heat 1 tablespoon of oil in the skillet over low heat. Place the sandwiches in the skillet, and put the cover directly on top of the sandwiches. Place a 2-pound weight on the cover and cook for about 5 minutes. Remove the cover, turn the sandwiches, and add the remaining 1 tablespoon oil. Replace the cover and press down with the weights. Cook another 5 minutes. Remove the sandwiches from the skillet and keep them warm in the oven while you cook the remaining sandwiches.

9. Cut each sandwich in half, then cut each half into two triangular pieces. Stand each triangle on end on a platter, and serve immediately.

## POTTED FISH AND MEATS

In the centuries before refrigeration, cooks could preserve meat, fish, or poultry for several months by cooking the liquid away and then packing the food into crocks, covering it with a layer of fat to seal out any air, and keeping it in a cool place. I don't trust this as a method of preserving but I do love the results, so I make them for the freezer.

Begin with either uncooked trimmings of meat, poultry, or fish or with cooked leftovers. This is a great way to stretch a small amount—say those two extra shrimp in a pound, or the livers and gizzards from a chicken you're roasting—because only 4 ounces of meat is needed to make elegant canapes for 4 people or a festive filling for 4 sandwiches.

# POTTED SHRIMP

You can also use lobster or crab to make this spread—or try smoked fish, such as salmon, trout, sturgeon, even oysters. Coarsely chopped clams or mussels work nicely, too. Add a cube of defrosted spread to enrich quick pan sauces for fish or poultry (page 239).

1 *pound large shrimp*

4 *cloves garlic, mashed*

1 *cup dry sherry*

¾ *cup (1½ sticks) unsalted butter or margarine*

*Salt and ground white pepper to taste*

1 *tablespoon unsalted butter or margarine, melted*

2 CUPS, 8 SERVINGS

1. Peel and devein the shrimp. (Save the shells for Shrimp Butter, page 236.)

2. Combine the peeled shrimp, garlic, sherry, and butter in a small saucepan and cook over high heat until the shrimp are cooked, about 5 minutes. Add the salt and white pepper.

3. Transfer the mixture to a food processor or blender, and purée. ▨ Scrape the purée into a ceramic or earthenware pot and refrigerate until set, about 2 hours. Seal the mixture by pouring the melted butter over the surface. (It will keep like this for 1 week in the refrigerator.)

4. Serve well chilled, on warm toast.

▨ To freeze, place all or some of the spread in a plastic container and cover the surface with the melted butter. Cover tightly, and freeze for up to 3 months. Defrost in the refrigerator. Do not defrost in the microwave.

Or place all or some of the spread in ice cube trays, and freeze. When the spread is frozen, remove it from the trays, wrap each cube individually with plastic wrap, place in a freezer bag, and freeze for up to 3 months.

# POTTED LIVER

**S**erve potted liver on toast points or crackers. Or spread it on bread for a sandwich. It also can be added to simple pan sauces for poultry or red meat.

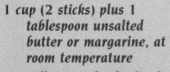

*1 cup (2 sticks) plus 1 tablespoon unsalted butter or margarine, at room temperature*

*1 small onion, finely diced (about ½ cup)*

*½ pound chicken livers, trimmed*

*¼ cup dry sherry or Madeira*

*¼ teaspoon salt*

*¼ teaspoon freshly ground black pepper*

*2 sprigs fresh thyme (leaves only), or ½ teaspoon dried*

**1.** Melt the 1 tablespoon butter in a medium-size skillet over medium heat. Add the onions and cook, stirring occasionally, about 3 minutes or until the onions soften. Add the livers and cook another 3 minutes.

**2.** Add the sherry, salt, pepper, and thyme. Raise the heat to high and cook another 5 minutes. Remove the skillet from the heat and transfer the contents to a mixing bowl. Let cool to room temperature, about 30 minutes.

**3.** Place the liver mixture, with any liquid, in a food processor or blender, and purée until smooth. Add the remaining 1 cup butter and blend until incorporated. ▨ Scrape the spread into a serving bowl and chill in the refrigerator until firm, about 30 minutes.

1¼ CUPS, 6 SERVINGS

▨ To freeze, place all or some of the spread in a plastic container, and pour 1 tablespoon melted butter over the surface. Cover tightly and freeze for up to 3 months. Defrost in the refrigerator. Do not defrost in the microwave oven. Let potted liver sit at room temperature for 30 minutes before serving.

Or place all or some of the spread an ice cube tray and freeze. When

(continued)

Potted Liver (continued)

the mixture is frozen, remove it from the trays, wrap each cube individually with plastic wrap, and place in a freezer bag. Freeze for up to 3 months. Add a cube of defrosted spread to enrich quick pan sauces for meat or poultry (page 239).

# RILLETTES

Rillettes are bits of pork, goose, or duck cooked in fat until they fall apart. Traditionally they were made with a fatty cut of meat, since the fat provided both the creamy texture and the airtight seal that preserved the meat. Delicious, but not very healthful. Instead, let the freezer preserve the meat and use butter or margarine to cream the texture. Make rillettes from lean pork, or from duck or goose legs. Spread them on toast, or serve a dollop in a spear of Belgian endive.

You'll need to start this recipe two days before you plan to serve the rillettes.

*1½ pounds pork loin roast, or goose or duck legs*

*2 tablespoons kosher salt*

*1 head garlic, whole and unpeeled*

*3 tablespoons fresh thyme leaves, or 1 tablespoon dried*

*6 bay leaves*

*1 teaspoon whole black peppercorns*

*1½ cups (3 sticks) unsalted butter or margarine*

3 CUPS, 12 SERVINGS

1. Cut the meat into 2-inch pieces and place them in a glass or ceramic bowl. Sprinkle the meat with the salt, cover the bowl, and chill in the refrigerator for 24 hours, or up to 3 days.

2. Remove the bowl from the refrigerator, and rinse the meat under cold running water. Pat it dry and place it in a 4-inch-deep baking dish. Cut the garlic head in half crosswise and add it to the meat. Add the thyme, bay leaves, and peppercorns. Add the butter, and cover the dish tightly with aluminium foil. Place it in the oven, turn the heat to 300°F, and cook for 3 hours.

3. Remove the dish from the oven. Using a slotted spoon, transfer the meat to the bowl of a food processor, making sure no peppercorns are adhering to the meat. (Reserve the

fat in the baking dish.) Process the meat lightly to shred it.

**4.** Transfer the meat to two ceramic crocks, and use a fork to pack it down firmly. Strain the reserved fat over the meat. Cover the surface with a round of wax paper, and place it in the refrigerator until well chilled, at least 12 hours, or up to 5 days. ▨

**5.** Serve the rillettes in their crocks, slightly chilled or at room temperature, accompanied by some crusty French or Italian bread, mustard, and cornichon pickles.

---

▨ To freeze, wrap crocks in plastic wrap and overwrap with freezer paper. Freeze for up to 3 months. Defrost in the refrigerator. Do not defrost in the microwave oven.

---

# RILLETTES SALAD

1½ *cups Rillettes (page 210), frozen or fresh*

1 *teaspoon Dijon mustard*

⅓ *cup red wine vinegar*

½ *cup olive oil*

½ *teaspoon salt, or as desired*

**Freshly ground black pepper** *to taste*

1 *bunch watercress*

1 *head curly endive*

SERVES 4 AS AN APPETIZER

**1.** Defrost the rillettes if frozen.

**2.** Combine the mustard and vinegar in a large salad bowl and mix well. Slowly beat in the oil until incorporated. Add the salt and pepper.

**3.** Trim and discard any yellow leaves and large stems from the watercress. Place the trimmed sprigs in the salad bowl. Remove and discard the outer leaves from the curly endive. Cut out and discard the core. Tear the trimmed endive into 1½-inch pieces, and add them to the salad bowl.

**4.** Toss the lettuces with the vinaigrette to coat evenly. Mound the lettuces on individual plates, place a large dollop of rillettes on top of each one, and serve immediately.

# ABOUT PÂTÉS AND FREEZERS

Pâtés are more interesting when they consist of chunky morsels in a smooth-textured base. Use one of the following recipes as a model and add cooked or uncooked morsels from the freezer to vary your pâtés. Bind meat pâtés with fat, fish pâtés and mousses with eggs and cream, and poultry pâtés with fat and eggs.

The breast meat of all fowl, especially chicken, tends to make a dry pâté because it has so little fat. But if you grind some sinewy and fatty dark meat in a meat grinder and use it for the base, you can then use a ½-inch dice of the white meat for the chunky garnish.

Meat pâtés can be made out of almost anything. Do not buy an expensive cut, because there will be less fat in it and the pâtés will be dry. Pâté is an invention for using the trimmings and the least desirable parts of an animal, so this is no time to be fancy. Pâté is usually made with pork, but of course you can use beef, veal, or lamb. (The distinction between meat loaf and pâté is in the amount of fat that gives the pâté a smooth texture. Meat pâtés are made with up to equal parts fat and meat.) Fat freezes better than water because it forms no ice crystals and does not expand, allowing the smooth texture to be maintained.

Seafood pâtés obtain their texture from the eggs and cream in the mixture. Egg whites hold the ingredients together; yolks and cream form a custard liaison and make the mixture richer. Each fish has its own properties. Whitefish is albuminous and needs very little binder; ground, it has a wonderful texture. Salmon, although naturally fatty, needs albumin to keep it from being crumbly and dry, so mix it with whitefish or add additional egg whites. Sinewy fish such as tuna and swordfish become dry and stringy when ground; instead, dice them, cooked or uncooked, and fold in as garnish to the background mixture. Raw scallops release an enormous amount of liquid, so they should be puréed to a smooth paste. Or use cooked chunks as garnish. They, too, have a lot of albumin and will make a pâté rubbery—add extra cream when using them. Uncooked shrimp and lobster pose little problem for the pâté maker—grind them or purée into a paste. They tend to make a rubbery pâté, so add extra cream and yolks and use fewer whites.

Because ground ingredients provide a favorite breeding ground for bacteria, be careful to freeze them quickly and defrost them in the refrigerator rather than at room temperature. And cook them as soon as possible after defrosting.

I find it more convenient to freeze cooked pâtés (make two—serve one and freeze one), but you can successfully freeze uncooked pâté mixture for up to 2 months. Defrost the uncooked mixture in the refrigerator; then add eggs to bind and any desired garniture.

# CHICKEN PÂTÉ

Using leg and thigh meat for the background creates a richer, moister texture. You can vary this recipe by substituting duck, goose, squab, or turkey for the chicken.

3 pounds boneless, skinless dark chicken meat

1 pound fatback

½ pound bacon

2 tablespoons cooking oil

1 large onion, finely diced (about 1 cup)

2 tablespoons finely minced garlic

1 teaspoon salt

2 teaspoons ground white pepper

½ teaspoon ground cloves

1 tablespoon chopped fresh thyme leaves, or 1 teaspoon dried

½ cup brandy

½ cup Madeira or dry sherry

¼ cup coarsely chopped pistachio nuts or walnuts

1 pound chopped cooked or uncooked white chicken meat; cooked or uncooked tongue, sweetbreads, chicken livers; cooked shrimp, crab, lobster, or scallops; cooked or uncooked foie gras; or a combination

8 eggs, lightly beaten

2 PÂTÉS, 15 SERVINGS EACH

1. At least 1 day before cooking the pâté, cut the chicken, fatback, and bacon into 1-inch pieces and place them in a nonreactive bowl.

2. Heat the oil in a small skillet over medium heat. Add the onions and garlic and cook, stirring, for about 5 minutes or until the onions are soft. Remove the skillet from the heat and scrape the onions and garlic into the bowl with the meat.

3. Add the salt, white pepper, cloves, thyme, brandy, and Madeira. Mix thoroughly, then cover and refrigerate overnight or for up to 4 days.

4. Fit a meat grinder with a medium blade and grind the mixture twice. Then mix well to ensure a uniform mixture. (Clean hands work better than a large spoon for this.) Add the chopped nuts to the mixture.

5. Preheat the oven to 325°F.

6. Combine the pâté mixture with your chosen garniture and the eggs. Mix well, and pack it into two 9 × 5 × 3-inch glass, ceramic, or metal loaf pans. Tap the pans on a counter to firmly pack the mixture. Cover the pans tightly with a double layer of aluminum foil.

7. Place the loaf pans in a larger baking pan, and fill the larger pan with boiling water until it rises halfway up the sides of the loaf pans. Bake for 2 hours.

8. Remove the loaf pans from the water bath and place them on a baking sheet or on wire racks. Allow them to cool for 1 hour. Then remove the aluminum foil wrapping and replace it with a clean sheet of foil. Place a 2-pound weight on each pâté (3 or

(continued)

Chicken Pâté   (continued)

4 cans from the supermarket or 2 or 3 cartons of milk will work well), and refrigerate overnight. (Cooked pâté will keep for up to 5 days, covered, in the refrigerator.)

**9.** To serve, remove the weights and foil. Dip each loaf pan in hot water for a minute, and then turn them out onto a plate. Accompany with some good French or Italian bread.

---

⊠ To freeze uncooked pâté, place all or half the mixture in a freezer bag, squeeze out as much air as possible, and seal. Or place it in a plastic container, cover the surface with freezer paper, and seal. Freeze for up to 2 months. Defrost in the refrigerator or microwave oven. To finish, proceed with Steps 5 through 9.

To freeze cooked pâté, wrap the loaf in plastic wrap, place it in a freezer bag, and freeze for up to 2 months. Defrost overnight in the refrigerator. Do not defrost in a microwave oven.

---

# COUNTRY PÂTÉ

So-called country pâtés are more coarsely ground mixtures than the smooth loaves served in most restaurants. They are no less elegant, but they are more easily prepared. This pâté consists of a background mixture combined with a medium dice of various meats. The diced meats—the "garniture," as it's called—identify the pâté. Add diced sweetbreads for a sweetbread pâté, for example. Indeed, sometimes the difference between a venison pâté and a country pâté is simply the diced venison garniture that is added to the pork "background."

That is not to say that you shouldn't make pâté out of ground venison—or any other meat. Just follow my recipe, substituting a selected meat for all or some of the pork, and improvise a garniture by selecting other meats, cooked or uncooked, from the freezer. Let common sense guide you.

2 *pounds lean pork*

1 *pound fatback*

1 *pound bacon*

1 *pound chicken livers or beef liver, trimmed*

2 *tablespoons cooking oil or margarine*

1 *large onion, finely diced (about 1 cup)*

2 *tablespoons finely minced garlic*

1 *tablespoon salt*

2 *teaspoons ground white pepper*

½ *teaspoon ground cloves*

1 *tablespoon chopped fresh thyme leaves, or 1 teaspoon dried*

½ *cup brandy*

½ *cup Madeira or dry sherry*

1 *pound chopped tongue, ham, venison, veal, rabbit, or sweetbreads, or a combination, cooked or uncooked*

6 *eggs, lightly beaten*

2 PÂTÉS, 15 SERVINGS EACH

**1.** Cut the pork into 2-inch cubes and place them in a nonreactive bowl. Cut the fatback and bacon into small pieces and add them to the pork. Trim the liver of any veins or greenish areas, and combine with the other meat.

**2.** Heat the oil in a small skillet over medium heat. Add the onions and garlic and cook, stirring occasionally, for about 5 minutes or until the onions are soft. Remove the skillet from the heat and scrape the onions and garlic into the bowl with the meat.

**3.** Add the salt, white pepper, cloves, thyme, brandy, and Madeira. Mix thoroughly, then cover and refrigerate overnight or for up to 4 days.

**4.** Fit a meat grinder with a medium blade and grind the mixture twice. Then mix well to ensure a uniform mixture. (Clean hands work better than a large spoon for this.) ▨

**5.** Preheat the oven to 325°F.

**6.** Combine the pâté mixture with your chosen garniture and the eggs. Mix well, and pack it into two 9 × 5 × 3-inch glass, ceramic, or metal loaf pans. Tap the pans on a counter to firmly pack the mixture. Cover the pans tightly with a double layer of aluminum foil.

**7.** Place the loaf pans in a larger baking pan, and fill the larger pan with boiling water until it rises halfway up the sides of the loaf pans. Bake for 2 hours.

**8.** Remove the loaf pans from the water bath and place them on a baking sheet or a wire rack. Allow them to cool for 1 hour. Then remove the aluminum foil wrapping and replace it with clean sheets of foil. Place a 2-pound weight on each pâté (3 or 4 cans from the supermarket or 2 or 3 cartons of milk will work well), and refrigerate overnight. (Cooked pâté will keep for up to 5 days, covered, in the refrigerator.)

**9.** To serve, remove the weights and foil. Dip each loaf pan in hot water for 1 minute,

(continued)

Country Pâté   (continued)

and then turn them out onto a plate. Accompany with some good French or Italian bread.

---

⊠ To freeze uncooked pâté, place all or half the mixture in a freezer bag, squeeze out excess air, and seal. Or place it in a plastic container, cover the surface with freezer paper, and seal. Freeze for up to 2 months. Defrost in the refrigerator or microwave oven. To finish, proceed with Steps 5 through 9.

To freeze cooked pâté, wrap the loaf in plastic wrap, place it in a freezer bag, and freeze for up to 2 months. Defrost in the refrigerator. Do not defrost in a microwave oven.

---

# SEAFOOD PÂTÉ

Seafood pâtés can be an elegant fish mousse or homey fare like croquettes. Either way they're savory, delectable, and easy to prepare. Just don't skimp on the seasonings—or on the eggs and cream, which keep them from falling apart.

2 slices white bread

2 tablespoons unsalted butter or margarine

1 medium onion, coarsely chopped

½ cup dry white wine

4 eggs, beaten

1 pound whitefish

1 pound salmon

1 teaspoon salt

1 teaspoon ground white pepper

1 teaspoon ground coriander

¼ teaspoon ground nutmeg

4 eggs

6 egg whites

1 cup whipping cream

1½ pounds chopped cooked seafood, such as sole, flounder, tuna, swordfish, salmon, whitefish, shrimp, scallops, lobster, crab, oysters, clams, or a combination; or smoked fish

2 PÂTÉS, 15 SERVINGS EACH

1. Remove and discard the bread crusts, and tear the bread into pieces. Set aside.

2. Melt the butter in a skillet over medium heat, and add the onions. Cook, stirring, for 5 minutes or until softened. Add the wine, bring to a boil, and cook for 1 minute. Add the bread and cook, stirring, 5 minutes. Scrape the mixture into a mixing bowl, and stir in the eggs.

3. Cut the whitefish and salmon into 1-inch pieces, and add them to the mixing bowl. Add the salt, white pepper, coriander, and nutmeg. Mix well.

4. Transfer the mixture to a food processor and process until smooth. Or fit a meat grinder with a medium blade and grind the mixture twice. ▨

5. Preheat the oven to 325°F.

6. Place the pâté mixture in a mixing bowl, and set the bowl in a pan of ice water. Add the eggs and the whites, and mix well. Slowly add the cream; then mix in your chosen garniture. Pack the mixture into two 9 × 5 × 3-inch glass, ceramic, or metal loaf pans. Tap the pans on a counter to firmly pack the mixture. Cover the pans tightly with a double layer of aluminum foil.

7. Place the loaf pans in a larger baking pan and fill it with boiling water until it reaches halfway up the sides of the loaf pans. Bake for 1 hour.

8. Remove the loaf pans from their water bath and place them on a baking sheet or wire racks. Allow to cool for 1 hour. Then refrigerate for at least 3 hours before serving (or up to 5 days).

9. To unmold the pâté, run a knife around

(continued)

Seafood Pâté   (continued)

the edges of the loaf pans. Dip each pan in hot water for a minute, and then turn the pâté out onto a plate. Accompany it with toast or crackers.

---

▧ To freeze uncooked mixture, place all or half in a freezer bag, squeeze out as much air as possible, and seal. Or place it in a freezer container, cover the surface with freezer paper, and seal. Freeze for up to 3 months. Defrost in the refrigerator or microwave oven. To finish, proceed with Steps 5 through 9.

To freeze cooked pâté, wrap it in a double layer of plastic freezer wrap, and freeze for up to 2 months. Defrost in the refrigerator. Do not defrost in a microwave oven.

---

# BRANDADE

Classic brandade consists of boiled salt cod that is pounded with the pulp of a baked potato, bound with olive oil, and strongly flavored with garlic. Served with crusty bread and accompanied by a simple green salad, it is a wonderfully satisfying meal. Served on its own, it makes a salty beginning that gets the juices flowing. It has the same appeal as meat loaf and mashed potatoes.

Because many Americans are unfamiliar with salt cod, and since so many people are salt sensitive, you can make this brandade using other fish. The more "fishy" fish—such as salmon, bluefish, carp, pompano, or mackerel—taste better than the milder ones. Or try finnan haddie or smoked salmon, trout, eel or sturgeon. Brandade offers an ideal use for those fish trimmings you have stored in the freezer.

It's impossible to give an exact measurement for the olive oil because the amount you will need depends on the other ingredients you use. Leftover mashed potatoes and cooked unsalted fish will require less olive oil than will the baked potato combined with salted or smoked fish. The important thing to know is that all the ingredients must be hot before you combine them.

1½ *pounds salt cod, smoked*
   *fish, or other raw or*
   *cooked fish*

1 *large baking potato (about*
   *¾ pound) or ¾ pound*
   *leftover cooked potatoes*

½ *to ¾ cup olive oil*

2 *tablespoons finely minced*
   *garlic*

**Toast**

SERVES 8 AS APPETIZERS

**1.** Two days before you plan to serve the brandade, place the salt cod in a shallow bowl, cover it with water, and place it in the refrigerator. Chill for 2 days, changing the water two or three times. The third day, drain the salt cod and discard the water. (If you are using other fish, omit this step.)

**2.** Wash the potato. Bake in a 375° oven for 45 minutes or until the potato is soft. Remove the potato from the oven, cut it in half, and scoop the pulp into a mixing bowl. (If you are using cooked potatoes from the refrigerator or freezer, place them in a small baking dish, cover, and heat in a 350°F oven until warmed through.)

**3.** While the potato is baking, place the cod or uncooked fish in a medium saucepan and cover with cold water. Place over medium heat and bring the water to a boil. Remove from the heat and let stand 10 minutes. Drain the fish and discard the water. (If you are using smoked fish, omit this step.) Remove and discard any skin and bones. (If you are using cooked fresh or smoked fish from the refrigerator or freezer, place it in a small ovenproof dish, cover, and heat in a 350°F oven until hot.)

**4.** Place the fish in the mixing bowl and mash it with the potato—a large wooden pestle works best. Or use a heavy-duty mixer fitted with a paddle, and mix until fluffy.

**5.** Combine the oil and garlic in a small saucepan, and cook over medium heat until the oil begins to bubble around the garlic, about 5 minutes. Remove the pan from the heat and slowly pour the oil and garlic into the bowl, mixing vigorously until incorporated. The mixture should be fluffy and shiny.

**6.** Mound the brandade on a serving platter and surround it with toast. ▧

**Brandade Croquettes:** Roll tablespoon balls of brandade in beaten egg, then in bread crumbs. Deep-fry until golden, and serve hot. (continued)

Brandade   (continued)

⊠ To freeze, transfer the brandade to a plastic container and allow it to cool completely. Seal, and freeze for up to 3 months. Defrost it in the refrigerator, or microwave oven. Reheat in a 375°F oven in a covered dish, stuff into peppers, or make croquettes.

# COMPOTE OF BEEF AND CARROTS

**A** compote should give the impression of things melting into each other—specifically, onions and root vegetables melting into meat. So, start with cooked meat (I like cooked brisket or pot roast, either veal or beef), and use vegetables that are high in fiber, full of moisture, and that contain a lot of natural sugar—turnips, parsnips, rutabagas, beets, carrots, salsify.

1½ *pounds cooked brisket, frozen or fresh*

4 *large onions, coarsely chopped (about 4 cups)*

10 *medium carrots, sliced into ¼-inch rounds (about 8 cups)*

½ *teaspoon salt, or to taste*

*Freshly ground black pepper to taste*

¼ *cup (½ stick) unsalted butter or margarine*

1½ *tablespoons flour*

½ *cup All-Purpose Broth (page 222) or canned low-sodium chicken broth*

1½ *tablespoons finely chopped fresh dill, or 1½ teaspoons dried*

**1.** Defrost the meat if frozen. Slice it into ½-inch-thick pieces, and remove any large veins of fat.

**2.** Place the onions, carrots, salt, pepper, and 2 tablespoons of the butter in a 2-quart Dutch oven or heavy roasting pan and stir well. Place the meat on top of the vegetable mixture, tightly cover the pan, and place it on the middle rack of the oven. Turn the oven on to 300°F, and cook for 1 hour.

**3.** Remove the pan from the oven, and stir in the flour and broth. If you are using dried dill, add it now. Cover, and bake for 1 hour more, or until the meat is falling apart.

**4.** Before serving, add the fresh dill and stir in the remaining 2 tablespoons butter.

SERVES 4

# FROZEN HELPERS

Whe we prepare a dish from scratch, we are usually conscientious about the little things that make it delicious—an added tablespoon of chopped shallots, perhaps, or cooking the puréed mushrooms an extra 5 minutes until they are concentrated in flavor. When we pull food out of the freezer, however, we usually want to get a meal on the table in a hurry and with a minimum of fuss. Food from the freezer suffers not from having been frozen, but from the (understandable) inattention of the cook. Freezing a variety of "helpers" enables us to complete a recipe quickly *and* diligently when we might have time for only the most basic cooking.

Extract a special dressing or sauce from the freezer to quickly transform a meal of simple grilled chicken or lamb chops from ordinary fare to the stuff of epicures. Keep homemade condiments and ingredients like basil pesto or exotic chutneys to add to sauces or to serve over grilled meats or vegetables. Fillings for pastas and stuffings for birds are also helpful to have around.

The freezer can also supply many of the building blocks for more complicated recipes. For example, most dishes are tastier when moistened with broth rather than water. It's not practical to make a few cups of broth each time you decide to cook a stew, but you can keep frozen broth in the freezer for up to 6 months. Fresh tomato sauce is not complicated to prepare, but you might omit it from a recipe if it adds 15 minutes to the cooking time. So prepare and freeze batches of sauce in late summer when tomatoes are at their best (and least expensive). It then can become a key ingredient for a bouillabaisse, a sauce, or the base of a tomato vinaigrette for chilled seafood. Why annoy yourself every time a recipe calls for chopped onions or shallots? A frozen cube of onion marmalade means one less chore when you want to put a meal on the table quickly.

A stockpile of these freezer helpers allows us to toss together a seemingly complicated meal with very little effort.

# ALL-PURPOSE BROTH

All-Purpose Broth is just that: all-purpose. Although based on chicken, it doesn't have the strong poultry flavor that a rich chicken stock has, and so when you moisten a beef stew with it or use it as the base for clam chowder, it takes on the character of that dish. Because the bones are already roasted and flavorful, it takes only 45 minutes to prepare this broth, as opposed to the 3 hours needed to make stock from uncooked bones.

When you have other cooked bones in the freezer—from a steak, veal chop, or even a short rib—add them to the all-purpose broth for a meatier flavor in meat dishes and sauces.

Bones of 2 cooked chickens
2 medium onions, quartered
2 medium carrots, cut into chunks
4 stalks celery, cut into chunks
1 teaspoon whole black peppercorns
2 bay leaves
4 sprigs fresh thyme, or 1 teaspoon dried
2 quarts water

1. Combine all the ingredients in a 5-quart stock pot, cover, and place over high heat. When it comes to a boil, remove the cover, reduce the heat to medium, and simmer for 45 minutes.

2. Strain the liquid, discarding the bones and vegetables. Let the broth cool to room temperature, and then refrigerate for 1 hour. Skim off any fat that has collected on the surface. (The broth can be kept, tightly covered, in the refrigerator for up to 1 week without freezing.) ☒

6 CUPS

☒ To freeze, pour chilled broth into 1-cup plastic containers, leaving ½ inch headroom. Cover tightly and freeze for up to 6 months.

Defrost in the refrigerator or microwave oven, or in a covered pot over medium heat. If not using immediately, boil for 2 minutes, covered, then refrigerate until ready to use.

## TOMATO SAUCES

There are two core sauces here: Tomato Concassée, which is uncooked, and Fresh Tomato Sauce, which is cooked. Both are invaluable kitchen helpers.

# TOMATO CONCASSÉE

Make concassée in August and September when tomatoes are plentiful, inexpensive, and have more flavor than at any other time of the year.

This preparation—basically chopped fresh tomatoes—is a versatile ingredient that can really help you out of a bind. Making tomatoes into concassée also improves even the mediocre flavor of most winter tomatoes.

*6 pounds ripe plum tomatoes*
*¼ teaspoon salt*
*Freshly ground black pepper to taste*

4 CUPS

1. Fill a medium-size saucepan three-quarters full with water, and bring it to a boil over high heat. Meanwhile remove the stems from the tomatoes and cut a small X at the tip.

2. Add 3 or 4 tomatoes to the pan, let the water return to the boil, and cook for 1½ minutes or until the skins start to crack. Remove them from the water and let cool until they can be handled comfortably. Repeat with the remaining tomatoes.

3. Using a small knife, peel the skins from the tomatoes and cut the pulp in half crosswise. Gently squeeze to remove the seeds. Chop the pulp finely, and add the salt and pepper.

4. Place the tomato pulp in a strainer over a bowl, and let it drain for 45 minutes. Discard the liquid. ▨

▨ To freeze, divide the concassée into 1-cup portions and place in freezer bags or containers. Seal, and freeze for up to 6 months.

Defrost in a strainer. Allow it to drain, pressing gently against the side of the strainer. Discard the liquid.

# SUN-DRIED TOMATO SAUCE

This thick, chunky sauce can be dolloped over grilled or roasted fish, shellfish, poultry, or white meats. It transforms baked potatoes and is also great for tossing with pasta.

1 cup Tomato Concassée
(page 223)

2 ounces dehydrated
tomatoes, coarsely
chopped (about 1 cup)

1 teaspoon minced garlic

½ cup dry white wine

8 tablespoons (1 stick)
unsalted butter

1½ CUPS

1. Defrost the concassée if frozen. Combine with dried tomatoes, garlic, and wine in a small saucepan over medium heat. Cook, uncovered, for 5 minutes or until the wine has evaporated and the mixture has begun to thicken slightly.

2. Remove the pan from the heat and whisk in the butter, a tablespoon at a time. Transfer the mixture to a blender or food processor, and blend until chunky-smooth. ▨

3. Return the sauce to the saucepan, and keep it warm in a larger pan of hot water for up to 30 minutes before serving.

**Sun-Dried Tomato Butter:** Extra sauce may be frozen and later used to make a flavored whipped butter. Let the frozen sauce defrost at room temperature. Place in a food processor and blend until whipped smooth. Let guests dollop spoonfuls of the butter over grilled foods.

# TOMATO CAPER SAUCE

This sauce looks almost separated, but don't worry, it's not. Use it over grilled meat, seafood, poultry, or vegetables.

Any extra sauce can be frozen and used as a base for a flavored whipped butter. Whip ⅓ cup of the defrosted sauce with 2 tablespoons room-temperature butter, and serve. Or chill it and cut into slices.

1 cup *Tomato Concassée* (*page 223*)

3 tablespoons olive oil

3 tablespoons capers, drained and chopped

1 medium onion, finely chopped (about ¾ cup)

½ cup milk

1. Defrost the concassée if frozen.
2. Combine the olive oil, capers, and onions in a medium-size saucepan over medium heat and cook, stirring, for 1 minute. Add the concassée and milk. Raise the heat to high and cook, stirring constantly, until the sauce has thickened, about 5 minutes.
3. Remove the skillet from the heat and transfer the sauce to a sauceboat. Serve immediately.

1½ CUPS

# TOMATO BALSAMIC VINAIGRETTE

Toss this vinaigrette with a green salad or use it on chilled steamed vegetables. The dressing is also terrific with poached fish, chilled sliced veal, mozzarella cheese, and pasta salads. It can be refrigerated, tightly covered, for up to 2 weeks (but not in a silver, aluminum, or copper container, or oxidation will give it an odd taste).

1 cup *Tomato Concassée* (*page 223*)

⅓ cup balsamic vinegar

1 tablespoon Dijon mustard

½ cup olive oil

1. Defrost the tomato concassée if necessary. Combine with vinegar in a small saucepan over medium heat and cook, uncovered, for 5 minutes. Remove the pan from the heat, pour the mixture into a mixing bowl, and add the mustard. Cool to room temperature.
2. Stir in the oil and serve.

1½ CUPS

## PICO DE GALLO

Serve this fresh South American salsa as a dip or as an accompaniment to fish, meat, poultry, or eggs.

1 *cup Tomato Concassée*
  *(page 223)*
¼ *cup olive oil*
2 *cloves garlic, finely minced*
2 *serrano chiles, finely*
  *chopped*
6 *tablespoons finely minced*
  *red onion*
3 *tablespoons fresh lime juice*

**1.** Defrost concassée if frozen.

**2.** Combine the olive oil, garlic, and chiles in a small saucepan, and cook over medium heat, stirring, for 3 minutes.

**3.** Place the concassée in a mixing bowl, and stir in the chile mixture, the red onion, and the lime juice. Chill before serving. ▨

1½ CUPS

▨ Freeze extra salsa in a freezer bag or container for up to 3 months.

# FRESH TOMATO SAUCE

Cooked tomato sauces are among the easiest sauces to prepare. They freeze well and their texture does not change in the freezer. Because of the highly acidic nature of tomatoes, their flavor remains fresh even after having been frozen and defrosted. Fresh tomato sauce is indispensable in the kitchen—use it as an addition to braises and stews to make their sauces richer, use it in pasta dishes, and use it as a base for other sauces. You can also add it to mayonnaise to make Russian dressing or to eggs for a wonderful frittata.

¼ *cup olive oil*

2 *large onions, diced (about 2 cups)*

2 *tablespoons minced garlic*

10 *pounds ripe plum tomatoes, cut in half*

2 *cups dry white wine*

2 *sprigs fresh thyme, or 1 teaspoon dried*

2 *bay leaves*

2 *teaspoons whole black peppercorns*

2 QUARTS

**1.** Combine the olive oil and onions in a large stainless steel or enamel saucepan, and place over medium-low heat. Cook, stirring occasionally, about 10 minutes or until the onions are soft and beginning to become translucent. Add the garlic, tomatoes, wine, thyme, bay leaves, and peppercorns. Cover and cook for 20 minutes.

**2.** Raise the heat to high and cook another 15 minutes. Then remove the pan from the heat and remove the bay leaves from the sauce. Place the sauce, in batches, in a food processor or blender and purée. Pass the purée through a strainer (or a food mill fitted with medium holes) to remove the skins, seeds, and herbs.

**3.** Return the sauce to the saucepan and cook over low heat, uncovered, for 1 hour, stirring occasionally and checking that the sauce doesn't burn on the bottom while it reduces in volume. ▨

▨ Pour 1½ cups of sauce into pint containers, filling them three quarters full. Cool completely in the refrigerator. Then cover tightly and freeze for up to 6 months. Defrost in the refrigerator, at room temperature, in the microwave oven, or under cool running water.

# FRESH TOMATO PASTE

Tomato paste, which is simply concentrated tomato sauce, is always useful for invigorating lackluster dishes. I didn't use any for years because I always felt that I was cheating—so I solved the problem by making my own. And the freezer lets me keep it fresh and store it in convenient quantities. Don't be put off by the long cooking this paste requires—it's well worth it. If you have a microwave oven it'll cook faster, of course. Just remember that in either oven, standard or microwave, you have to do a lot of stirring.

(continued)

Fresh Tomato Paste   (continued)

1 quart Fresh Tomato Sauce
(page 226), frozen or
fresh

2 CUPS

**1.** Defrost the tomato sauce if frozen.

**2.** Preheat the oven to 250°F.

**3.** Place the tomato sauce in a heavy ovenproof skillet or casserole—stainless steel, lined copper, enamel, or Pyrex. Bake, uncovered, for 5 hours, stirring occasionally for the first hour, then every 20 minutes as the mixture becomes more pastelike. Or cook in a full-power microwave oven for 1½ hours, stirring occasionally.

**4.** Remove from the oven and transfer the tomato paste to a bowl to cool. ▨

▨ To freeze, fill ice cube trays with cooled tomato paste and place in the freezer. When they are frozen, remove the cubes of paste and place them in airtight freezer bags. Freeze for up to 6 months.

# TOMATO FENNEL CREAM SAUCE

This is a rich sauce that should accompany a simple dish—roasted chicken, for example, or a whole poached fish. Or serve it with sautéed fennel, zucchini, or eggplant.

1½ cups Fresh Tomato Sauce
(page 226), frozen or
fresh
2 tablespoons olive oil
2 tablespoons finely minced
onion
½ cup whipping cream
¼ cup Pernod
1 teaspoon chopped fresh
tarragon leaves, or ½
teaspoon dried

1½ CUPS

**1.** Defrost the tomato sauce if frozen.

**2.** Combine the olive oil and onions in a medium-size stainless steel or enamel skillet over medium heat, and cook 1 minute.

**3.** Add the tomato sauce, bring to a boil, and cook 7 minutes. Then add the cream and Pernod. If you are using dried tarragon, add it now. Continue to cook, stirring occasionally, for another 5 minutes or until the sauce is thick enough to coat the back of a wooden spoon. Remove it from the heat and add the fresh tarragon.

**4.** Transfer the sauce to a sauceboat, and serve immediately.

# COARSE TOMATO AND OLIVE SAUCE

Serve this over pasta, or with vegetables, chicken, or seafood.

1½ cups Fresh Tomato Sauce
(page 226), frozen or
fresh
2 tablespoons olive oil
½ cup finely minced onion
12 pitted green olives, finely
chopped

1. Defrost the tomato sauce if frozen.
2. Combine the olive oil, onions, and olives in a medium-size stainless steel or enamel skillet over medium heat, and cook for 2 minutes. Add the tomato sauce and cook until the sauce is boiling and starting to thicken, about 7 minutes.
3. Pour the sauce into a sauceboat and serve immediately.

1 CUP

# CURRIED YOGURT TOMATO SAUCE

Yogurt simulates the richness of cream in a sauce, but once it has been added, the sauce cannot be reheated. So serve it immediately or keep it warm by sitting the pan in a larger pan of hot water for up to 30 minutes.

1 cup dry white wine
1 cup All-Purpose Broth
(page 222) or canned
low-sodium chicken broth
1 tablespoon curry powder
½ teaspoon ground cumin
½ teaspoon salt
Large pinch of cayenne
pepper
6 tablespoons Fresh Tomato
Paste (page 226) or
canned
½ cup plain yogurt

1. Combine the wine, broth, curry, cumin, salt, cayenne, and tomato paste in a small saucepan over medium heat. Cook, uncovered, until the mixture has thickened and reduced by two thirds, about 15 minutes. (You can prepare the sauce up to 3 hours in advance to this point, and leave it at room temperature. Reheat gently before proceeding.)
2. Remove the pan from the heat and whisk in the yogurt (do not reheat the sauce or it will curdle). Serve immediately.

1 CUP

## CHUTNEYS, PESTOS, AND SALSAS

In recent years American chefs have begun to use uncooked, or barely cooked, condiments as alternatives to rich sauces. And grilling, which has become not merely a respectable method of restaurant cooking but a national rage, gives us tasty morsels that call out for light, fresh, barely cooked accompaniments. So, with typical American disregard for tradition, we have adopted the classic chutney, pesto, and salsa and have created variations unheard of in their native lands—and they're divine.

Here are three classics, followed by some variations. Simply remember that to adapt them for the freezer, you must first rid the ingredients of some of their water.

# FRESH MANGO CHUTNEY

This is a traditional Indian chutney—lightly cooked, lightly sweetened—that is closer to a Latin American salsa than it is to an English pickled chutney, which is more like a sweet and sour relish. Serve this chilled or at room temperature, as an accompaniment for white meats, poultry, or shellfish.

*3 ripe medium mangoes, cut into ¼-inch dice (about 3 cups)*

*1 small onion, finely chopped (about ½ cup)*

*¼ cup fresh lemon juice*

*¼ teaspoon kosher salt*

*2 tablespoons sugar*

*½ tablespoon curry powder*

*Tabasco sauce to taste*

*2 tablespoons cold-pressed peanut or flavorless salad oil*

1. Combine the mangoes, onions, lemon juice, and kosher salt in a glass or stainless steel mixing bowl. Cover and set aside at room temperature for 3 hours.

2. Place a strainer or colander over a bowl, and drain the mango mixture, pressing gently to extract the juice. Transfer the juice to a small saucepan, and place the mango and onion in the bowl.

3. Place the saucepan over low heat and cook until the liquid has reduced and begun to thicken, 5 to 7 minutes. Immediately remove it from the heat and pour into the mixing bowl.

4. Add the curry powder, Tabasco sauce, and oil. Stir well. ▨

2 CUPS

**Mint and Apple Chutney:** Substitute 2

apples for the mangoes, and add 2 table-spoons finely chopped fresh mint leaves when you add the curry powder.

**Papaya Chutney:** Substitute 1 large papaya for the mangoes.

**Tomato Chutney:** Substitute 4 chopped, seeded, peeled tomatoes for the mangoes.

▨ To freeze, fill freezer bags or containers three quarters full. Freeze for up to 6 months.

# BASIL PESTO

Although fresh herbs generally freeze well and are better than dried, they do lose some of their flavor. A pesto-style sauce maintains the flavor of a fresh herb. Add a spoonful to salad dressings, sauces, and unbaked bread doughs; or use as a sauce for pasta, chicken, or fish. Usually a better result is obtained by freezing a pesto made from fresh herbs than by preparing a pesto using previously frozen herbs.

3 tablespoons pine nuts

3 tablespoons grated Romano or Parmesan cheese

2 teaspoons minced garlic

6 anchovy fillets

½ cup olive oil

4 cups tightly packed fresh basil leaves (about 6 ounces)

1½ CUPS

**1.** Combine the pine nuts, cheese, garlic, and anchovies in a food processor or blender, and purée into a coarse meal. With the motor still running, add the olive oil in a slow, steady stream.

**2.** Add the basil leaves and purée until chunky-smooth. (If you are using a blender, you will have to add the leaves in two or three batches.) ▨

**Walnut and Parsley Pesto:** Substitute walnuts (chopped) and parsley for the pine nuts and basil.

(continued)

Basil Pesto (continued)

**Black Olive Pesto:** Add ¼ cup puréed Calamata or Niçoise olives to the purée before you add the basil.

⊠ To freeze, place the pesto in ice cube trays, cover with plastic wrap, and place in the freezer. When they are solid, remove the cubes from the trays and place them in a freezer bag. Freeze for up to 3 months.

# TOMATILLO SALSA

It is important to let the moisture drain out of the chopped tomatillos before combining them with the other ingredients. You can substitute other vegetables (such as cucumber or roasted peppers) or fruits (such as apples or papaya) for the tomatillo. Use salsa as a dip for chips and as accompaniment to plainly cooked fish, poultry, and meat.

*2 pounds tomatillos, papery husks removed*

*¼ cup flavorless cooking oil*

*3 serrano chiles, slit lengthwise and seeded*

*¼ cup fresh lemon juice*

*2 tablespoons kosher salt*

*2 large onions, finely diced (about 2 cups)*

*¼ cup finely chopped cilantro leaves*

1. Wash the tomatillos under cold water and pat dry. Cut them in half.

2. Heat the oil in a medium-size saucepan over medium heat and add the tomatillos, chiles, lemon juice, and kosher salt. Cover and cook for 5 minutes or until the tomatillos begin to compote.

3. Remove the pan from the heat. Press the mixture into a mixing bowl through a food mill or a large-mesh sieve. Add the onions and cilantro, and stir well.

4. Chill completely before serving. ⊠

2 CUPS

⊠ To freeze, place in freezer bags or containers, and seal. Freeze for up to 6 months.

# TOMATILLO AND MUSTARD SALSA

**F**oods that are cooked and then puréed are good freezer candidates because their texture doesn't change once they have been defrosted. But uncooked vegetables and fruits—because of their liquid, which expands during freezing—turn to mush. However, you can avoid a soggy mess by chopping and salting ("degorging") the fruits and vegetables, thereby ridding them of much of their liquid, before freezing them. If a salsa seems too liquid after defrosting, simply drain it and adjust the seasonings to taste.

Serve this salsa with grilled seafood, poultry, and red or white meats.

*2 pounds tomatillos, papery husks removed*

*2 large onions, finely chopped (about 2 cups)*

*1½ teaspoons kosher salt*

*¼ cup whole-grain mustard*

*¼ cup fresh lemon juice*

*¼ cup olive oil*

2 CUPS

**1.** Chop the tomatillos into ¼-inch dice, and combine them with the onions and the salt in a colander. Place the colander over a plate or in the sink, and degorge for 30 minutes.

**2.** Place the tomatillos and onions in a clean kitchen towel, and gently wring them out over the sink to get rid of more water.

**3.** Transfer the tomatillos and onions to a mixing bowl, and add the mustard, lemon juice, and olive oil. Mix well. ▨

▨ To freeze, place the salsa in freezer bags or containers. Seal, and freeze for up to 3 months.

## WARM BUTTER SAUCES

Shallots or onions cooked with vinegar and wine until dry is the basis for quick sauces. Freeze the concentrate in ice cube trays, then transfer to a freezer bag. Each cube of reduction plus 6 tablespoons of butter should yield about ½ cup of sauce, or enough for 3 to 4 people.

# SHALLOT REDUCTION

6 *cups dry white wine*

6 *cups white wine vinegar*

3 *cups finely minced shallots or onions*

2 *tablespoons salt*

1 *teaspoon cayenne pepper*

2½ CUPS

1. Combine the wine, vinegar, shallots, salt, and cayenne in a stockpot over high heat and boil for 20 minutes. Reduce the heat to medium and continue to simmer another hour or until the mixture is bubbling and thick—about 2½ cups should remain.

2. Remove the pot from the heat and pack the mixture into ice cube trays. Let cool and place trays in the freezer until mixture is frozen. Transfer the cubes to freezer bags, seal, and freeze for up to 9 months.

**Red Wine Reduction:** Substitute red vinegar and red wine for white. This is a red sauce that is delicious both on seafood and meat.

**Muscat:** Substitute muscat or other sweet white wine for total amount of vinegar and wine. Serve over scallops and encourage guests to use lots of freshly cracked black pepper.

# BEURRE BLANC

**A** classic fish sauce from Brittany, this sauce does not require stock. It's also good on vegetables and poultry as well as seafood.

1 *cube shallot reduction*

6 *tablespoons butter*

SERVES 3 TO 4

**1.** Defrost concentrate if frozen and place it in a small saucepan, covered, over medium heat until hot. Reduce heat to low, remove cover, and whisk in the butter a tablespoon at a time.

## CHILLED WHIPPED BUTTERS

Butter flavored with fresh or dried herbs and liquid flavorings are chilled until firm. Melt slices of these butters over grilled steaks and poultry, and over steamed, baked, or grilled fish and vegetables. Or use them in soufflé bases (pages 185–187), on sandwiches (pages 205–206), and in Quick Pan Sauce (page 239).

## HERB BUTTER

For fish, poultry, meats, and vegetables.

2 *tablespoons chopped fresh parsley*

2 *tablespoon finely chopped shallots*

¼ *teaspoon salt*

¼ *teaspoon freshly ground black pepper*

1 *tablespoon fresh lemon juice*

½ *cup (1 stick) unsalted butter, room temperature*

½ CUP

Combine all the ingredients in a food processor or mixing bowl, and purée or mix until smooth and homogeneous. Place on a sheet of plastic wrap or freezer paper, and roll up to form a log shape. Refrigerate until chilled. ▨

**Rosemary Butter:** Add 2 teaspoons chopped fresh rosemary leaves to the herb butter.

▨ To freeze, place the wrapped log in a freezer bag, or wrap with a second piece of plastic wrap or freezer paper. Freeze for up to 6 months.

# SHELLFISH BUTTER

For seafood and white meats.

**1 cup (2 sticks) unsalted butter**

**Shells from 24 cooked or raw shrimp, 1 cooked lobster, or 1 cooked crab (6 to 7 ounces)**

**¼ teaspoon salt**

**Pinch of cayenne pepper**

¾ CUP

**1.** Preheat the oven to 325°F. Cut the butter into 8 pieces.

**2.** Place the seafood shells in a small baking dish or ovenproof skillet, and bake for 15 minutes, or until the raw shrimp shells turn light pink. Add the butter and bake for another 10 minutes

**3.** Transfer the butter and shells to a food processor, and pulse to break up the shells. Place the mixture in a strainer over a small bowl and strain, pressing the shells to extrude all flavor and butter. Discard the shells and refrigerate the butter, covered, until set but not hard, about 2 hours.

**4.** Transfer the chilled butter to a food processor and whip until smooth. Then place it on a piece of plastic wrap or freezer paper, and roll up to form a log shape. Refrigerate until serving time, or as long as 2 weeks. ▨

▨ To freeze, place the wrapped log in a freezer bag, or wrap it with a second piece of plastic wrap or freezer paper. Freeze for up to 6 months.

# FENNEL BUTTER

For white meats, fish, asparagus, and broccoli.

½ cup (1 stick) unsalted
    butter
2 tablespoons fresh lemon
    juice
2 tablespoons Pernod
¼ cup All-Purpose Broth
    (page 222) or canned
    low-sodium chicken broth
½ teaspoon celery seeds
½ teaspoon fennel seeds
¼ teaspoon salt
⅛ teaspoon cayenne pepper

1. Cut the butter into ½-tablespoon pieces, and set them aside.

2. Combine all the remaining ingredients in a small saucepan, and cook over medium heat until only 2 tablespoons remain, 5 to 10 minutes. Remove the pan from the heat, and using a wire whisk or wooden spoon, add the butter a piece at a time, swirling to incorporate.

3. Refrigerate the butter until set but not hard, about 2 hours, then transfer to a food processor and whip until smooth. The butter can be refrigerated for up to 2 weeks. Whip until smooth before serving. ▨

½ CUP

▨ To freeze, place butter on a piece of plastic wrap or freezer paper, and roll it up to form a log shape. Place the wrapped log in a freezer bag or wrap it with a second piece of plastic wrap or freezer paper. Freeze for up to 6 months.

# DIJON BUTTER

For meats, fish, and poultry.

¼ cup dry white wine
3 tablespoons Dijon mustard
½ cup (1 stick) unsalted
    butter

1. Combine the wine and mustard in a small saucepan and cook over low heat for 3 minutes. Pour into a food processor, add the butter, and whip until smooth.

2. Serve at room temperature, or place the butter on a sheet of plastic wrap or freezer paper and roll up to form a log shape. Refrigerate until chilled. ▨

½ CUP

(continued)

Dijon Butter   (continued)

**Mustard and Green Peppercorn Butter:** Add 1½ tablespoons bottled green peppercorns (drained) to the Dijon butter.

**Mustard and Herb Butter:** Add 1½ tablespoons chopped fresh tarragon, rosemary, thyme, chervil, or sage to the Dijon butter. Or add 2 teaspoons of the dried herb to the wine before cooking.

⊠ To freeze, place the wrapped log in a freezer bag, or wrap it with a second piece of plastic wrap or freezer paper. Freeze for up to 6 months.

# ONION MARMALADE

**S**pread this sweet onion concoction on sandwiches, add it to butter sauces, or use dollops of it to accompany grilled meats. It can also stand in for chopped onions or shallots in a recipe. You can even moisten it with a little All-Purpose Broth or milk and create a simple onion soup!

*2 pounds onions (about 6
    medium), finely chopped*

*⅓ cup olive oil*

*½ cup All-Purpose Broth
    (page 222) or canned
    low-sodium chicken broth*

*½ teaspoon salt*

3 CUPS

**1.** Combine the onions, oil, broth, and salt in a medium-size noncorrosible saucepan or skillet. Cook over medium heat, stirring occasionally, until the liquid has evaporated and the onions are golden, about 1 hour. Remove from heat and transfer to a mixing bowl to cool. (The marmalade will keep, covered, in the refrigerator for up to 1 week.) ⊠

**Shallot Marmalade:** Substitute shallots for the onions.

**Garlic Marmalade:** Substitute finely sliced or chopped garlic for the onions.

**Ginger and Garlic Marmalade:** Use equal parts chopped fresh ginger and garlic in place of the onions.

⊠ To freeze, place the chilled marmalade in freezer bags or containers. Freeze for up to 6 months.

# QUICK PAN SAUCE

Use fresh or flavored butters, or potted meat and fish, along with wine or another alcohol to deglaze a roasting or sauté pan and make a quick sauce for meats, fish, and poultry. Whenever possible, make a pan sauce in the same pan in which the food has cooked, so you can take advantage of the flavorful juices that have concentrated on the bottom of the pan. The method is to dissolve these with liquid, reduce it, and then replace the evaporated liquid with butter—easy!

½ cup All-Purpose Broth (page 222) or canned low-sodium chicken broth

½ cup dry white wine

¼ cup finely minced shallots

½ teaspoon salt, or as desired

Freshly ground black pepper to taste

¼ cup chilled whipped butter (pages 235–237)

**1.** Combine the broth, wine, shallots, salt, and pepper in a skillet or saucepan over medium heat. Cook until the liquid has reduced by about three quarters and the mixture appears thick.

**2.** Remove the skillet from heat and swirl in the butter, frozen or unfrozen, a tablespoon at a time, until incorporated. Serve immediately.

½ CUP (SERVES 3 TO 4)

# MUSHROOM DUXELLES

Add this to stuffings, sauces, and mayonnaise; use it in meat loaf; or simply serve it as a vegetable side dish—you'll never be sorry you have duxelles—puréed mushrooms cooked until dry—in your freezer.

Try adding a little milk to some duxelles to make a soup. Cook ¼ cup of duxelles with ½ cup cream, whisk in ¼ cup butter, and you have a sauce to accompany fish or poultry. Mix with some bread crumbs to stuff a leg of lamb. It makes a better binder in meat loaf than bread crumbs: add 1 cup of duxelles to 3 cups of meat. Improvise a mushroom soufflé (page 186) or pancake (pages 181–182).

*2 pounds mushrooms*
*1 medium onion, quartered*
*½ teaspoon salt*
*¼ teaspoon freshly ground*
  *black pepper*
*2 tablespoons unsalted butter*

2½ CUPS

**1.** Wash the mushrooms well. Place them, in batches, in a food processor with the onions, salt, and pepper, and purée until chunky-smooth.

**2.** Heat the butter in a medium-size skillet over medium heat, and when it has melted, add the purée. Cook, stirring occasionally, until the mixture is dry, 25 to 30 minutes. Remove the skillet from the heat and transfer the duxelles into a mixing bowl to cool. (The duxelles will keep covered, in the refrigerator for up to 1 week.)

⊠ To freeze, place chilled duxelles in ice cube trays, and freeze. When they are solid, transfer the cubes to freezer bags or containers, and freeze for up to 6 months.

# MUSHROOM AND CORIANDER SAUCE

This is a wonderful recipe. If your guests surprise you by not mopping up all their sauce, freeze the leftovers; the defrosted sauce can be served as a chilled whipped butter: Place it in a food processor or blender and whip; serve in a small bowl to accompany fish, poultry, or veal.

¼ cup **Mushroom Duxelles,**
    **or 1 frozen duxelles cube**
    **(above)**
**2 teaspoons ground coriander**
¼ **cup dry white wine**
¼ **cup fresh lemon juice**
¼ **cup (½ stick) unsalted**
    **butter**

1. Combine the duxelles, coriander, wine, and lemon juice in a small saucepan over medium heat. Bring to boil and cook for 10 minutes, or until reduced by one third.

2. Remove the pan from the heat and swirl in the butter, a tablespoon at a time. Serve immediately, or keep warm in a larger pan of hot water for up to 30 minutes. ⊠

½ CUP

⊠ To freeze, place the sauce in an airtight freezer bag or container, and seal. Freeze for up to 3 months. Defrost at room temperature in the refrigerator.

# MUSHROOM GRAVY

**3 teaspoons unsalted butter**
**1 tablespoon flour**
**1 cup All-Purpose Broth**
    **(page 222) or canned**
    **low-sodium chicken broth**
¼ **cup Mushroom Duxelles,**
    **or 1 frozen duxelles cube**
    **(page 240)**
**Salt and freshly ground**
    **black pepper to taste**

1. Melt the butter in a medium-size saucepan over medium heat, and add the flour. Stir together until smooth, and then cook 1 minute.

2. Add the broth and duxelles, and cook until the mixture is reduced and saucelike, about 4 minutes. Transfer to a sauceboat and serve immediately.

½ CUP

## STUFFINGS

When you prepare stuffing, make extra for freezing. This is a basic recipe that can be tarted up to flatter many different dishes—try stuffing and rolling skirt steak, boneless lamb shoulder, veal scallops, and pork cutlets.

# BASIC BREAD STUFFING

For poultry, veal, and lamb.

½ cup olive oil, or ½ cup (1 stick) unsalted butter

4 large onions, finely diced (about 4 cups)

4 stalks celery, finely sliced (about 3 cups)

8 cups coarsely chopped stale bread (½-inch pieces)

2 cups All-Purpose Broth (page 222) or canned low-sodium chicken broth

2 teaspoons salt

2 teaspoons freshly ground black pepper

2 tablespoons fresh thyme leaves, or 1 teaspoon dried

2 tablespoons chopped fresh sage leaves, or 1 teaspoon dried

6 CUPS

1. Heat the olive oil or butter in a large saucepan over medium heat. Add the onions and cook 5 minutes, stirring occasionally. Add the celery and continue to cook, stirring occasionally, for 10 minutes.

2. Add the bread, broth, salt, pepper, thyme, and sage. Cook 5 minutes, mixing well. Remove the pan from the heat and transfer the mixture to a large mixing bowl.

3. Place the mixing bowl, covered, in the refrigerator and completely chill the stuffing before stuffing a bird or freezing the stuffing. ▨

**Chicken Liver Stuffing:** Cook ¼ cup chicken livers in 1 tablespoon flavorless oil or unsalted butter and ¼ cup dry sherry. Coarsely chop and add to 1 cup stuffing.

**Chestnut Stuffing:** Add ¼ cup chopped roasted chestnuts to 1 cup of stuffing.

**Apple Stuffing:** Cook 1 apple (peeled, cored and diced) in 1 tablespoon butter, and add to 1 cup stuffing.

**Oyster Stuffing:** Coarsely chop 12 fresh or smoked oysters and add to 1 cup stuffing.

Mushroom Stuffing: Add 1 cup Mushroom Duxelles (page 240) to 1 cup stuffing.

▨ To freeze, divide the stuffing among 1-cup freezer containers or freezer bags, and seal. Freeze for up to 12 months. Defrost in the refrigerator or microwave oven.

# BASIL PASTA STUFFING

You can bake this stuffing by itself and serve it as a side dish, but it is more flavorful when used to stuff a bird.

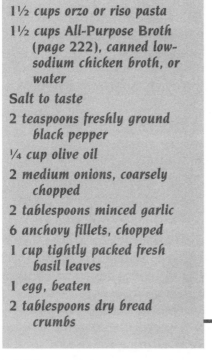

1½ cups orzo or riso pasta
1½ cups All-Purpose Broth (page 222), canned low-sodium chicken broth, or water
Salt to taste
2 teaspoons freshly ground black pepper
¼ cup olive oil
2 medium onions, coarsely chopped
2 tablespoons minced garlic
6 anchovy fillets, chopped
1 cup tightly packed fresh basil leaves
1 egg, beaten
2 tablespoons dry bread crumbs

6 CUPS

1. Combine the pasta and broth in a small saucepan, place over medium-high heat, and bring to a boil. Cook for 5 minutes or until the pasta is barely soft. Remove from the heat and transfer the contents of the pan to a mixing bowl. Stir in the salt and pepper.

2. Meanwhile, heat the olive oil in a medium-size skillet over medium heat. Add the onions, garlic, and anchovies. Cook, stirring occasionally, until the onions are soft, 8 to 10 minutes. Transfer the mixture to a food processor, add the basil, and process until coarsely ground.

3. Add the onion mixture to the pasta, and add the egg and bread crumbs. Mix well, and set aside for 15 minutes. Then refrigerate the stuffing, covered, until completely chilled before stuffing a bird or freezing the stuffing. ▨

Cheese Stuffing: Crumble or dice ¼ pound of blue, Gruyère, or Gouda cheese and add to 1 cup of stuffing.    (continued)

Basil Pasta Stuffing   (continued)

▬▬▬▬▬

**Sausage Stuffing:** Add 3 ounces un-cooked sausage meat to 1 cup stuffing.

▬▬▬▬▬

**Pâté Stuffing:** Add 1 cup cooked or un-cooked pâté (pages 212–218) to 1 cup stuffing.

▨ To freeze, divide the stuffing among 1-cup freezer containers or freezer bags. Seal and freeze for up to 6 months. Defrost in the refrigerator or microwave oven.

## FILLINGS FOR LASAGNA AND OTHER STUFFED PASTAS

Collect your bits of frozen meat, fish, or poultry, or fresh vegetables or cheese, to make a filling to use now or later in pasta dishes like lasagna, manicotti, canneloni, and stuffed shells. Pull a filling out of the freezer, defrost it, and use it to dress a bird. Roll and tie a boneless leg of lamb, breast of veal, or butterflied flank steak around a filling. Or make your own versions of egg rolls and wontons. The following recipes don't need to be adhered to faithfully—in fact you'll get more satisfaction if you adapt them to the contents of your freezer. But remember, the ingredients that give a filling its structure should remain pretty constant: flour and broth to bind a meat filling; flour, milk, and eggs to bind a vegetable filling; eggs to bind a cheese filling.

# MEAT FILLING

4 *pounds frozen cooked beef,*
  *veal, pork, or chicken*
  *(about 3 cups), finely*
  *chopped or ground*

¼ *cup olive oil*

2 *large onions, coarsely*
  *chopped (about 2 cups)*

2 *tablespoons finely minced*
  *garlic*

2 *tablespoons chopped fresh*
  *oregano leaves, or 1*
  *tablespoon dried*

1 *teaspoon ground coriander*

¼ *cup flour*

1 *cup All-Purpose Broth*
  *(page 222) or canned*
  *low-sodium chicken broth*

½ *teaspoon freshly ground*
  *black pepper*

½ *teaspoon salt, or as*
  *desired*

6 CUPS
(ENOUGH FOR 2 LASAGNAS)

**1.** Defrost the meat in the refrigerator or microwave oven.

**2.** Heat the oil in a medium-size skillet over medium heat. Add the onions, garlic, oregano, and coriander. Cook, stirring, for 5 minutes. Then sprinkle the flour over the onions and mix well. Add the broth and meat and cook, stirring, until the mixture is thickened and bubbling, 3 minutes. Stir in the pepper and salt.

**3.** Remove the skillet from the heat and transfer the mixture to a bowl. Refrigerate, uncovered, until cool. (This filling can be stored, covered, in the refrigerator for up to 5 days.) ▨

▨ To freeze, place 1-cup amounts of filling in freezer bags or containers. Seal, and freeze for up to 3 months. Defrost in the refrigerator or microwave oven.

# VEGETABLE FILLING

4 cups finely chopped
    assorted vegetables (such
    as artichoke hearts,
    asparagus, eggplant,
    mushrooms, broccoli,
    cauliflower), frozen or
    fresh, cooked or uncooked

2 tablespoons olive oil

2 large onions, coarsely
    chopped (about 2 cups)

2 cups chopped cooked
    spinach

6 tablespoons flour

1 cup milk

1 egg, beaten

½ teaspoon salt, or as
    desired

½ teaspoon ground white
    pepper

1 teaspoon fresh rosemary
    leaves, or ½ teaspoon
    dried

1. Defrost the vegetables if frozen.

2. Heat the oil in a large skillet over medium heat. Add the onions and cook, stirring, for 5 minutes. Decrease the heat to low and add the mixed vegetables and spinach. If you are using uncooked vegetables, cover and cook for 10 minutes. If cooked, cook uncovered for 5 minutes. Sprinkle the flour over the vegetables and stir well. Add the milk and cook, stirring, another 2 minutes or until the mixture has thickened.

3. Remove the skillet from the heat and stir in the egg. Add the salt, pepper, and rosemary. Transfer the mixture to a bowl to cool. (This filling can be stored, covered, in the refrigerator for up to 7 days.) ▨

6 CUPS

▨ To freeze, place 1-cup amounts of filling in freezer bags or containers. Seal, and freeze for up to 3 months. Defrost in the refrigerator or microwave oven.

# CHEESE FILLING

¼ cup olive oil

2 large onions, coarsely chopped (about 2 cups)

2 tablespoons minced garlic

1 teaspoon salt, or as desired

½ teaspoon ground white pepper

¼ teaspoon ground mace

1 tablespoon chopped fresh thyme leaves, or 1 teaspoon dried

1 pound cottage cheese

1 pound hoop or pot cheese

1 pound mozzarella cheese, grated or shredded

6 eggs, lightly beaten

6 CUPS
(ENOUGH FOR 2 LASAGNAS)

1. Heat the oil in a small saucepan over medium heat. Add the onions and garlic and cook, stirring, 5 minutes.

2. Transfer the onion mixture to a large bowl, and add the salt, white pepper, mace, thyme, and three cheeses. Mix well. Add the eggs and mix to incorporate. (This filling can be stored, covered, in the refrigerator for up to 5 days.) ▨

▨ To freeze, place 1-cup amounts of filling in freezer bags or containers. Seal, and freeze for up to 3 months. Defrost in the refrigerator or microwave oven.

# DESSERTS

In restaurants it's common for cooks and pastry chefs to have a chilly relationship because the nature of their work is so different. Cooks are always under fire to get a dish out of the kitchen quickly. They know how to substitute ingredients on a moment's notice, speed up or slow down the cooking, perform all sorts of culinary "white lies" in the face of hungry, demanding customers. It's all part of giving good service. At heart, all cooks like throwing things together "by feel."

Pastry chefs, on the other hand, work with a different craziness—they must be neat and organized. Unlike the cook, they must measure everything. They can't throw a large pinch of baking powder into a cake and call it a teaspoon. They can't turn the oven higher to make a cake cook faster. They must plan so that desserts that need to chill—cold mousses, for example— are prepared early in the day. Pastry crusts need to rest in the refrigerator to firm for an hour before they can be rolled. Dessert making requires exactitude.

At home, most of us resemble cooks, not pastry chefs. We don't usually have the time or energy, in the middle of preparing meals for family or company, to cook desserts from scratch with the attention that they so often require. So, instead of recommending that you find a good bakery and buy all your desserts, I've included some freezer desserts that will help your meals finish with a flourish. The freezer can store prepared items, such as cheesecake and frozen zabaglione, as well as building blocks for desserts that you can assemble without much trouble.

Freezer cheesecake, for instance, needs assembling only, no baking. You can partially defrost it to serve as is; it will have the delightful consistency of an Italian *semifreddo* dessert—creamy but icy. The mixture can become the filling of a frozen pie or a sponge cake. Or you can defrost it completely and serve it as a beautiful cheesecake terrine with fruit sauce—also from the freezer.

As you no doubt already know, frozen cookie dough allows you to produce fresh, warm, fragrant cookies to guests on very short notice. I also use frozen cooked cookie crumbs to make the streusel topping for fruit pies. And I love dunking frozen cookies in hot tea. Frozen butter cakes—pound cake and chocolate brownie cake—actually develop a finer, firmer texture after freezing. A frozen pound cake can be turned into an ice cream sandwich made of cake slices piled with ice cream or frozen coffee zabaglione.

Frozen chocolate soufflé batter turns out to be a real surprise: When you take it from freezer to oven, it puffs nicely (although not as high as the traditional kind), forms a crust, and tastes delicious.

So this is not a comprehensive chapter on desserts. I have included only those preparations that are versatile enough to warrant taking up valuable freezer space. With these preparations stored in your freezer, you'll be able to throw sweet concoctions together with the same confidence that you do ingredients for a stew or a roast.

## COOKIES

There are thousands of recipes for cookies and almost all of them can be frozen. Here are a few of my favorites to add to your list. Although they don't give way to reveries on quite the same level as Marcel Proust's madeleines, they're special to me. And they're easy.

## SHORTBREADS

**2 cups (4 sticks) unsalted butter**

**1 cup sugar**

**½ teaspoon salt**

**¼ cup sweetened condensed milk**

**½ teaspoon vanilla extract**

**3½ cups flour**

**½ cup cornstarch**

4 DOZEN

**1.** Combine the butter, sugar, and salt in a mixer bowl, and beat at medium speed until creamy. Add the condensed milk and vanilla, and beat until incorporated. Reduce the speed to low and slowly add the flour and then the cornstarch. Beat until incorporated.

**2.** Divide the dough into 4 balls, and wrap each one in plastic wrap. Refrigerate for 1 hour or until firm (or for up to 3 days) or freeze. ▨

**3.** Lightly flour a work surface, and roll out the dough until ¼ inch thick. Keep lifting the dough, and if it sticks to the surface, sprinkle with a little more flour.

**4.** Preheat the oven to 300°F.

**5.** Using a 2½-inch round cookie cutter,

cut out circles of dough; or use a knife to cut into 2-inch squares. Place them on nonstick or lightly buttered cookie sheets, and refrigerate until chilled, about 15 minutes.

**6.** Bake the shortbread on the middle rack of the oven for 15 to 20 minutes, until only slightly colored. Cool completely.

---

▨ To freeze the dough, overwrap with freezer paper, and freeze for up to 3 months. Defrost for 6 hours in the refrigerator or for 45 minutes at room temperature.

To freeze baked cookies, place in freezer bags for up to 3 months. Remove cookies from bag before defrosting.

---

# GINGERSNAP COOKIES

I like gingersnaps to be hard and crisp and very gingery. If you like them less crisp, add 2 egg yolks to the recipe when you cream the butter and sugar together.

2 cups (4 sticks) unsalted
    butter, room temperature
2 cups firmly packed dark
    brown sugar
1 cup molasses
½ teaspoon vanilla extract
2 teaspoons baking soda
¼ cup powdered ginger
¼ teaspoon ground cloves
1 teaspoon salt
6 cups flour
3 tablespoons sugar

**1.** Using an electric mixer, cream the butter and brown sugar together in a bowl. Add the molasses, vanilla, baking soda, ginger, cloves, and salt; beat until incorporated. Slowly add the flour, beating until just combined.

**2.** Divide the dough into 10 pieces, and roll them into logs 2 inches in diameter and about 7 inches long. Wrap each log in a piece of plastic wrap or wax paper, and refrigerate for at least 1 hour (or up to 3 days), or freeze. ▨

**3.** Preheat the oven to 325°F.

**4.** Working on a marble or wooden surface, unwrap the dough logs and cut them into rounds about ¼ inch thick. Sprinkle each

10 DOZEN

(continued)

Gingersnap Cookies  (continued)

round with a little sugar, and lightly flatten them with a rolling pin.

**5.** Place the rounds on unbuttered cookie sheets, and chill in the refrigerator until firm, about 10 minutes.

**6.** Bake the cookies on the middle rack of the oven for about 10 minutes or until the surface has started to crack slightly. Remove from the oven and let cool. The cookies will be chewy at first, but will harden as they cool.

⊠ To freeze the dough, overwrap with freezer paper, and freeze for up to 3 months. Defrost for 6 hours in the refrigerator or for 45 minutes at room temperature.

To freeze baked cookies, place in freezer bags for up to 3 months. Remove cookies from bag before defrosting.

# POPPYSEED COOKIES

These are "drop" cookies—the dough is too sticky to roll into a log. They are great for dipping in tea, or for crumbling to make streusel topping for fruit pies.

1 cup (2 sticks) unsalted
  butter, room temperature

½ cup sugar

¼ teaspoon salt

2 eggs

1½ cups prepared poppyseed
  paste

2¾ cups flour

¼ cup powdered sugar

8 DOZEN

**1.** Combine the butter, sugar, and salt in a mixer bowl, and beat at medium speed until creamy. Add the eggs and poppyseed paste, and beat until incorporated. Reduce the speed to low and slowly add the flour, beating until incorporated.

**2.** Drop tablespoon-size dollops of batter 1 inch apart on lightly buttered or nonstick cookie sheets. The cookies can be covered and refrigerated for up to 1 day at this point, or frozen. ⊠

**3.** Preheat the oven to 350°F.

**4.** Bake the cookies on the middle rack

of the oven for 15 minutes. The edges should be light golden brown. Remove from oven and let cool completely. Sprinkle the cookies with powdered sugar.

---

⊠ To freeze the unbaked cookies, place the cookie sheets in the freezer for 2 hours. When they are frozen, place in a freezer bag, seal, and freeze for up to 3 months. To defrost, place the cookies 1 inch apart on a buttered or nonstick cookie sheet, and leave at room temperature for 2 hours before baking.

To freeze baked cookies, place in freezer bags for up to 3 months. Remove cookies from bag before defrosting.

---

# LEMON SEMOLINA COOKIES

Although they probably lend themselves to numerous variations, these tart, chewy cookies disappeared too quickly from my kitchen to find out. I had to cook a second batch to make icebox cake (page 275).

*1 cup (2 sticks) unsalted butter*

*¼ teaspoon vanilla extract*

*1 teaspoon salt*

*2¼ cups sugar*

*1 egg*

*½ cup fresh lemon juice*

*2 teaspoons grated lemon rind (yellow part only)*

*3 cups semolina*

*1 cup flour*

7 DOZEN

1. Combine the butter, vanilla, salt, and 2 cups of the sugar in a mixer bowl, and beat at medium speed until creamy. Add the egg, lemon juice, and grated rind; beat until incorporated. Decrease the speed to slow and add the semolina and then the flour, beating until just incorporated.

2. Divide the dough into 2 balls and roll each ball into log shapes 2 inches in diameter. Wrap in plastic wrap or wax paper and refrigerate for at least 1 hour (or up to 3 days), or freeze. ⊠ When they are chilled, remove the balls from the refrigerator and roll them into log shapes 2 inches in diameter.

3. Preheat the oven to 325°F.

(continued)

Lemon Semolina Cookies   (continued)

**4.** Working on a marble or wooden surface, unwrap the logs and cut them into rounds about ½ inch thick. Sprinkle each round with a little of the remaining sugar, and lightly flatten them with a rolling pin.

**5.** Place the rounds on unbuttered cookie sheets, and refrigerate until firm, about 10 minutes.

**6.** Bake the cookies on the middle rack of the oven for about 10 minutes or until the surface has started to crack slightly. Remove from the oven and let cool. The cookies will be chewy at first, but will harden as they cool.

▨ To freeze the dough, overwrap logs with freezer paper, and freeze for up to 3 months. Defrost for 6 hours in the refrigerator or for 45 minutes at room temperature.

To freeze baked cookies, place in freezer bags for up to 3 months. Remove cookies from bag before defrosting.

# CAKES

These are hearty cakes that I make especially for the freezer. I don't think you'd believe me if I gave you recipes for fancy frosted or decorated cakes and told you to freeze them—and I wouldn't blame you. It's crazy to waste your freezer for things like that, and besides, when you decorate a beautiful dessert, it's usually done for a special occasion—pulling a beautiful cake out of the freezer for someone's birthday is like recycling a Christmas present into a birthday gift.

Cakes freeze pretty well, though. Just remember to unwrap them before defrosting so that they don't get soggy from the condensation that collects inside the wrapper. And cakes should be completely chilled before going into the freezer.

# SOUR CREAM POUND CAKE

This is moister and denser than most pound cakes and makes great ice cream sandwiches.

1 cup (2 sticks) unsalted
　　butter, room temperature
¾ cup sugar
4 eggs
¾ cup sour cream
1 teaspoon vanilla extract
½ teaspoon ground nutmeg
¼ teaspoon baking soda
¼ teaspoon salt
2 cups flour

SERVES 8

1. Cream the butter and sugar together with an electric mixer at high speed.

2. Add the eggs one at a time, as each one is absorbed. Add the sour cream, and mix until incorporated. Then add the vanilla, nutmeg, baking soda, and salt. Decrease the speed to medium, add the flour, and mix for 1 minute.

3. Preheat the oven to 350°F.

4. Spoon the batter into a 1-quart loaf pan, round, or rectangular cake pan, leaving ½ inch at the top. Bake the cake on the middle rack of the oven for 50 to 60 minutes. It is done when the surface has cracked and a toothpick inserted into the center comes out clean.

5. Remove the cake from the oven and let it cool in the pan for 15 minutes before unmolding onto a rack. (The cooled pound cake will keep, tightly wrapped in plastic, at room temperature for up to 2 days or refrigerated for up to 1 week.) ▨

**Pound Cake Toasts:** Slice pound cake and toast it like bread in a toaster. Serve buttered toasted pound cake with coffee in the morning. Or serve unbuttered pound cake toast with ice cream and fruit sauce.

▨ To freeze, wrap tightly in plastic wrap, overwrap with freezer paper, and freeze for up to 3 months. Unwrap and defrost at room temperature or in the refrigerator.

# CHOCOLATE BROWNIE CAKE

The texture of this dense, rich, moist cake resembles pound cake.

8 ounces semisweet baking
   chocolate

½ cup sweetened condensed
   milk

3 eggs

2 egg yolks

¾ cup sugar

1 teaspoon vanilla extract

12 tablespoons (1½ sticks)
   unsalted butter, room
   temperature

1 teaspoon baking powder

1½ cups flour

Powdered sugar

Whipped cream

SERVES 8

1. Preheat the oven to 350°F.

2. Butter and flour a 12-cup bundt pan or fluted tube pan.

3. Melt the chocolate in the top of a double boiler. Stir in the condensed milk until incorporated. Remove from the heat and set aside.

4. Combine the whole eggs, yolks, sugar, and vanilla in a mixer bowl, and beat on high speed until the mixture is pale, about 3 minutes. Add the butter and beat until the mixture is smooth.

5. Reduce the speed to low and add the melted chocolate. Mix, scraping down the sides of the bowl, until blended. Add the baking powder, and then slowly add the flour. Continue to mix for 1 minute.

6. Spoon the batter into the prepared pan, and tap it gently on the counter to eliminate any air bubbles. Bake on the middle rack of the oven for 25 minutes. When the cake is done, a toothpick or wire cake tester will come out clean when inserted in the center, and the cake will be springy to the touch.

7. Remove the cake from the oven and let it cool in the pan for 15 minutes. Then invert it onto a wire cake rack and let cool completely.

8. To serve the cake, dust it with powdered sugar and accompany with whipped cream. ▨

▨ To freeze, wrap tightly in plastic wrap, then overwrap with freezer paper. Freeze for up to 3 months. Defrost in the wrapping at room temperature or in the refrigerator.

# PEARL'S CHIP SPONGE CAKE

Grating the chocolate and mixing it into the batter allows the cake to rise to an airy height; the results are light and wonderful.

**2 ounces unsweetened baking chocolate**

**2 egg yolks**

**⅔ cup sugar**

**½ teaspoon vanilla extract**

**¼ cup water**

**1¼ cups sifted cake flour**

**2 teaspoons baking powder**

**4 egg whites**

**¼ teaspoon cream of tartar**

**2 tablespoons powdered sugar**

**Powdered sugar for dusting**

SERVES 8

1. Preheat the oven to 350°F. Butter a 4-inch-deep, 10-inch round tube cake pan.

2. Grate the chocolate with a hand grater or in a food processor, and set aside.

3. Combine the egg yolks, sugar, and vanilla in a mixer bowl, and beat at high speed until the mixture lightens to a light lemony yellow. Add the water and grated chocolate, and mix for 1 minute. Add the cake flour and baking powder, and mix until incorporated. Set the batter aside.

4. Beat the egg whites in another mixer bowl on medium speed until foamy. Add the cream of tartar, raise the speed to high, and beat until soft peaks form. Add the powdered sugar and beat until stiff peaks form.

5. Stir one fourth of the stiff whites into the batter. Spoon the rest of the whites over the batter and gently fold together. Pour into the buttered tube cake pan.

6. Bake on the middle rack of the oven for 25 to 30 minutes or until golden brown. When the cake is done, a toothpick inserted into the center will come out dry and the cake will have pulled away from the sides of the pan.

7. Remove the pan from the oven and immediately invert it over a wire rack. Let the cake cool for 1 hour before unmolding. To unmold the cake, loosen the sides with a thin knife or long metal spatula, and invert onto a plate. Sprinkle with powdered sugar and serve. ▨

▨ To freeze, wrap in plastic wrap, then overwrap with freezer paper and place in the freezer for up to 3 months. To defrost, unwrap for 3 hours at room temperature, then in a preheated 350°F oven for 5 minutes to crisp.

## MOUSSES, SOUFFLÉS, AND WHIPPED PUDDINGS

Mousses, soufflés, and whipped puddings are smooth desserts that can sometimes resemble cafeteria food—something people either love or hate. I find them more comforting than elegant, especially when all I have to do is pull them out of the freezer a few hours before serving.

# CHESTNUT MOUSSE

*1 teaspoon powdered gelatin*

*¼ cup brandy*

*¾ cup sweetened chestnut purée (8-ounce can chestnut spread)*

*½ teaspoon vanilla extract*

*¼ teaspoon ground allspice*

*½ cup whipping cream*

SERVES 4

**1.** Combine the gelatin and brandy in the top of a double boiler, stir, and set aside for 5 minutes. Then place the pan over simmering water and cook, stirring occasionally, for about 5 minutes to burn off the alcohol. Remove from the heat and cool to room temperature.

**2.** Combine the chestnut purée, vanilla, and allspice in a mixing bowl, and add the cooled brandy mixture.

**3.** Place the cream in a chilled mixing bowl, and whip until you can see the path of the mixer in the stiff cream and peaks form.

**4.** Stir a quarter of the whipped cream into the chestnut mixture. Spoon the remaining whipped cream over the mixture and gently fold the two together. ▨

**5.** Spoon the mousse into wine glasses, cover, and refrigerate for about 6 hours, or up to 2 days, before serving.

▨ Place the mousse in plastic freezer containers, seal, and freeze for up to 1 month. Defrost for 4 hours in the refrigerator.

# FROZEN COFFEE ZABAGLIONE

¾ *cup whipping cream*

½ *teaspoon vanilla extract*

4 *egg yolks*

1 *tablespoon instant coffee powder*

⅔ *cup sweet white wine*

⅓ *cup sugar*

SERVES 4

1. Combine the cream and vanilla in a large chilled bowl, and using a whisk or hand-held electric beater, whip until the cream is stiff. Cover, and set aside in the refrigerator.

2. Fill a large bowl with ice cubes and add a little water. Set aside.

3. Combine the yolks, instant coffee, wine, and sugar in the top of a double boiler (or in a bowl set over gently boiling water). Using a beater or whisk, beat vigorously until the mixture is frothy and has started to thicken slightly, about 8 minutes with a hand-held electric beater.

4. Transfer the pot to the ice-water bath and continue to beat until the mixture has cooled, about 10 minutes. Remove the bowl of whipped cream from the refrigerator, spoon the coffee mixture onto the cream, and fold the two together.

5. Fill coffee cups with the zabaglione, and freeze for 6 hours. Let the zabaglione soften for at least 30 minutes, or up to 1 hour in the refrigerator, before serving. ▨

▨ Freeze the zabaglione, double-wrapped in plastic wrap, for up to 3 months. Defrost as in Step 5.

# INDIVIDUAL CHOCOLATE SOUFFLÉS

These individual soufflés are not as light as traditional ones, but they have the advantage of durability. The mixture can be frozen and cooked directly from the freezer, as long as they're in freezer-to-oven containers. The result is quite delicious, although it is more a soufflé pudding than a true soufflé.

(continued)

Individual Chocolate Soufflés   (continued)

3 *tablespoons unsalted
  butter, melted*

3 *tablespoons powdered
  sugar*

2 *ounces semisweet baking
  chocolate*

1 *cup milk*

1 *teaspoon instant coffee
  powder*

3 *egg yolks*

¼ *cup sugar*

¼ *teaspoon vanilla extract*

1 *tablespoon cornstarch*

¼ *teaspoon baking powder*

4 *egg whites*

¼ *teaspoon cream of tartar*

¼ *teaspoon salt*

SERVES 8

1. Lightly butter eight 1-cup soufflé dishes. Then sprinkle them with the powdered sugar. Set aside in the refrigerator.

2. Melt the chocolate in the top of a double boiler. Set it aside.

3. Combine the milk and instant coffee in a small saucepan, bring to a boil, and immediately remove from the heat. Set it aside.

4. Preheat the oven to 425°F.

5. Combine the egg yolks, sugar, vanilla, and cornstarch in a large mixing bowl and whisk together until smooth. Add the melted chocolate and stir to incorporate. Slowly pour in the hot milk, stirring.

6. Pour the mixture into a saucepan and place over low heat. Stir constantly until thick, about 5 minutes. Remove the pan from the heat and pour the mixture back into the mixing bowl. Mix in the baking powder.

7. Place the egg whites and cream of tartar in a mixer bowl and whip until stiff. Stir one fourth of the whites into the chocolate mixture. Spoon the remainder of the whites over the chocolate mixture and gently fold together. Fill the prepared soufflé dishes three-quarters full. ▨

8. Place the soufflés on the middle rack of the oven, lower the heat to 375°F, and bake until the soufflés rise, about 20 minutes.

9. Remove the soufflés from the oven and serve immediately.

**White Chocolate Amaretto Soufflés:** Substitute white chocolate for the dark, 1 teaspoon amaretto for the instant coffee powder.

▨ Spoon all or some of the soufflé into freezer-to-oven custard cups, cover, and freeze for up to 1 month.

To serve, preheat the oven to 375°F and cook the soufflés, without defrosting, for 30 to 35 minutes. Serve immediately.

# FRIED COCONUT CUSTARD WITH FRUIT SAUCE

8 eggs

1 tablespoon flour

⅓ cup sugar

1 teaspoon vanilla extract

½ cup light rum

1 cup whipping cream

1 cup sweetened condensed milk

½ cup sweetened shredded coconut

2 eggs, beaten

1 cup graham cracker crumbs

2 tablespoons unsalted butter

1 cup strawberry sauce (page 269)

Powdered sugar

SERVES 10

1. Preheat the oven to 350°F.

2. Beat the 8 eggs, flour, and sugar together in a large bowl until smooth. Add the vanilla, rum, cream, condensed milk, and coconut. Mix until incorporated.

3. Pour the mixture into a 9-by 11-inch buttered baking dish; the custard should be about 1 inch deep. Cover with aluminum foil, and bake for 20 minutes.

4. Remove the baking dish from the oven and let the custard cool. Then refrigerate it for 2 hours, until set. Cut the custard into 2-inch squares, and unmold.

5. Place the beaten eggs in a bowl, and the crumbs on a plate. Dip squares of custard in the egg, then in the crumbs, pressing to coat well. Repeat with egg, then crumbs. Set aside until all the custard squares are coated. ⊠

6. Melt the butter in a nonstick skillet over medium heat. Add the custards and cook until both sides are golden, about 4 minutes per side.

7. To serve, pour strawberry sauce onto individual plates and arrange pieces of custard on top. Dust lightly with powdered sugar, and serve immediately.

⊠ To freeze, place all or some of the custard squares between pieces of freezer paper, and wrap tightly in plastic wrap, freezer paper, or freezer bags. Seal, and freeze for up to 3 months.

Defrost unwrapped at room temperature for 1 hour before proceeding with Steps 6 and 7.

# STEAMED BANANA DATE PUDDING

Even those people who detest fruitcake and Christmas pudding seem to adore this dessert.

¾ cup (1½ sticks) unsalted butter, room temperature

¼ cup dark brown sugar

2 eggs

2 overripe bananas

1 cup dry bread crumbs

1 cup graham cracker crumbs

2 teaspoons baking powder

½ cup dark rum

1½ cups chopped pitted dates

Whipping cream

SERVES 10

1. Butter a pudding mold or 1-pound coffee can. Set it aside.

2. Fill a 3-quart saucepan with water and bring it to a boil over high heat.

3. Meanwhile cream the butter and the brown sugar together in a mixer bowl on medium speed. When the mixture is smooth, add the eggs and mix until incorporated. Then add the bananas and mix until smooth.

4. Turn the speed to low and add the bread crumbs, cracker crumbs, baking powder, rum, and dates. Mix for 1 minute, until incorporated.

5. Spoon the pudding mixture into the prepared mold (no more than three-quarters full). Cover with a cloth and secure it with string. Wrap the cover with aluminum foil. Place the mold in the saucepan so that the water reaches three-quarters of the way up the sides, and simmer for 1½ hours. ▨

6. Remove the pudding from the water and let it cool for 10 minutes before unmolding. Serve warm or at room temperature, and accompany with a pitcher of cream.

▨ To freeze, cool the pudding completely. Leave in the mold or unmold, then wrap in plastic wrap, and overwrap with freezer paper, or place in a large freezer bag. Seal, and freeze for up to 6 months.

Defrost unmolded pudding at room temperature or in the refrigerator. Unwrap and cover with foil. Bake in a 250°F oven for 45 minutes before serving.

If the frozen pudding is still in its mold, place the mold in simmering water and steam for 1½ hours before serving.

## PIES AND PASTRY

Pastries depend on flour and fat to bake together into a stiff but flaky holder for sweet creams, fruits, pastes and other delicious things. Cooked or uncooked, they are perfect candidates for freezing. Follow the recipe guidelines for freezing the dough in Nut Pie Crust (page 264) or Cream Cheese Pie Crust (page 266) and freeze your own favorite pastry.

# APPLE CRUMBLE PIE

**W**hether defrosted or freshly made, use well-chilled dough. Work quickly and rechill before adding the filling.

⅓ recipe **Nut Pie Crust** (recipe follows)

¼ cup (½ stick) unsalted butter

4 cups thinly sliced peeled green apples

½ cup sugar

2 tablespoons fresh lemon juice

⅛ teaspoon ground mace

½ tablespoon cornstarch

1 cup poppyseed cookie crumbs (page 252)

¼ cup (½ stick) unsalted butter, melted

2 tablespoons dark brown sugar

SERVES 8

1. Place the ball of chilled dough on a piece of lightly floured wax paper, and pound it with a rolling pin to flatten and soften it. Roll the dough out to form an 11-inch circle. Lift it with the wax paper and invert it onto a 9-inch pie dish. Press the dough firmly into the dish, and gently remove and discard the wax paper. Chill the crust in the refrigerator for 1 hour.

2. Preheat the oven to 400°F.

3. Melt the butter in a medium-size skillet over medium heat. Add the apples, cover, and cook for 5 minutes. Remove the cover and add the sugar, lemon juice, mace, and cornstarch. Cook 2 minutes, stirring. Remove the skillet from the heat and set it aside.

4. Meanwhile, bake the pie shell for 10 minutes.

5. While the pie shell is baking, combine the cookie crumbs, melted butter, and brown sugar in a bowl, and mix well.

6. Remove the pie shell from the oven and fill it with the cooked apple mixture. Sprinkle the cookie crumble evenly over the apples.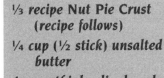

7. Bake the pie for 20 minutes. Allow it to cool to room temperature before serving.

(continued)

Apple Crumble Pie   (continued)

⊠ To freeze, wrap the pie in plastic wrap, overwrap with freezer paper, and freeze for up to 2 months.

To serve, unwrap the pie and place it directly in a preheated 400°F oven. Bake for 35 minutes.

# Nut Pie Crust

**2 cups flour**

**1 cup ground blanched almonds**

**½ teaspoon ground cinnamon**

**½ teaspoon ground cloves**

**½ teaspoon salt**

**2 tablespoons unsweetened cocoa powder**

**1 cup sugar**

**1 teaspoon grated lemon rind**

**1½ cups (3 sticks) unsalted butter**

**1 egg, beaten**

**1.** Combine the flour, almonds, cinnamon, cloves, salt, cocoa, sugar, and lemon rind in a mixer bowl, and mix well on low speed.

**2.** Increase the speed to medium and add the butter, a tablespoon at a time. Mix until the dough begins to form a ball. Add the egg and mix until just incorporated.

**3.** Divide the dough into thirds, form into 3 balls, and wrap each one in plastic wrap. ⊠ Chill for 1 hour before using.

3 CRUSTS

⊠ Freeze the uncooked pie dough for up to 2 months, either in 3 balls or rolled out and fitted into 3 pie tins, each double-wrapped in plastic wrap. Defrost the wrapped balls in the refrigerator or at room temperature. Bake formed shells from the freezer.

# BLUEBERRY BUTTER PIE

The berries melt into the butter filling and create something gooey and wonderful. Be sure to use well-chilled dough.

⅓ recipe **Cream Cheese Pie Crust (recipe follows)**

5 tablespoons unsalted butter

2 eggs, beaten

1 cup sugar

½ cup flour

4 cups blueberries

Powdered sugar

SERVES 8

1. Place the ball of chilled dough on a piece of lightly floured wax paper, and pound it with a rolling pin to flatten and soften it. Roll the dough out to form an 11-inch circle. Lift it with the wax paper and invert it onto a 9-inch pie dish. Press the dough firmly into the dish, and gently remove and discard the wax paper. Chill the crust in the refrigerator for 1 hour.

2. Preheat the oven to 375°F.

3. Place the butter in a small saucepan over medium heat, and cook until it turns hazelnut brown. Remove the pan from the heat and set aside to cool slightly.

4. Meanwhile, combine the eggs and sugar in a mixer bowl, and mix until smooth. Add the flour and continue to beat until incorporated. Pour in the brown butter, and mix.

5. Remove the pie shell from the refrigerator. Fill it with the berries, and carefully pour in the butter mixture. Bake on the middle rack of the oven for 35 to 40 minutes or until golden and puffed.

6. Remove the pie from the oven and let it cool to room temperature. Sprinkle with powdered sugar and serve. ▨

▨ To freeze, wrap the baked pie in plastic wrap, overwrap with freezer paper, and freeze for up to 3 months. Defrost, unwrapped, in the refrigerator. Then bake in a preheated 375°F oven for 10 minutes to refresh. Allow it to cool before serving.

## CREAM CHEESE PIE CRUST

1 cup (2 sticks) unsalted
   butter, cut into pieces
½ pound cream cheese
2 teaspoons vanilla extract
2 cups flour

3 CRUSTS

1. Cream the butter, cream cheese, and vanilla together in a mixer bowl on medium speed or in a food processor. Reduce the speed to low and add the flour. Mix just until incorporated.

2. Divide the dough into thirds, form into 3 balls, and wrap each in plastic wrap. ⊠ Chill for 1 hour before using.

⊠ Freeze uncooked pie dough for up to 2 months, either in 3 balls of dough or rolled out and fitted into 3 pie tins, each double-wrapped in plastic wrap. Defrost the wrapped balls in the refrigerator, or for 6 hours at room temperature. Bake formed shells from the freezer.

## CHOUX PUFF SHELLS

Fill these cream puff shells with flavored whipped cream, ice cream, frozen zabaglione (page 259), or freezer cheesecake (page 268). Or omit the sugar and after baking, make cocktail teasers by filling the shells with savory mixtures such as pâté (pages 212–217), brandade (page 218), or potted meats or fish (page 208). These little pastry cases are actually better when cooked after freezing.

2 cups water
¼ teaspoon salt
3 tablespoons sugar
10 tablespoons unsalted butter
1½ cups flour
8 eggs

8 DOZEN

1. Combine the water, salt, sugar, and butter in a 2-quart saucepan and bring to a boil over high heat. Reduce the heat to medium and add the flour all at once. Using a large wooden spoon, stir vigorously until the mixture pulls away from the sides of the pan and forms a ball.

2. Remove the pan from the heat and place the dough in a mixer bowl or food processor. Running the mixer on medium

speed, add the eggs one at a time, beating until incorporated after each addition. Transfer the dough to a pastry bag or mixing bowl.

**3.** Preheat the oven to 425°F.

**4.** Squeeze or spoon 1-inch mounds of choux paste about 1½ inches apart on ungreased cookie sheets. Dip a brush or the back of a spoon in water, and lightly smooth the surface of the mounds. ▨

**5.** Place the cookie sheets on the middle rack of the oven, and bake for 10 minutes. Then reduce the temperature to 375°F and continue to bake until golden, another 25 to 30 minutes. The puffs will be about 2 inches across and they should be very firm to the touch. Remove from the oven and let cool completely before using.

---

▨ To freeze uncooked choux paste, place the cookie sheets in the freezer and chill for 1 hour. When the mounds are frozen, place them in a plastic freezer bag or container, and freeze for up to 3 months. To cook, bake frozen choux paste (do not defrost) in a preheated 375°F oven until golden and firm to the touch, about 45 minutes.

Freeze baked choux puffs for up to 6 months in a plastic freezer bag or container. Bake the frozen puffs (without defrosting) in a preheated 375°F oven for 10 minutes to refresh before using.

---

## OTHER DESSERTS

This is by no means the end of the dessert line as far as the freezer goes. Among the following recipes are many traditional favorites, some of which are actually "cooked" by the freezer, such as Freezer Cheesecake, Lemon Icebox Cake, and Chocolate Truffles.

# FREEZER CHEESECAKE

**S**erve this unbaked cheesecake mixture in a baked pie shell, in choux puffs, or as chilled slices topped with berry sauce. Or simply freeze the cheesecake, then let it partially defrost in the refrigerator for 4 hours, and serve it like a Italian *semifreddo* dessert.

1 *envelope powdered gelatin*

¼ *cup milk*

6 *egg yolks*

½ *cup sugar*

3 *tablespoons flour*

2 *cups cottage, hoop, or ricotta cheese*

½ *pound cream cheese, room temperature*

1 *tablespoon grated lemon rind*

½ *teaspoon vanilla extract*

*Pinch of mace*

½ *recipe Berry Sauce (recipe follows)*

SERVES 10

**1.** Combine the gelatin and the milk in a small bowl, and set aside for 5 minutes to soften.

**2.** Beat the egg yolks and sugar together in a mixer bowl at high speed until they turn a light lemon-yellow. Add the flour and mix to incorporate. Add the softened gelatin, cottage cheese, cream cheese, lemon rind, vanilla, and mace. Beat until smooth.

**3.** Pour the mixture into the top of a double boiler, and cook over simmering water, stirring continuously, until the mixture has thickened, about 15 minutes.

**4.** Line a 1-quart loaf pan with wax paper or plastic wrap, leaving about 6 inches hanging over on all sides. Pour in the cheesecake mixture, and let it cool to room temperature, about 1 hour. Then cover the top with the overhanging wrap, and refrigerate for at least 6 hours. ▨

**5.** Remove the cheesecake from the loaf pan by lifting it out by its wrapper. Using a knife, carefully slice the cheesecake. Lay a slice on each plate, spoon some berry sauce over the slice, and serve.

▨ To freeze, remove the chilled cheesecake from the loaf pan by lifting it out with its wrapping. Cut the cake into 1-inch slices, wrap each slice in plastic wrap, and place the slices in a freezer bag or container. Freeze for up to 3 months.

Partially defrost in the refrigerator for 1 hour, and serve semi-frozen.

# BERRY SAUCE

1 pound (2 pints) fresh
   strawberries, raspberries,
   blueberries, or
   blackberries
½ cup sugar
2 tablespoons fresh lemon
   juice

Pick through the berries, discarding any rotten ones and removing any stems. Combine the berries, sugar, and lemon juice in a food processor or blender and purée until smooth. Strain to remove any seeds. ▨

2 CUPS

▨ Fill 1-cup freezer bags or containers three quarters full, seal, and freeze for up to 6 months.

# BROWN BUTTER PEACH CHARLOTTE

6 to 8 peaches
¼ cup dark brown sugar
20 baked Lady Fingers
   (recipe follows), fresh or
   frozen (do not defrost)
3 eggs
1 cup sugar
½ cup flour
½ cup (1 stick) unsalted
   butter
½ teaspoon vanilla extract
Whipped cream

1. Preheat the oven to 350°F.
2. Bring a medium pot of water to a boil over high heat. Add the peaches and cook for about 2 minutes. Then remove the pan from the heat, drain the peaches and cool them under cold running water. Using a small knife, remove and discard the skin. Cut the peaches in half from tip to stem, and remove the pits. Chop the peaches into ½-inch pieces; you should have about 5 cups. Combine the brown sugar and the peaches in a medium-size saucepan and cook over medium heat for 5 minutes.
3. Remove the pan from the heat and set it aside.
4. Butter a 3-inch-deep, 8-inch round

SERVES 8

(continued)

Brown Butter Peach Charlotte   (continued)

baking dish, and arrange the lady fingers on the bottom and sides. Set the dish aside.

**5.** Whisk the eggs, sugar, and flour together in a mixing bowl and set aside. In a small saucepan, heat the butter and vanilla extract over medium heat until the butter is foamy and has turned nut-brown. Remove the pan from the heat and slowly pour the butter into the egg mixture, stirring continuously. Stir in the peaches.

**6.** Spoon the mixture carefully into the prepared baking dish, and place it on the middle rack of the oven. Bake for 45 minutes. The charlotte is done when the top is crusty and the inside is smooth but not runny. Let it cool completely. ▨

**7.** To serve, invert the charlotte onto a platter and accompany with whipped cream.

---

▨ Wrap the charlotte in plastic wrap, overwrap with freezer paper, and freeze for up to 3 months. Defrost, unwrapped, in the refrigerator or at room temperature.

---

# LADY FINGERS

6 egg whites

¼ teaspoon cream of tartar

Small pinch of salt

¾ cup powdered sugar

¼ teaspoon vanilla extract

¼ teaspoon baking powder

2 egg yolks

⅔ cup flour

3 DOZEN

**1.** Preheat the oven to 350°F.

**2.** Place the egg whites in the bowl of an electric mixer and mix on low speed for 2 minutes. Add the cream of tartar and raise the speed to high. When the whites are stiff, reduce the mixer speed to medium and slowly add the salt, powdered sugar, vanilla, baking powder, and egg yolks while mixing continuously. Reduce the speed to low and add the flour. Mix until just incorporated.

**3.** Line a cookie sheet with parchment paper, or use a nonstick sheet. Using a soup spoon, shape heaping tablespoon amounts of batter onto the cookie sheet in strips about 1 inch wide and 3 inches long.

**4.** Bake for 8 to 10 minutes or until golden. Let the lady fingers cool before removing them from the paper or pan. ▨

▨ To freeze, let the lady fingers cool completely. Then place them in a freezer bag or container, seal, and freeze for up to 3 months.

To serve, remove from the bag and defrost at room temperature. Bake on a cookie sheet in a preheated 350°F oven for 5 minutes to refresh. Allow to cool.

# FIGS IN PHYLLO

**P**hyllo dough is easy to work with if you lay the sheets on a slightly damp towel and work rapidly. You can store uncooked phyllo in the freezer for up to 6 months, keeping it on hand to pull out in an emergency. Wrap little bits of prepared foods like pâté, meat loaf, and brandade in phyllo and create an impromptu cocktail party.

*8 ripe fresh figs*

*½ cup sugar*

*1 vanilla bean, slit lengthwise*

*½ cup water*

*¼ cup (½ stick) unsalted butter*

*4 sheets phyllo dough, defrosted*

*2 tablespoons powdered sugar*

*4 scoops vanilla ice cream (optional)*

SERVES 4

**1.** Remove and discard the stems from the figs. Combine the sugar, vanilla bean, and water in a small saucepan and bring to a boil over high heat. Add the figs, cover, and reduce the heat to medium. Cook for 5 minutes. Then remove the figs and let them cool to room temperature on a plate. Continue to cook the liquid until it has reduced by about half and is syrupy, 5 to 10 minutes. Remove the syrup from the heat and pour it into a bowl. Add any juice that has escaped from the figs. Set the vanilla bean aside for another use. (The syrup will keep in the refrigerator for up to 1 year.)

**2.** Melt the butter in a small saucepan. Remove it from the heat and set aside.

**3.** Lay a sheet of phyllo on a work sur-

(continued)

Figs in Phyllo (continued)

face, and using a small brush, lightly brush it with melted butter. Then sprinkle with powdered sugar. Lay another sheet of phyllo over the first one; brush with butter and sprinkle with sugar. Repeat until the 4 sheets are stacked.

**4.** Cut the stack of phyllo into 8 squares. Place a fig on each square. Gather up the corners of each square and give them a twist to close. Brush the surface with a little melted butter. ▨

**5.** Preheat the oven to 375°F.

**6.** Place the phyllo bundles on a cookie sheet and bake for 12 to 15 minutes or until golden. Remove from the oven and let cool slightly.

**7.** Serve the warm phyllo bundles on individual plates. Place a scoop of ice cream next to each one, and spoon some vanilla syrup over the top.

---

▨ To freeze the uncooked figs in phyllo, chill on a cookie sheet in the freezer for 1 hour. Then transfer them to a freezer bag or container, seal, and freeze for up to 4 months. To serve, bake the frozen bundles (do not defrost) in a preheated 375°F oven for 20 to 25 minutes.

To freeze cooked figs in phyllo, let the bundles cool completely. Then wrap in plastic wrap and place in a freezer bag or container. Freeze for up to 4 months. To serve, bake without defrosting in a preheated 375°F oven for 15 to 20 minutes.

---

# STRAWBERRY SHORTCAKES

Use this recipe to take advantage of other fruits in season—blueberries, raspberries, peaches, and nectarines are all delicious in a shortcake.

2 cups flour

2 tablespoons baking powder

¼ cup sugar

½ teaspoon salt

½ cup (1 stick) unsalted
   butter

1 egg yolk

½ teaspoon vanilla extract

¾ cup sweetened
   condensed milk

2 cups whipping cream

⅔ cup powdered sugar

1 teaspoon orange blossom
   water (optional)

4½ cups sliced strawberries

½ recipe strawberry sauce
   (page 269)

6 SHORTCAKES

1. Preheat the oven to 425°F.

2. Combine the flour, baking powder, sugar, and salt in a mixer bowl. With the mixer on low speed, add the butter, 2 tablespoons at a time, mixing until just incorporated. Do not overmix.

3. Add the egg yolk, vanilla, and condensed milk. Mix until just incorporated.

4. Turn the dough out onto a well-floured board, and roll it out until it is ½ inch thick. Cut the dough into rounds with a 3-inch cookie cutter. ▨

5. Place the rounds on a lightly greased baking sheet, and bake for 15 minutes or until golden around the edges. Transfer the shortcakes to a plate, and let them cool for 30 minutes.

6. Place the cream in a chilled mixing bowl, and whip until you can see the path of the beater in the stiff cream. Continue to whip while adding the powdered sugar and orange blossom water. Stop whipping as soon as stiff peaks form.

7. Split the shortcakes in half with a knife, and sprinkle the centers with a few drops of orange blossom water. Place the bottom halves of the shortcakes on individual plates. Cover each with a dollop of whipped cream, and then with 2 tablespoons sliced strawberries. Replace the top crusts, and cover them with strawberries. Top with whipped cream. Ladle some strawberry sauce over the top, and serve at once.

**Fruit Cobbler:** Place an unsplit shortcake in a bowl, add ½ cup hot cooked apples or peaches (pages 263, 269), and top with a scoop of vanilla ice cream. (continued)

Strawberry Shortcakes    (continued)

⊠ To freeze unbaked shortcake, wrap each round in plastic wrap, then place them in freezer bags. Seal, and freeze for up to 2 months. To serve, bake frozen rounds (do not defrost) in a preheated 425°F oven for 25 minutes.

To freeze baked shortcakes, wrap each in plastic wrap, then place them in freezer bags. Seal, and freeze for up to 3 months. To serve, defrost unwrapped at room temperature. To refresh, bake in a preheated 350°F oven for 5 minutes before serving.

# CHOCOLATE TRUFFLES

Hide these truffles in the freezer so you don't eat them all at once.

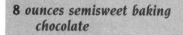

**8 ounces semisweet baking chocolate**
**1 egg yolk**
**¼ cup brandy**
**⅓ cup whipping cream**
**2 tablespoons unsalted butter**
**12 ounces bittersweet baking chocolate**
**¼ cup unsweetened cocoa powder**

20 TRUFFLES

1. Melt the semisweet chocolate in the top of a double boiler over simmering water. Whisk in the egg yolk. Remove the double boiler from the heat and set it aside.

2. Heat the brandy in a small saucepan over medium heat for 1 to 2 minutes to burn off the alcohol. Add the cream and cook until warm, about 2 minutes.

3. Stir the cream mixture into the melted chocolate. Add the butter and stir until incorporated. Pour the mixture into a shallow pan, forming a layer about 1 inch thick, and refrigerate until set, about 45 minutes.

4. Remove the chocolate cream from the refrigerator, and form the truffles: Using a tablespoon or melon baller, dip the spoon in hot water and scoop out spoonfuls one by one. Quickly form them into 1-inch balls with your hands. Place them on a tray in the refrigerator. After all the truffles have been formed, freeze them for 30 minutes.

5. Melt the bittersweet chocolate in the top of the double boiler over simmering water. Place the cocoa powder in a small bowl. Remove the chocolate balls from the

freezer, and drop them one at a time into the melted chocolate. Immediately retrieve the ball by spearing it with a toothpick. Shake off any excess chocolate, and roll the ball in the cocoa powder. Place each truffle on a plate as it is coated. Refrigerate to set for at least 10 minutes before serving. ▨

**Cinnamon Nut Truffles:** Substitute amaretto for the brandy, and add ½ cup ground nuts to the chocolate cream. Roll the truffles in a mixture of cinnamon and powdered sugar instead of cocoa powder.

**Chocolate Mint Truffles:** Use crème de menthe in place of the brandy.

▨ To freeze, place layers of truffles between sheets of freezer paper in a plastic container. Seal, and freeze for up to 3 months. To serve, let the truffles defrost for 30 minutes in the refrigerator.

# LEMON ICEBOX CAKE

The cookies plump up from the moisture in the whipped cream and become cakelike. Make the recipe a day ahead.

2 cups whipping cream
¼ cup powdered sugar
¾ teaspoon vanilla extract
24 Lemon Semolina Cookies
    (page 253)

SERVES 6

1. Place the cream in a chilled mixing bowl, and beat until you can see the path of the beater in the cream. Slowly add the powdered sugar, whipping continuously until peaks form. Add the vanilla and mix just until incorporated.

2. Line a cookie sheet or loaf pan with wax paper. Using a rubber spatula, spread out a 1-inch layer of whipped cream 2 inches wide and 9 inches long. Place a teaspoon-size dollop of whipped cream on a cookie,

(continued)

Lemon Icebox Cake  (continued)

and stand it up in the whipped cream. Repeat with all the cookies. Spread the remaining cream over the top of the cookies so that they are completely covered.

**3.** Place the cake in the freezer and freeze completely, about 6 hours. ⊠

**4.** Remove the cake from the freezer and place it on a serving platter. Defrost for 3 hours in the refrigerator. To serve, cut diagonal slices approximately 1 inch thick.

⊠ When the cake is frozen solid, wrap it in plastic wrap, overwrap with freezer paper, and seal. Freeze for up to 3 months. Proceed with Step 4.

# ICE CREAM SANDWICHES

*2 to 3 cups ice cream, any flavor*

*1 Pearl's Chip Sponge Cake (page 257), partially defrosted if frozen*

*6 ounces semisweet baking chocolate*

SERVES 4

**1.** Place the ice cream in the refrigerator and let it soften slightly, about 30 minutes.

**2.** Cut the cake into 8 equal slices, about ½ inch thick.

**3.** Spread a ¾-inch-thick layer of ice cream over 4 cake slices. Place the remaining slices on top, and press down lightly. Use a spatula to smooth any ice cream that squeezes out the sides. Place the sandwiches in the freezer for 30 minutes.

**4.** Melt the chocolate in the top of a double boiler over simmering water. Dip one end of each sandwich in the melted chocolate about a third of the way up, then place the sandwiches on a cookie sheet. Put back in freezer until the chocolate is set and the ice cream is completely hardened, about 30 minutes. ⊠

⊠ Wrap the sandwiches individually in plastic wrap, overwrap with freezer paper, and freeze for up to 3 months.

# FREEZER DICTIONARY

## A

**ACORN SQUASH** See Squash.

**ALMONDS** See Nuts.

**APPLES** Generally poor candidates for freezing uncooked, and since there is always some variety available, it's senseless to waste valuable freezer space. However, leftover baked apples, sautéed apples, applesauce, and apple chutney freeze perfectly well in freezer containers or bags for up to 6 months. Can be cooked directly from freezer, or defrosted in containers in the refrigerator, at room temperature, or in the microwave oven.

**ARTICHOKES** Remove outer leaves, trim stem, and blanch before freezing; boil for 10 minutes in a large pot of water containing half a lemon; drain and let cool. Or wrap individual artichokes in plastic wrap and cook in a microwave oven for 7 minutes; unwrap and let cool. Freeze in individual freezer bags for up to 1 year. Cook blanched artichokes without defrosting. Completely cooked artichokes can be frozen for up to 1 year, but are better used to prepare a purée or a soup.

**ASPARAGUS** Peel large asparagus; don't peel medium or thin asparagus. Trim off tough bottom of stalk. Soak in salted water for 10 minutes. Open-freeze, transfer to a freezer bag, and freeze for up to 8 weeks. Can be cooked directly from freezer, or defrost and serve chilled uncooked asparagus.

## B

**BACON** Smoked or salted meats change flavor in the freezer. Slab bacon is generally a better candidate for freezing than presliced packaged bacon: Remove and discard the tough bottom skin. Chill the bacon in the refrigerator, then slice to desired thickness —about ⅜-inch-thick slices. Wrap serving portions in plastic wrap and then in freezer paper. Seal tightly and freeze for up to 1 month. Defrost, still wrapped, in the refrigerator.

**BANANA** Frozen bananas are mushy when defrosted and are good only in cooked desserts or blender drinks. Freeze the whole fruit in its peel for up to 1 year; defrost before removing peel, then purée. Or purée the fresh fruit, mix with sugar and a little lemon juice, and freeze for use in breads or cakes. Can be cooked directly from freezer, or defrosted in containers in the refrigerator, at room temperature, or in the microwave oven.

**BARLEY** Drain any liquid from cooked pearl barley, place in a freezer bag or container, and freeze for up to 1 year. Freeze soup containing barley, and thin with stock after defrosting if necessary. Defrost cooked barley or barley soup in the refrigerator, at room temperature, or in the microwave oven.

**BASIL** Do not freeze fresh basil leaves. Instead, remove stems, add 1 tablespoon oil for each ¼ cup leaves, and purée, or make pesto (page 231). Freeze in ice cube trays; then wrap cubes individually, place in freezer bag or container, and freeze for up to 1 year. Can be added frozen to sauces and soups. Can be cooked directly from freezer, or defrosted in containers in the refrigerator, at room temperature, or in the microwave oven.

**BASS** Striped bass don't freeze well. Sea bass, including tile fish and black bass, freeze for up to 2 months. See also Fish.

**BEANS, DRIED** Soak dried beans overnight; then drain and open-freeze on a cookie sheet. Transfer to freezer bags or containers, and keep frozen for up to 1 year. Or freeze cooked beans in freezer bags for up to 6 months. Can be cooked directly from freezer, or defrosted in containers in the refrigerator, at room temperature, in the microwave oven.

**BEANS, FRESH** Green beans, wax beans, haricots verts: blanch for 2 minutes in salted water, or cook in a microwave oven on high setting for 3 minutes per ½ pound. Plunge immediately in ice water; then drain on absorbent towels. Place in freezer bags or containers and freeze for up to 1 year.

Limas, butter beans, flageolets, fava beans: Freeze cooked or blanched (as above) in freezer bags for up to 1 year. Can be cooked directly from freezer, or defrosted in containers in the refrigerator, at room temperature, or in the microwave oven.

**BEEF** See page 116 for specific directions. See also Meat.

**BEETS** Raw beets change texture in the freezer, becoming grainy. Wrap whole cooked beets individually in plastic wrap and place in freezer bags. Freeze for up to 1 year. Can be cooked directly from freezer, or defrosted in containers in the refrigerator, at room temperature, or in the microwave oven.

# BLANCHING TIMETABLE

| ARTICHOKES | 10 minutes |
|---|---|

| BEANS, FRESH, including pods | |
|---|---|
| small | 2 minutes |
| medium | 3 minutes |
| large | 4 minutes |

| BOK CHOY | 4 minutes |
|---|---|

| BROCCOLI FLORETS | 3 minutes |
|---|---|

| BRUSSELS SPROUTS | |
|---|---|
| small | 3 minutes |
| medium | 4 minutes |
| large | 5 minutes |

| CARROTS | |
|---|---|
| diced, sliced, julienned | 2 minutes |
| small whole | 5 minutes |

| CAULIFLOWER FLORETS | 3 minutes |
|---|---|

| CELERIAC | |
|---|---|
| ½-inch cubes | 2 minutes |

| FENNEL | |
|---|---|
| thick slices | 2 minutes |
| paper-thin slices | 30 seconds |

| GREENS | |
|---|---|
| beet, chard, kale, mustard, spinach, turnip | 1 minute |
| collards | 3 minutes |

**BERRIES** All berries freeze well in terms of flavor, but they are mushy when defrosted. You can freeze them in syrup or packed in sugar, but your product will be no better than a commercially prepared one. Instead, purée the fresh fruit and freeze it in containers for up to 9 months; use defrosted purée for sauces or jams. Defrost the purée for 8 to 12 hours in the refrigerator, 8 to 10 minutes in a microwave oven, or 1 to 2 hours at room temperature.

### KOHLRABI

| | |
|---|---|
| ½-inch cubes | 1 minute |
| whole small or medium | 3 minutes |

### OKRA

| | |
|---|---|
| small | 3 minutes |
| large | 4 minutes |

### PARSNIPS

| | |
|---|---|
| cubed or sliced | 2 minutes |

### PEAS

| | |
|---|---|
| black-eyed | 2 minutes |
| green | 1½ minutes |

### PEPPERS

| | |
|---|---|
| halves | 3 minutes |
| slices | 2 minutes |

### PUMPKIN

| | |
|---|---|
| | until barely soft |

### RUTABAGAS

| | |
|---|---|
| ½-inch cubes | 2 minutes |

### SNOW PEAS

| | |
|---|---|
| | 1 minute |

### SQUASH

| | |
|---|---|
| summer | 2 minutes |
| winter | until barely soft |

### SWEET POTATOES

| | |
|---|---|
| | until almost tender |

### TURNIPS

| | |
|---|---|
| ½-inch cubes | 2½ minutes |

**BLANCHING** A brief scalding in boiling water, essential before freezing vegetables. The process cleans the food and kills any organisms on the surface. It also retards the action of enzymes that would rob the vegetables of their color, vitamins, and flavor after a month or so in the freezer. The better the flavor and quality when blanched, of course, the better the defrosted vegetable will be.

Wash and trim the vegetables as you would if you were cooking them fresh. Sort them into similar sizes to cook uniformly. Use 4 quarts of lightly salted water for each pound of vegetables, more for leafy greens. When the water comes to a rapid boil, place the vegetables in a wire basket and lower into the water. Begin timing as soon as the vegetables enter the water. Cover or stir while cooking. Remove promptly at the proper time and plunge into ice water to stop the cooking process. You can reuse the water for subsequent batches, but be sure to return it to a rapid boil, and replenish with boiling water from a tea kettle when necessary. Stir vegetables in the ice water as they cool; they should cool about the same length of time they cooked. Dry thoroughly on absorbent towels. Then pack into freezer bags or containers, one serving per pack. Seal, and freeze for up to 1 year.

**BLUEFISH** Freezes for up to 2 months, cooked or uncooked. *See also* Fish.

**BONES, FISH** Raw fish bones, along with heads, tails, and other trimmings, can be frozen for fish stock; freeze for up to 3 months in freezer bags.

**BONES, MEAT, AND POULTRY** Freeze uncooked or cooked bones to use in stocks, soups, and sauces. Place in a freezer bag, close tightly, and freeze for up to 6 months. Add more bones to the bag as you accumulate them.

Cut a chicken carcass into 3 or 4 pieces for easier storage. Beef, veal, and pork bones may be stored together for use in All-Purpose Broth. Lamb bones should be stored and used separately because of their strong flavor, but they make an excellent broth for lamb stew.

**BRAINS** Do not freeze uncooked; they will fall apart. Wrap cooked brains tightly in plastic wrap, then in freezer paper, and freeze for up to 3 months. Defrost, still wrapped, in the refrigerator or microwave oven.

**BREAD** Freeze only the freshest bread, and wrap it tightly in plastic freezer wrap or freezer paper. To defrost, unwrap, rewrap with aluminum foil, and heat in a 250°F oven until warm. After defrosting, place French or Italian loaves in a preheated 350°F oven for 5 minutes to recrisp the crusts.

Bread doughs can also be frozen. Yeast-bread doughs should be frozen after the first rise. When preparing the dough, add 50 percent more yeast than the recipe calls for. Defrost, loosely wrapped, at room temperature for 5 to 6 hours. Freeze 1-loaf quantities for up to 3 months.

Quick-rising bread doughs should be frozen after rising. Defrost at room temperature for 3 hours; then cook semidefrosted dough in a 350°F oven until baked.

**BROCCOLI** Cut the tops off and cut into serving pieces. Peel the long woody stem and cut into rounds. Blanch both stems and florets for 3 minutes. Or cook, covered, in a microwave oven for 2 minutes per pound. Freeze in freezer bags or containers for up to 1 year. Can be cooked directly from the freezer, or defrosted in freezer containers or freezer in the refrigerator, at room temperature, or on the defrost setting of a microwave oven.

**BROTHS** All broths freeze well for up to 6 months. Make certain that they have been completely degreased and well chilled before freezing. Freeze in plastic containers leaving 1 inch of space at the top, or in plastic bags, flat on a baking sheet. When frozen, they can be removed from sheet and stacked neatly. Freeze in most con-venient batch size for you. Defrost for 8 to 12 hours per pint in the refrigerator, 1 to 2 hours at room temperature, or 8 to 10 minutes on the defrost setting of a microwave oven.

**BRUSSELS SPROUTS** Remove and discard outer leaves and cut an X in the root tip. Blanch for 3 to 5 minutes in lightly salted water, or cover tightly and cook in a microwave oven for about 2 minutes per pint. Open-freeze on a baking sheet, then seal in freezer bags or containers and freeze for up to 1 year. Do not defrost before cooking.

**BUTTER** Butter is a sponge for freezer odors so it must be tightly wrapped; leave in its original wrapping and overwrap with a double layer of plastic wrap. Salted butter changes flavor after 3 months, but unsalted can be frozen for up to 6 months. Defrost for 2 hours in the refrigerator or 1 hour at room temperature. Do not defrost in a microwave oven.

**BUTTERS, FLAVORED** Freeze flavored butters for up to 3 months. Defrost for 2 hours at room temperature; then whip in a food processor until creamy. (See pages 235–237.)

# C

**CABBAGE** Remove any bruised outer leaves, and cut out the center core. Blanch whole head in a large pot of boiling water for 5 minutes. Drain, and carefully remove as many large outer leaves as you can without tearing. Repeat blanching until all large leaves are removed. Pile large leaves together, seal in a freezer bag, squeezing out as much air as possible, and freeze for up to 3 months. Cut the remainder of the head in half and shred the cabbage. Place in plastic freezer bags or containers, and freeze for up to 1 year. Defrost 4 hours in refrigerator or 2 to 3 hours at room temperature. *See also* Napa cabbage.

**CAKES** It's possible to decorate cakes and then freeze them, but I find that they never look or taste as appealing as cakes that are decorated after defrosting. Avoid synthetic flavorings such as imitation vanilla—they change in the freezer. Wrap cake in a double layer of plastic wrap and then in freezer paper. Freeze for up to 3 months. Defrost, wrapped (unless frosted), at room temperature for 2 to 3 hours. Sponge cakes freeze best.

**CARROTS** Peel carrots and cut into ½-inch rounds or ½-by 2-inch sticks. Blanch for 2 minutes in lightly salted water, or cook, covered, in a microwave oven for 3 minutes per ½ pound. Open-freeze on a baking sheet, then place in plastic containers or bags and freeze for up to 1 year. Do not defrost before cooking.

**CATFISH** When completely fresh, farm-raised catfish doesn't change much when frozen and defrosted. Freeze individual fillets, cooked or uncooked, between sheets of freezer paper in freezer bags for up to 2 months. See also Fish.

**CAULIFLOWER** Young compact heads freeze better than more mature large ones. Break into 2-inch florets and blanch for 3 minutes in lightly salted water. Pat dry. Place serving-size portions in freezer bags, and freeze for up to 1 year. Can be cooked directly from freezer, or defrosted in containers in the refrigerator, at room temperature, or in the microwave oven.

**CAVIAR** Most fish roes—especially lumpfish, whitefish, flying fish, and salmon—freeze well provided they have not come into contact with water. Freeze in a tightly sealed container. Defrost in the refrigerator. Don't freeze the more delicate roes (Ossetra, Sevruga, Beluga); their texture is ruined by the process.

**CELERIAC** Excellent in the freezer. Peel, cut into ½-inch dice, and immediately toss with a little lemon juice to prevent discoloration.

Cook 1 cup (about 10 ounces) diced celeriac, covered, in a microwave oven, for 3 minutes; or blanch in lightly salted boiling water for 2 minutes. Cool, pat dry, seal in freezer containers, and freeze for up to 1 year. May be cooked directly from freezer, or defrosted in containers in the refrigerator, at room temperature, or in the microwave oven.

**CELERY** Celery can be frozen raw; after defrosting, use it only in cooked dishes. I prefer to freeze braised celery hearts: chill, wrap in plastic wrap, and place in a container; freeze for up to 1 year. Can be cooked directly from the freezer, or defrosted in containers in the refrigerator, at room temperature, or in the microwave oven.

**CHEESE** How a cheese freezes depends on the percentage of butterfat and water it contains. Hard grating cheeses such as Parmesan or Romano freeze perfectly well for up to 9 months. Hard cheeses such as Cheddar, Gouda, Edam, Gruyère, Morbier Emmenthal, Raclette Tomme de Savioe, and Tomme de Pyrenées freeze well for up to 6 months but don't melt nicely after defrosting. Semi-soft cheeses with 60 percent butterfat like Brie, Camembert, Pont l'Evêque, and Port Salut generally suffer from being frozen for up to 2 months, and can be used only in cooking after defrosting. Fresh Italian mozzarella freezes quite well for up to 6 weeks. Crumbly blue cheeses such as Roquefort become more crumbly after defrosting, but creamier Stilton and Bleu de Bresse maintain character. All goat cheeses freeze well. Cottage cheese cannot be frozen, as it loses its fresh taste and its texture is ruined. Don't freeze cream cheese, either. However, cooked dishes containing cottage or cream cheese are perfectly fine to freeze. Defrost cheese for 8 hours per ½ pound in the refrigerator or 2 hours at room temperature. Do not defrost in a microwave oven.

**CHERRIES** Pit the cherries, open-freeze on a baking sheet, then seal in freezer bags and freeze for up to 1 year. Use defrosted cherries only for cooking. Can be cooked directly from the freezer, or defrosted in containers in the refrigerator, at room temperature, or in the microwave oven.

**CHESTNUTS** Cut an X in the flat side of fresh chestnuts. Blanch in boiling water for 5 minutes, or cook 1 pound of nuts in a microwave oven for 5 minutes. Drain, peel, and seal in freezer bags. Freeze for up to 1 year. Can be cooked directly from freezer, or defrosted in containers in the refrigerator, at room temperature, or in the microwave oven.

**CHICKEN** Do not freeze uncooked chicken in its supermarket wrapping. Rinse the bird and dry it well. Remove giblets and freeze them separately for up to 6 months. Then double-wrap the bird with plastic wrap and overwrap with freezer paper. Freeze for up to 1 year. I prefer to marinate or season the bird before freezing (see pages 95–96). Defrost for 12 hours in the refrigerator or for 20 minutes in the microwave oven. Do not defrost at room temperature.

Cooked chicken freezes well for up to 3 months. It can be safely frozen for up to 6 months, but it begins to take on a stale flavor, so use it in dishes where it is disguised, such as a chicken hash. The dark meat of all poultry freezes better than the white.

**CHICK-PEAS** See Beans, dried.

**CHIVES** Do not freeze. They lose their oniony tang and their crispness.

**CHOCOLATE** There's no reason to freeze chocolate, as it keeps perfectly well in a cool place in the cupboard.

**CHOUX PASTE (CREAM PUFF DOUGH OR PÂTE À CHOUX)** Freeze both baked and unbaked. To freeze unbaked, line a tray with nonstick paper and pipe out 2-inch dots of paste for puffs, 5-inch lengths of paste for éclairs. Freeze baked or unbaked choux uncovered, then pack into bags or containers for up to 6 months for baked, 3 months for unbaked. Place unbaked frozen paste on an ungreased cookie sheet and place in a 375°F preheated oven for 5 minutes. Reduce heat to 350° and continue to bake until done. Place baked frozen choux on an ungreased cookie sheet and reheat for 7 minutes in a 400° oven.

**CHUTNEY** Freezes perfectly. Freeze in ice cube trays; then place cubes in freezer bags, and freeze for up to 6 months. Can be cooked directly from freezer, or defrosted in containers in the refrigerator, at room temperature, or in the microwave oven.

**CILANTRO** (fresh coriander) Trim off long stems. Purée 1 cup of leaves with 2 tablespoons flavorless oil such as corn, safflower, or soy. Place in ice cube trays and freeze. Remove from trays, place in freezer bags, and freeze for up to 4 months. Add frozen cubes to sauces and soups. To add to a cold dish, defrost at room temperature or in the microwave oven.

**CLAMS** Freeze shucked raw clams for up to 3 months, submerged in their liquor in freezer bags. Freeze steamed clams, with or without their steaming liquid, for up to 6 months. Defrost for 8 hours in refrigerator or add frozen to soups.

**CLOVES** Do not freeze; turn bitter in the freezer.

**COCONUT** Freeze fresh coconut in chunks or shredded, in its milk, for up to 6 months. Or freeze toasted shreds for up to 3 months, sweetened for up to 6.

**COD** Freeze lightly salted fresh cod (see page 74) for up to 3 months. See also Fish.

**COFFEE** Freeze whole beans to retain freshness for up to 6 months. Can be ground without defrosting.

**COLLARDS** Cut out thick center stem. Blanch leaves in lightly salted boiling water until just wilted. Cool in ice water. Dry thoroughly and freeze in a plastic container for up to 1 year. May be cooked directly from freezer, or defrosted in containers in the refrigerator, at room temperature, or in the microwave oven.

**CORN** Shuck corn on the cob and immediately blanch for 1 minute. Cool, and dry thoroughly. Seal in freezer bags and freeze for up to 1 year. Can be cooked directly from freezer, or defrosted in containers in the refrigerator, at room temperature, or in the microwave oven.

**CORNISH GAME HEN** See Chicken.

**CORNSTARCH** Since cornstarch lacks gluten, cornstarch-thickened soups and gravies maintain a smooth texture when frozen and defrosted. They may look curdled, but upon reheating their texture will be restored. Use ¾ tablespoon cornstarch to thicken a cup of liquid.

**CRAB** Freeze cooked hard-shell crabmeat in plastic containers. Once frozen, add water to cover the flesh, seal, and freeze for up to 3 months. Defrost in the refrigerator (allowing crabmeat to drain) or microwave oven. Use crabmeat as soon as possible after defrosting.
Do not freeze soft-shell crabs.

**CRANBERRIES** Freeze cooked cranberry sauces or jellies for up to 1 year. Freeze uncooked cranberries, in their original supermarket bag or in a freezer bag, for up to 1 year. Can be cooked directly from the freezer.

**CREAM** Whipping (heavy) cream can be frozen for up to 3 months. After defrosting it cannot be used for whipping but will be fine for cooking.
Half-and-half and light cream can be frozen for up to 3 months. Defrost all types of cream for 8 to 12 hours in the refrigerator, 1 to 2 hours at room temperature, or 8 to 10 minutes on the defrost setting of a microwave oven.

Cream sauces and soups usually break when they are frozen and then defrosted. So wherever possible, freeze a soup or sauce before adding cream. If you have added cream, add some milk to the defrosted soup or sauce before reheating, then bring almost to a boil as boiling will cause curdling. In recipes for cream soups I often use milk, or a combination of milk and cream, and this seems to solve the problem in many cases—it's also more healthful.

**CROISSANTS** Wrap freshly baked croissants individually in foil and freeze for up to 3 months. Do not defrost; unwrap and bake in a preheated 350°F oven for 15 minutes. Unbaked croissants can be frozen, individually wrapped, for up to 2 weeks. Unwrap and defrost in the refrigerator to complete the rise, then bake in a 375°F oven.

**CUCUMBERS** There's no reason to freeze them since they're available year-round. They cannot be eaten uncooked in salads once frozen, but can be used marinated or cooked.

**CUSTARDS AND CUSTARD DESSERTS** Do not freeze.

# D

**DEFROSTING** Though you can defrost at room temperature or in the microwave, whenever possible defrost slowly in the refrigerator.
**Large blocks of frozen food,** such as roasts or family size quantities of soup, defrost unevenly in the microwave, heating on the outside before thawing on the inside. Partially defrost any block weighing over 3 pounds for 2 hours at room temperature before completely defrosting in the microwave. Or partially defrost in the microwave and finish defrosting in the refrigerator.
**Smaller pieces of frozen food:** Partially defrost boneless chicken breasts, fillets of

# Defrosting Timetable

| FOOD | IN REFRIGERATOR | AT ROOM TEMPERATURE | IN MICROWAVE OVEN |
|---|---|---|---|
| BUTTER | 2 hours per ¼-pound stick | 1 hour | not recommended |
| CHEESE | 8 hours per half pound | 2 hours | not recommended |
| CHICKEN (under 4 pounds) | 5 hours per pound | not recommended | 8 to 10 minutes per pound |
| DUCKLING (4 to 5 pounds) | 12 hours | not recommended | 40 minutes |
| FISH, steak or fillets | 2 hours per 8 ounces | 1 hour | 2 minutes |
| FISH, whole | 3 hours per pound | not recommended | 10 minutes per pound |
| GROUND MEAT | 6 hours per pound | 2 hours | 5 minutes |
| MEAT (under 4 pounds) | 4 hours per pound | 2 hours per pound | 15 minutes per pound |
| MEAT (over 4 pounds) | add 1 hour per pound | add 30 minutes per pound | add 2 minutes per pound |
| PURÉE, LIQUIDS | 8 to 12 hours per pint | 1 to 2 hours | 8 to 10 minutes |
| TURKEY (10 pounds) | 20 to 24 hours | not recommended | 10 hours in refrigerator, then 10 minutes per pound |

fish, or individual steaks on the high setting of the microwave oven for a short amount of time (check the surface to ensure that it is not cooking), then finish defrosting in the refrigerator. Some foods, such as small cuts of meat or poultry, blanched vegetables, uncooked pastry can be cooked from frozen.

**Portion-size quantities:** Defrost at room temperature or in a microwave oven, then cook immediately to prevent bacterial growth. Do not defrost perishable or easily spoilable items such as poultry and seafood at room temperature.

**Liquids** can be defrosted under warm or cold running water and should be immediately boiled for 3 minutes to kill bacteria. Pureed items and ground meat, fish and poultry should also be cooked immediately.

**DEGORGE** Salt degorges vegetables such as cucumbers and cabbage by drawing water from the flesh. The freezer can perform the same function: Cut the vegetable into the size and shape desired for a recipe, and open-freeze. The vegetable will degorge as it defrosts. Drain, blot with paper towels, and proceed with recipe.

**DOUGHNUTS** Home-cooked and commercially prepared doughnuts freeze well, except for filled jelly doughnuts. Defrost, wrapped, in the refrigerator, then revive in a 350° for 5 minutes if not glazed.

**DRIED FOODS** Although they do freeze well, dried fruits and vegetables don't need freezing if they are kept in plastic containers.

**DUCK** Choose young ducklings, under 5 pounds, to freeze. Remove giblets, rinse duck, pat dry. Double-wrap in plastic wrap, overwrap with freezer paper, and freeze for up to 4 months. (Steaming before freezing greatly facilitates cooking; see page 108.) Freeze giblets separately for up to 6 months. Defrost for 12 hours in the refrigerator in wrapping, or for 40 minutes on the defrost setting of a microwave oven. Do not defrost at room temperature.

# E

**EGGPLANT** Sprinkle slices or cubes with salt and allow to drain for 1 hour before freezing; or roast whole eggplant, scrape out the insides, and purée. Freeze for up to 6 months. Defrost the purée for 8 to 12 hours per pint in the refrigerator, 8 to 10 minutes on the defrost setting of a microwave oven, or 1 to 2 hours at room temperature.

**EGGS, RAW** Separate yolks and whites. Freeze yolks in ice cube trays, one yolk to a niche; then place in freezer bags. (A yolk equals 1 tablespoon.) Freeze whites in the same manner. (One white equals 2 tablespoons.) Yolks and whites can be frozen for up to 6 months. Defrost, still wrapped, in the refrigerator. Yolks thicken after defrosting. Defrosted egg whites are easier to beat than fresh and attain a greater volume, but make a less stable meringue. Preparations containing stiffly beaten egg whites can be frozen and should be cooked without defrosting.

# F

**FAT** Fat doesn't expand in volume when frozen, so fatty foods maintain good texture in the freezer. However, since fat reacts with oxygen and gives foods a rancid flavor, do not freeze uncooked fatty meats such as lamb or pork for more than 4 months, or beef for more than 6 months. Trim meat of any excess layer of fat before freezing. Stews and broths should be chilled and skimmed of fat before freezing. Food cooked in fat—potted meats, fish, poultry, and pâtés—freeze perfectly well when tightly wrapped, but for only 3 months.

**FENNEL** Discard feathery leaves and hard root tip. Sliver the bulb into ¼-inch cross-sections. Blanch for 2 minutes in boiling water; or cook, covered, in a microwave oven for 1 minute. Cool, and dry thoroughly. Freeze in freezer containers or bags for up to 4 months. Can be cooked directly from freezer, or defrosted in containers in the refrigerator, at room temperature, or in the microwave oven.

**FIGS** Fresh figs can be frozen for up to 6 months but must be cooked after defrosting. Wash and dry fresh figs. Place on a baking sheet, then store in freezer bags. Can be cooked directly from freezer, or defrosted in containers in the refrigerator, at room temperature, or in the microwave oven. It's pointless to freeze dried figs—keep them in a plastic container.

**FISH** See also individual varieties. Best freezer candidates are scallops and crustaceans, fatty fish such as whitefish and salmon, and meaty fish such as swordfish and tuna. Smaller fillets of lean fish—flounder, sole, turbot—freeze poorly. Be absolutely certain that seafood is completely fresh and that the grocer has not sold you defrosted fish. Freeze uncooked, unprepared fish for no longer than 1 month. (See pages 74, 82, 86, 89, 90 for preparing fish for freezing.)

Defrost whole fish for 3 hours per pound

in the refrigerator or 10 minutes on the defrost setting of a microwave oven (but not at room temperature). Defrost steaks or fillets for 2 hours per ½ pound in the refrigerator, 2 minutes in a microwave, or 1 hour at room temperature.

**FLAGEOLETS** See Beans, dried.

**FLOUNDER** Freezes very poorly. Grind defrosted flounder to use in a loaf or pâté, or stuff it to disguise its frozen nature. See also Fish.

**FOIE GRAS** Fresh livers freeze well for up to 1 month, cooked whole livers for up to 3 months. Defrost, still wrapped, in the refrigerator. Canned pâtés and terrines should not be frozen once they are opened.

**FRUIT** Freeze uncooked fruit for up to 3 months, cooked fruit preparations—pie fillings, for example—for up to 6. Fruit should be frozen and defrosted only if intended for cooked preparations. Freeze only ripe or overripe fruit. Small fruits, such as berries, should be rinsed, dried, and placed on a baking sheet in the freezer for 2 hours; then pack into freezer bags and freeze for up to 6 months. Cut large fruits into 2-ounce pieces and open-freeze. Apples and pears should be peeled and cored. Stone fruits—peaches, apricots, plums, and nectarines—should be peeled, halved, and pitted. Melons should be peeled and seeds removed. Freeze citrus fruit juice, but not the fruit. Freeze grated citrus rind in freezer bags. Can be cooked directly from the freezer, or defrosted in containers in the refrigerator, at room temperature, or in the microwave oven. All fruits can be cooked with sugar without defrosting.

# G

**GARLIC** Purée peeled garlic cloves, mix with a little olive oil, and freeze, covered, in ice cube trays. Remove cubes, double-wrap individually with plastic wrap, and freeze in a freezer bag for up to 1 year. Can be cooked directly from freezer, or defrosted in containers in the refrigerator, at room temperature, or in the microwave oven.

**GELATIN** Recipes that call for gelatin, usually creamy mousses, freeze well for up to 3 months. Defrost, still wrapped, in the refrigerator.

**GINGER, FRESH** Young ginger (you'll recognize it by its thin skin) is preferable to the more commonly found older root, which has a thick outer skin. Freeze it when you find it because it's not around much of the time. Scrub and finely chop fresh young ginger. Place in ice cube trays, cover, and freeze. Wrap the individual cubes in plastic wrap and seal in freezer bags. Freeze for up to 1 year. Can be cooked directly from freezer, or defrosted in containers in the refrigerator, at room temperature, or in the microwave oven.

**GOOSE** See Duck.

**GRAPES** Do not freeze.

**GRITS** Spread cooked grits 1 inch thick on a buttered baking sheet, and when cool, cut into 2-inch squares. Wrap individually in plastic wrap and place in a freezer bag or container. Freeze for up to 1 year. Defrost at room temperature; or in the microwave oven; or bake, covered, without defrosting. Once frozen, cooked grits become soggy when defrosted, but can be reheated in butter or cream.

**GROUPER** Freeze uncooked for up to 2 weeks. Use salting or marinating method (see pages 74, 82) for freezing up to 1 month. See also Fish.

# H

**HADDOCK** Bread and freeze for up to 2 months, or salt and freeze for up to 3 months (see pages 74, 89 for techniques). *See also* Fish.

**HAKE, WHITING** Freeze for up to 2 weeks. Treat by lightly salting or marinating (see pages 74, 82), and freeze for up to 3 months. Cook without defrosting.

**HALIBUT** I don't know why this fish is so prevalent in the frozen cases of super-markets—it just doesn't freeze well. Do not freeze fresh halibut unless you salt it first (see page 74), and don't freeze for more than 2 weeks. Even freezer-marinating ruins it. *See also* Fish.

**HAM** Salted and smoked meats change flavor in the freezer if frozen for too long. Do not freeze for more than 1 month.

**HERBS** Frozen herbs generally taste more like their fresh version than do dried. Remove the stems, and freeze the leaves in plastic containers for up to 6 months. Use without defrosting. More delicate leaves like basil tend to become mushy and can discolor; purée them and mix with a little flavorless oil before freezing. See Basil, Parsley, Sage. May be cooked directly from the freezer, or defrosted in containers in the refrigerator, at room temperature, or in the microwave oven.

**HERRING** This versatile fish is often pickled, salted, smoked, and marinated or cooked; can be frozen for up to 6 months. Fresh, it freezes well for up to 1 month. *See also* Fish.

**HONEY** There's no reason to freeze honey since it keeps in a cool place almost indefinitely. Cakes prepared with honey freeze well and remain moist after defrosting.

**HORSERADISH** Remove and discard the peel, cut root into 1-inch chunks, and place in a food processor. Add 2 tablespoons white vinegar for every cup of horseradish, and purée. Place in plastic containers, and freeze for up to 3 months. Can be cooked directly from freezer, or defrosted in containers in the refrigerator, at room temperature, or in the microwave oven.

# I

**ICE CREAM** Of course it freezes. But changes in temperature form ice crystals and ruin it. Keep it well sealed at a constant freezer temperature. Freeze ice cream cakes, tightly wrapped, for up to 3 months, and unwrap before softening in the refrigerator.

# J

**JAM** Sugar preserves the fruit in jam, so there's no reason to put it in a freezer.

**JICAMA** Freeze cooked puréed jicama in freezer bags or containers for up to 4 months. Many people find this a lovely accompaniment for white meats. Defrost the purée for 8 to 12 hours per pint in the refrigerator, 8 to 10 minutes in the microwave oven, or 1 to 2 hours at room temperature.

# K

**KALE** Cut out the large center rib and slice it into ½-inch pieces. Blanch the cubed ribs with the leaves in boiling water until the leaves wilt, about 1 minute. Dry thoroughly and freeze for up to 1 year. Can be cooked directly from freezer, or defrosted in containers in the refrigerator, at room temperature, or in the microwave oven.

**KIWI** Freeze puréed kiwi for up to 6 months. Defrost for 8 to 12 hours per pint in the refrigerator, 8 to 10 minutes on the defrost setting of a microwave oven, or 1 to 2 hours at room temperature. Use as an alternative to berries in berry sauce.

# L

**LAMB** Trim excess fat, and freeze for up to 4 months. Much of the lamb we buy today comes frozen from New Zealand. See also Meat.

**LEMONGRASS** A woody Southeast Asian grass. It's very aromatic. Sometimes you can find young tender leaves that can be chopped and added to a dish. But most likely you'll buy large woody stems that you cook into a dish and discard before serving. Freeze (chopped) for up to 3 months. Add to stews and sauces without defrosting.

**LEMONS** Freeze the juice of lemons, limes, and oranges, but not the fruit. Fresh grated zest (yellow part of rind) can be frozen in freezer containers for up to 1 year; use without defrosting to flavor sauces and desserts.

**LENTILS** See Beans, dried.

**LIMA BEANS** See Beans, fresh.

**LIMES** See Lemons.

**LIVER** I find it risky to freeze calf's liver because it sometimes becomes grainy. Beef liver is less delicate and freezes well for up to 3 months.

Chicken, duck, and goose livers freeze well. Collect them as you buy whole birds and accumulate in a freezer bag. Trim off any purplish spots and membranes, place livers in freezer bags or containers, and freeze for up to 2 months. Defrost, still wrapped, in the refrigerator or on the defrost setting of a microwave oven.

**LOBSTER** The cooked meat of true lobsters from Maine and of spiny rock lobsters from South Africa, California, or the Mediterranean freezes well for up to 3 months. I don't recommend freezing uncooked meat because it doesn't cook well. If you are preparing lobsters for the freezer, undercook them (page 90) so they will not be tough when finished in a recipe. Defrost 3 hours per pound in the refrigerator, 1 hour at room temperature, or 2 minutes on the defrost setting of a microwave oven.

# M

**MACKEREL** Choose a freshly caught fish and freeze it whole or filleted for up to 3 months. See also Fish.

**MANGO** A good candidate to freeze. Peel the fruit and scrape off any flesh that adheres to the skin. Cut fruit away from the pit until it becomes too fibrous. Place fruit in a container and freeze for up to 1 year. Can be cooked directly from freezer, or defrosted in containers in the refrigerator, at room temperature, or in the microwave oven. Use in sweet sauces, sherbets, steamed pudding, fruit tarts.

**MARGARINE** See Butter.

**MARROW** Freezes remarkably well. Ask the butcher for 2-inch veal marrow bones. Soak them in ice water for 4 hours, drain, dry, and place in freezer bags, squeezing out as much air as possible. Freeze for up to 4 weeks. Defrost in the refrigerator, or cook in a microwave oven until the marrow just begins to soften. Remove the marrow from the bones and quickly sauté with herbs, or add to a meat sauce just before serving.

**MAYONNAISE** Forget it—it just won't freeze.

**MEAT** See individual entries. In general, defrost up to 4 pounds for 4 hours per pound in the refrigerator, 2 hours at room temperature, or 15 minutes on the defrost setting of a microwave oven. For over 5 pounds, 5 hours per pound in the refrigerator, 2½ hours at room temperature, and 17 minutes in a microwave.

**MEAT, GROUND** Defrost for 6 hours per pound in the refrigerator, 2 hours at room temperature, or 5 minutes on the defrost setting of a microwave oven.

**MILK** Don't freeze it; buy powdered instead.

**MINT** Loses much of its flavor when frozen. Since it's readily available throughout the year, use only fresh or dried.

**MONKFISH** One of the few fish whose frozen version is almost indiscernible from fresh. Place only very fresh tails in freezer bags, squeeze out as much air as possible, and freeze for up to 3 months. *See also* Fish.

**MUSHROOMS** Freeze fresh wild mushrooms such as porcini, chanterelles, and morels when they are in season for use throughout the year: Wipe them clean of any sand and debris, place in freezer bags or containers, and freeze for up to 1 year. May be cooked directly from the freezer, or defrosted in containers in the refrigerator, at room temperature, or in the microwave oven. (I prefer cooking frozen varieties rather than the dried. Dried mushrooms give a very delicious, strong flavor to any dish, but bear no resemblance to their fresh counterparts.) Japanese varieties such as oyster and shiitake are available nearly year-round, so don't bother to freeze them. Enoki mushrooms cannot be frozen. Common mushrooms cannot be served raw once they have been defrosted, and since they are always available, you don't have to freeze them. Cooked mushroom duxelles, however, is a very useful freezer item (see page 240). Defrost duxelles for 8 to 12 hours in the refrigerator, 1 to 2 hours at room temperature, or 8 to 10 minutes on the defrost setting of a microwave oven.

**MUSSELS** People used to avoid shellfish from May through August because of the risk of poisoning from so-called red tides. With many shellfish coming from colder waters around the world today, this is less of a problem, but I do find that mussels often develop a strong odor, like a harbor at low tide. So freeze a batch in April, when you are assured of briny, delicious mussels, and use them throughout the summer in soups and seafood salads: Steam mussels quickly in white wine and remove each one as it opens. Remove mussels from the shells when they are cool, and debeard them. Place on a baking sheet and open-freeze. When they are frozen, place in freezer bags, squeeze out as much air as possible, and freeze for up to 3 months. Strain the cooking liquid through a fine-mesh sieve or double layer of cheesecloth, pour into a plastic container leaving ½ inch headroom, and freeze for up to 3 months. Defrost mussels and broth in the refrigerator, or add frozen to soups and sauces.

**MUSTARD GREENS** Blanch small, young, tender leaves in lightly salted water until just wilted. Drain on absorbent towels, place in plastic containers, and freeze for up to 1 year. Defrost several hours in the refrigerator or 2 to 3 hours at room temperature.

# N

**NAPA CABBAGE** Freeze leftover cooked cabbage for up to 1 year. Defrost several hours in refrigerator or 2 to 3 hours at room temperature.

**NECTARINES** Like most other fruits, can be cooked or puréed and then frozen for up to 1 year. *See also* Fruit.

**NUTS** Although they stay moist and fresh for up to 9 months, this is a waste of good freezer space. Salted and roasted nuts freeze poorly, as the oil can become bitter very quickly; keep them in plastic containers in the refrigerator.

# O

**OCTOPUS** See Squid.

**OKRA** Blanch for 3 to 4 minutes in boiling salted water. Plunge into ice water to chill, dry on absorbent towels, and freeze in plastic freezer bags for up to 1 year. May be cooked directly from the freezer, or defrosted in containers in the refrigerator, at room temperature, or in the microwave oven.

**OLIVE OIL** Keep olive oil in the refrigerator. The addition of olive oil to a preparation does not alter the way it freezes.

**ONIONS.** Many people freeze minced raw onions in small packages. Don't do it. The flavor of onions and shallots changes when frozen, and although not distasteful, it's not the subtle one that we are looking for. Instead, cook onions in butter until soft; place them in ice cube trays, wrap the trays (so that the flavor and odor does not contaminate other foods in your freeze) and freeze. Then place the cubes in freezer bags, and freeze for up to 3 months. Use in sauces, soups, and vegetables.

**OPEN-FREEZING** When you want to freeze separate pieces of food so that they don't form into a solid block—scallops, shrimp, choux paste shells, diced peppers, kernels of corn—spread them on a baking sheet, uncovered, and freeze. Then pack convenient-sized portions into freezer bags, seal, and freeze.

**ORANGES** See Lemons.

**OYSTERS** Freeze only the freshest oysters, bought in the shell. (You won't want to eat them raw after defrosting, but they are great in other recipes.) Place the oysters, deep shell down, on a rimmed baking sheet, and cook in a preheated 500°F oven for about 7 minutes. The shells should open quite easily and the oysters will not be cooked. Remove them from the shells, being careful not to lose any juices. Place oysters and juice in plastic bags or containers, and freeze for up to 1 month. Defrost in a microwave oven or in the refrigerator, or add frozen to soups and sauces.

# P

**PANCAKES** Pancakes freeze well. Stack cooled cakes between sheets of freezer paper, place in freezer bags or containers, and freeze for up to 4 months. Defrost at room temperature for 20 minutes before reheating in the oven.

**PAPAYA** Freeze cooked papaya preparations, such as chutney or puréed fruit, for up to 1 year. Do not freeze fresh fruit.

**PARSLEY** Separate leaves from stems. Finely chop the leaves, place them in a freezer bag, and freeze for up to 1 year; use without defrosting to garnish soups, sauces, stews, and casseroles. Freeze the stems and use without defrosting to flavor stocks, stews, casseroles, and soups.

**PARSNIPS** Peel and cut into 1-inch cubes. Blanch in lightly salted boiling water for 1 minute. Drain, dry on absorbent towels, and freeze in freezer bags or containers for up to 1 year. Defrost at room temperature, under running water, or in the microwave oven; or use without defrosting.

**PARTRIDGE** See Chicken.

**PASTA** Fresh uncooked pasta freezes well in freezer bags for up to 6 months. Leftover cooked pasta can be frozen, unsauced, and used in pasta pancakes or casseroles (Chapter 8). Cooked or uncooked pasta casseroles such as lasagna (page 203) can be frozen for up to 3 months. Can be cooked directly from the freezer, or defrosted in containers in the refrigerator, at room temperature, or in the microwave oven.

**PEARS** Peel unripe pears, sprinkle with lemon juice, wrap in plastic wrap, and freeze for up to 1 year. Can be cooked directly from the freezer, or defrosted in containers in the refrigerator, at room temperature, or in the microwave oven. Once defrosted, use them for cooking (poached pears, chutney, pickled relish). Or purée peeled, cored ripe pears and freeze for up to 1 year. Use in steamed puddings or fruit sauce. *See also* Purées.

**PEAS, GREEN** I prefer frozen peas to fresh ones unless I pick them from the garden and cook them immediately. Like corn, the sugar in the vegetable turns quickly to starch after picking, so commercially flash-frozen ones are more likely to taste like fresh-picked. To freeze fresh peas, shell them, and blanch for 1 minute in lightly salted water. Drain, place in plastic containers, and freeze for up to 1 year. Cook without defrosting. *See also* Snow peas.

**PEEL, CITRUS.** See Lemons.

**PEPPER** Ground or whole pepper loses its spicy pungency and becomes acrid after 1 month in the freezer. Green peppercorns packed in water (not brine) can be frozen for up to 3 months; freeze them in tablespoon quantities. *See also* Spices.

**PEPPERS, ROASTED** Freeze well, for up to 1 year. By all means roast some extra when they're called for, and keep a stock on hand in the freezer. Can be cooked directly from freezer, or defrosted in the refrigerator or in the microwave oven.

**PERCH** Among the least freezable but most-oft-frozen fish. Buy only fresh whole perch, have the fishmonger fillet them, and salt before freezing for up to 2 months (see page 74). *See also* Fish.

**PHEASANT** See Chicken.

**PIKE** Buy a whole fish, have your fishmonger fillet it, and salt before freezing (see page 74) for up to 3 months. *See also* Fish.

**PINEAPPLE** Freeze slices in airtight plastic bags for up to 6 months. May be cooked directly from freezer, or defrosted in containers in the refrigerator, at room temperature, or in the microwave oven. Defrosted pineapple is good only for cooking.

**PLANTAIN BANANAS** Freeze only ripe ones (a little soft to the touch and the skin mottled with black spots) in their skins for up to 1 year. Defrost at room temperature, in the refrigerator, or in the microwave oven.

**PLUMS** See Fruit.

**POMEGRANATES** A fruit highly prized for its juice. To more easily obtain the juice, place the whole fruit in a plastic bag and freeze for at least 3 hours. Then defrost at room temperature, break open the fruit, and gently press all the seeds to extract the juice. Discard seeds and skin. Refreeze juice in a freezer container for up to 1 year. Defrost for 8 to 12 hours per pint in the refrigerator, 8 to 10 minutes on the defrost setting of a microwave oven, or 1 to 2 hours at room temperature.

**POMPANO** Wrap fillets in plastic freezer wrap and freeze for up to 2 weeks. For longer freezing (up to 2 months), marinate it first (see page 82). *See also* Fish

**PORK** Because of its high fat content, pork, both cooked and uncooked, freezes better than other meats, but for a shorter period of time—up to 3 months. Cured hams and bacon freeze for only 1 month because of the high salt content, which contributes to a rancid flavor. *See also* Meat.

**POTATOES** The combination of high water content and temperamental starch make potatoes difficult freezer candidates. Do not freeze raw potatoes; they cook up poorly and they discolor. Cooked baked potatoes freeze best. Freeze mashed potatoes, but add a little butter or margarine and some milk to reconstitute after defrosting; purée in a blender or processor to excite the starch, and then reheat. Fried potatoes, or potatoes otherwise cooked with fat or oil, freeze well. Freeze potato casseroles such as gratins. These will all freeze for up to 3 months. Soups made with a potato base often become grainy after defrosting.

**PUMPKIN** Cut the pumpkin in half, scoop out the seeds, and remove the peel with a sharp knife. Cut the flesh into 2-inch chunks, and blanch in boiling water until just soft. Dry thoroughly, place in a plastic container or freezer bag, and freeze for up to 1 year. Can be cooked directly from freezer, or defrosted in containers in the refrigerator, at room temperature, or in the microwave oven.

**PURÉES, FRUIT AND VEGETABLE** Purées freeze very well for up to 9 months in plastic containers. Freeze convenient batch sizes, or freeze the purée in ice cube trays and then transfer the cubes to freezer bags. Defrost for 8 to 12 hours per pint in the refrigerator, 8 to 10 minutes on the defrost setting of a microwave oven, or 1 to 2 hours at room temperature.

# Q

**QUAIL** See Chicken.

**QUINCE** Peel, quarter, and core the fruit. Cut into 1-inch chunks and blanch for 1 minute in boiling water. Cool, dry thoroughly, and open-freeze on a tray, then place in plastic bags and freeze for up to 1 year. Can be used without defrosting.

# R

**RABBIT** Place fresh rabbit quarters in freezer bags and squeeze out as much air as possible. Freeze for up to 4 months. Defrost in the refrigerator or in the microwave oven. Freeze and defrost cooked rabbit as you would poultry (see Chicken).

**RADICCHIO** Blanch whole heads of round red radicchio in boiling salted water for 10 minutes. Blanch long heads of Treviso radicchio in boiling salted water for 5 minutes. Place on absorbent towels until cool, wrap in plastic wrap, and freeze for up to 1 year. Defrost at room temperature.

**RANCIDITY** Fatty foods have a shorter freezer life than lean ones because oxygen reacts with the acids in the fat, changing both flavor and aroma. This change—rancidity—does not affect the safety of the food, although it is unappetizing. Salt speeds up rancidity, so cured meats such as corned beef, pastrami, and ham change flavor. Good airtight packaging helps salty and fatty foods such as bacon freeze better.

**RED SNAPPER** True red snapper is found on the Atlantic coast off Florida and in the Gulf of Mexico. Off the West Coast of the U.S., red snapper is actually rockfish—and bears no resemblance to the snapper. For best results, marinate snapper or rockfish (see page 82) and freeze for no longer than 2 weeks. See also Fish.

**REFREEZING** Don't refreeze foods that have completely defrosted at room temperature. Foods that have partially defrosted in the refrigerator can be refrozen. The exceptions are fish and poultry, which should never be refrozen once they have defrosted, although more from a quality standpoint than a health one. The bacterial action in ground meat is greater than in solid, so if refrozen from a partially defrosted state, use it as quickly as possible.

**RHUBARB** Remove and discard leaves. Cut young, tender stalks into 1-inch pieces, place in freezer bags or containers, and freeze for up to 1 year. Can be cooked directly from the freezer, or defrosted in containers in the refrigerator, at room temperature, or in the microwave oven.

**RICE** Leftover cooked rice freezes well for up to 1 year. Can be cooked directly from the freezer, or defrosted in containers in the refrigerator, at room temperature, or in the microwave oven. Rather than re-serve it as a vegetable dish, add cream and eggs and turn it into a savory pudding or rice pancake (see Index).

**RICE, WILD** See Rice.

**RIND, CITRUS** See Lemons.

**RUTABAGAS** See Turnips.

# S

**SAGE** Freeze fresh leaves in a freezer plastic bag for up to 6 months. Use without defrosting.

**SALMON** Freeze untreated uncooked salmon for only 2 weeks. Or salt it (see page 74) and freeze for up to 2 months—this actually produces a tastier salmon with no discernible loss of quality in the texture. See also Fish.

**SAUSAGE** All sausages freeze well, losing no quality of texture, for up to 2 months. If you make your own and use less salt than commercial makers do, you can freeze them for up to 3 months. Commercial sausages, whether smoked or fresh, should be frozen only if you know they are perfectly fresh and have not been previously frozen. Defrost, still wrapped, in the refrigerator or in the microwave oven.

**SCALLIONS** Do not freeze; they become soggy. Substitute onions for scallions if all or some of your recipe is destined for the freezer.

**SCALLOPS** Neither large sea nor small bay scallops freeze particularly well without some help: salt them lightly before freezing (page 74), or marinate them and make freezer seviche (page 82). Freeze for up to 4 weeks. Freeze leftover cooked scallops without sauce for up to 2 months and use for chilled salads. Defrost, still wrapped, in the refrigerator. See also Fish.

**SCROD** See Cod.

**SHAD, SHAD ROE** One of the few fish that benefit from freezing, its flesh becoming firmer. Freeze fillets of lightly salted (page 74) shad for up to 1 month. Defrost in the refrigerator or in the microwave oven.

Shad roe should be rinsed, patted dry, wrapped in plastic wrap, and placed in freezer bags. Freeze for up to 4 months. Defrost in the refrigerator or under cold running water—not in the microwave oven.

**SHALLOTS** See Onions.

**SHELLFISH.** See Fish, individual entries.

**SHIITAKE** See Mushrooms.

**SHRIMP** Most shrimp we find in the market were frozen on the boat when they were caught; do not refreeze them. Cook them in their shells in boiling water for 2 minutes, and freeze up to 3 months to use in salads or eat chilled with cocktail sauce.

To freeze absolutely fresh shrimp, remove the heads and rinse the tails. Pat the tails dry, and open-freeze on a tray. When they are frozen, dip each shrimp in icewater before placing in a container. Freeze for up to 4 months. Defrost overnight in the refrigerator, or microwave oven, or under cold running water.

**SMOKED FOODS** Smoking, a method of preserving meat and fish before there was refrigeration, causes a loss of texture because fibers in the flesh are broken down. Generally there are two kinds of smoked foods, those that are cold-smoked, like smoked salmon, and those that are cured and hot-smoked—bacon, frankfurters, and other sausages. Smoked foods generally suffer no loss of quality in the freezer as far as the texture is concerned, but they do change flavor after several months. Smoked fish fare well for up to 3 months, but smoked meats, probably because of the combination of fat, salt, and smoke, turn rancid after only 1 month. Defrost, still wrapped, in the refrigerator or microwave oven.

**SNAPPER** See Red snapper.

**SNOW PEAS** Remove strings from pods. Blanch pods in lightly salted boiling water for 1 minute. Plunge into ice water until chilled, and spread on absorbent towels to dry. Place in freezer bags and freeze for up to 1 year. Use without defrosting.

**SOLE** Best to prepare them breaded (see page 89). The extra work required pays off, however, because they freeze for up to 4 months. See also Fish.

**SORREL** (Also known as sour grass.) Best used fresh when it's at its most pungent, but you can freeze the purée and use it in fish sauces, or as a flavoring for potato or spinach soup: Remove and discard the center stem. Place leaves in a food processor along with a squeeze of lemon juice. Purée leaves, place in a plastic container, and freeze for up to 1 year. See also Purées.

**SOUR CREAM** Freeze for up to 6 months. Defrost and then whip back together if separated. Preparations using sour cream, such as coffee cakes, freeze well. Always try to find unstabilized sour cream—without gum additives. Defrost, still wrapped, in the refrigerator.

**SPICES** Most spices freeze well in foods and retain their potency for up to 3 months. After that, they tend to fade. Highly spiced foods change flavor and should not be frozen for longer than 2 months.

**SPINACH** To freeze spinach, wash it well and remove the stems. Sauté the leaves in olive oil until barely wilted or blanch in boiling salted water for 30 seconds. Place in a colander or strainer and drain thoroughly before placing in freezer bags. Freeze for up to 1 year. Can be cooked directly from freezer, or defrosted in containers in the refrigerator, at room temperature, or in the microwave oven.

**SQUAB** See Chicken.

**SQUASH** Winter squash (butternut, acorn, banana, spaghetti squash, pumpkin, etc.) should be peeled and seeded and the flesh diced; blanch until barely tender. Summer squash (zucchini, crookneck) should be diced and blanched for 2 minutes or placed, covered, in the microwave for 1 minute before freezing. Can be cooked directly from the freezer, or defrosted in containers in the refrigerator, at room temperature, or in the microwave oven. See also Pumpkin.

**SQUID** Squid and octopus freeze well for up to 6 months and are equally fine bought frozen or fresh. To prepare fresh squid for freezing, you must clean it: Hold the sac in one hand, the tentacles in the other, and gently pull apart. All or most of the contents of the sac should come away attached to the tentacles. Cut the tentacles above the eyes and discard the contents of the sac along with the hard "beak." Remove the thin bladelike cuttlebone from the sac, and using your finger, remove anything that may remain in the sac. Rinse both tentacles and sac under running water, pulling off the sac's thin outer skin and whatever skin you can easily remove from the tentacles. Place sac and tentacles in a lidded plastic container, cover with water, and freeze for up to 3 months. Defrost, still wrapped, in the refrigerator or microwave oven.

**SUGAR SNAP PEAS** See Beans, fresh.

**SWEETBREADS** Rinse under cold water, peeling and discarding the outer membrane. Cut away and discard any veins and fat. Place in a freezer bag, squeeze out as much air as possible, and freeze for up to 6 months. Or place in a saucepan of cold water, bring to a boil, and remove from the heat. Rinse under cold water and freeze for up to 6 months. Defrost, still wrapped, 6 to 8 hours in the refrigerator or in the microwave oven.

**SWEET POTATOES** Freeze only cooked sweet potatoes, Bake them in their skins, let cool to room temperature, wrap individually, and pack into a large plastic container or freezer bag. Defrost at room temperature for 2 hours. Unwrap and bake at 350°F for 20 minutes. Or freeze mashed sweet potatoes. Remove them, still frozen, from their freezer bag or container, place in a covered casserole with a few tablespoons of water, and bake at 350°F until hot.

**SWORDFISH** Thick steaks and large loin pieces freeze better than thin steaks or small pieces. The flavor remains remarkably fresh during freezing and defrosting. Wrap tightly in plastic wrap, then in freezer bags, and freeze for up to 2 months. See also Fish.

# T

**TOMATILLOS** Discard the papery husk and coarsely chop the fruit. Place in freezer containers, and freeze for up to 1 year. Can be cooked directly from freezer, or defrosted in containers in the refrigerator, at room temperature, or in the microwave oven.

**TOMATOES** Cut in half crosswise and squeeze out seeds. Salt, and leave to drain for 1 hour. Pat dry with paper towels. Place in freezer bags, and freeze for up to 6 months. Can be cooked directly from freezer, or defrosted in containers in the refrigerator, at room temperature, or in the microwave oven. Use for sauces, soups, stews.

**TONGUE** Freeze cooked fresh tongue for up to 3 months, uncooked fresh tongue for up to 6 months, pickled tongue for up to 2 months. Wrap tightly in 2 layers of plastic wrap, then overwrap with freezer paper. All tongues can be cooked directly from the freezer, or defrost, still wrapped, in the refrigerator or in the microwave oven.

**TROUT** Freeze cleaned, whole fish that are absolutely fresh. Wrap in plastic wrap, place in a plastic container, and freeze for up to 1 month. See also Fish.

**TRUFFLES** Do not freeze; it ruins their texture and flavor. Store truffles in a small container of uncooked rice in the refrigerator for up to 1 month. Not only do the truffles keep well, but the rice takes on a delicious truffle flavor when cooked.

**TUNA** Quickly freeze and immediately defrost fresh tuna before serving it raw, to destroy any parasites. It can be frozen for up to 2 weeks without losing quality. For freezing for up to 2 months, marinate (page 82) or salt (page 74) it first. See also Fish.

**TURBOT** Freezes best if lightly salted first (page 74). Freeze for up to 1 month. See also Fish.

**TURKEY** Although it takes up a lot of freezer space, you can freeze a whole turkey. An 11-pound bird will need 20 to 24 hours to defrost in the refrigerator; or defrost it for 10 hours in the refrigerator, then 30 minutes on the defrost setting of a microwave oven. Of course you can also freeze it in pieces (see Chicken). Never defrost turkey at room temperature. Cooked turkey freezes well for up to 6 months; though the white meat tends to become dry, so use it in pot pies or hash, or cook it in sauce.

**TURNIPS** Small ones the size of walnuts can be peeled, then blanched whole in boiling salted water for 3 minutes. Cut larger turnips and rutabagas into 2-inch pieces and blanch for 2 minutes. Dry on absorbent towels, place in a freezer bag or container, and freeze for up to 1 year. Can be cooked directly from the freezer, or defrosted in containers in the refrigerator, at room temperature, or in the microwave oven.

# V

**VANILLA** Beans keep perfectly well in plastic

bags in the refrigerator for a long time, so don't freeze them. Freeze natural vanilla extract and preparations that use it for up to 4 months. Do not freeze synthetic vanilla extract, which becomes bitter and loses its vanilla character.

**VEAL** Truly young milk-fed veal has very little fat and will lose its moisture when defrosted, so do not freeze it. The fattier, larger cuts such as breast or brisket freeze better than the lean ones. Freeze uncooked veal for up to 4 months. *See also* Meat.

# W

**WATERCRESS** Do not freeze, except after puréeing to be used in sauces or soups. It can be puréed without the addition of liquid. *See* Purées.

**WHITEFISH** The texture suffers after freezing. Light salting helps slightly (page 74), and breading solves the problem (page 89). Properly prepared, freeze for up to 2 months. *See also* Fish.

**WHITING** *See* Hake.

# Y

**YAMS** Do not freeze uncooked yams. Freeze baked yams to use in pie fillings, as puréed vegetable, or in soup. *See* Sweet potatoes.

# Z

**ZEST** *See* Lemons.

**ZUCCHINI** *See* Squash.

# INDEX

**Boldface** entries refer to master recipes.